W9-CEZ-583

Diversity & Women's Career Development

Women's Mental Health and Development

Series Editor: Barbara F. Okun, *Northeastern University*

Women's Mental Health and Development covers therapeutic issues of current relevance to women. This book series offers up-to-date, practical, culture-sensitive, professional resources for counselors, social workers, psychologists, nurse practitioners, family therapists, and others in the helping professions. Volumes in this series are also of significant value to scholars in gender studies and women's studies.

This series is designed to deal particularly with those issues and populations underrepresented in the current professional literature. Particular attention is paid to the sociocultural contexts of these issues and populations. While some of the volumes of this series cover topics pertinent to all women, others focus on topics applicable to specific groups. The series integrates material from established models, emerging theoretical constructs, and solid empirical findings in a format designed to be applicable for clinical practice. Professionals and trainees in a variety of mental health fields will find these readable, user-friendly volumes immediately useful.

Authors of volumes in this series are selected on the basis of their scholarship and clinical expertise. The editorial board is composed of leading clinicians and scholars from psychology, counseling, and social work.

Editorial Board

Diversity & Women's Career Development

From Adolescence to Adulthood

Helen S. Farmer
and Associates

Women's Mental Health & Development, Volume 2

SAGE Publications
International Educational and Professional Publisher
Thousand Oaks   London   New Delhi

Copyright © 1997 by Sage Publications, Inc.

For information address:

 SAGE Publications, Inc.
2455 Teller Road
Thousand Oaks, California 91320
E-mail: order@sagepub.com

SAGE Publications Ltd.
6 Bonhill Street
London EC2A 4PU
United Kingdom

SAGE Publications India Pvt. Ltd.
M-32 Market
Greater Kailash I
New Delhi 110 048 India

Printed in the United States of America

Library of Congress Cataloging-in-Publication Data

Diversity and women's career development: From adolescence to
adulthood / edited by Helen S. Farmer and associates.
    p. cm. — (Women's mental health and development; vol. 2)
  Includes bibliographical references and index.
  ISBN 0-7619-0489-1 (cloth). — ISBN 0-7619-0490-5 (pbk.)
  1. Vocational guidance for women—United States. 2. Career
development—United States. 3. Women in the professions—United
States. 4. Minority women in the professions—United States.
I. Farmer, Helen S. II. Series.
HF5382.65.D58 1997
331.7'02'082—dc21   97-4894

This book is printed on acid-free paper.

97 98 99 00 01 02 10 9 8 7 6 5 4 3 2 1

Acquiring Editor: Jim Nageotte
Editorial Assistant: Kathleen Derby
Production Editor: Diana E. Axelsen
Production Assistant: Karen Wiley
Typesetter & Designer: Laura Lawrie
Print Buyer: Anna Chin

Contents

Series Editor's Introduction

Work is a vital component of women's well-being. Therefore, clinicians of every discipline and modality need to keep abreast of contemporary theory and practice to help our clients make informed choices that will enhance rather than restrict their lives. We need to help our women clients value their career decisions and paths whether they choose to conform to or deviate from the male-dominant career tracks that prevail in career development theory and practice.

I am pleased to introduce Volume 2 of the Sage Women's Mental Health and Development series, *Diversity and Women's Career Development: From Adolescence to Adulthood,* which recognizes the importance of work to women. This volume was written by the renowned career development scholar Helen Farmer and her associates. The book is unique in its range of topics, including the impacts of gender, family, ethnicity, culture, and socioeconomic status on the career aspirations and development of women. Using social learning theory as a theoretical framework, the authors develop our awareness and understanding of the common career development issues experienced by women across race, ethnic, and class groups in our contemporary society from adolescence through adulthood.

Based on an integration of original qualitative and empirical data, current psychological theory, and personal stories, Farmer and her associates call our attention not only to the subtle interplay of investigators' background and attitudes and their lines of inquiry but also to the viability of current career development theoretical views for women. Challenging the inadequacy of current career counseling programs and practices, the authors offer concrete suggestions for remediating the lack of effective career and life planning programs in schools and throughout the life span.

The Sage Women's Mental Health and Development series seeks to contribute innovative, cutting-edge perspectives to the interdisciplinary mental health literature. As with Volume 1 of this series, Klonoff and Landrine's *Preventing the Misdiagnosis of Women,* Farmer's volume comprehensively explores and develops crucial areas pertaining to women's mental health and development that have heretofore been ignored or marginalized. Future volumes in this series will also focus on issues affecting women that are underrepresented in the current literature.

I am fortunate in having an enthusiastic, involved interdisciplinary editorial board of such renown. Forthcoming volumes in progress focus on women immigrants, women prisoners, breast cancer, health development, psychopharmacological issues for women, and cultural perspectives of women.

Barbara F. Okun, Ph.D.
Northeastern University

Preface

Several years ago, when the principal investigator, Helen Farmer, was examining the results of the longitudinal research project on women's persistence in science careers described in this book, she found what appeared to be inconsistencies in the data on what she termed "persisters and nonpersisters in science fields" and decided to heed the call of those results and investigate further. She knew, however, that more quantitative data would not suffice to unlock the meaning behind the inconsistencies. Explanations were needed from the people who had given their time to fill out the surveys. She needed their stories—the full stories of their career development—to find the connections that would make the "inconsistent" data more meaningful.

The research team conducted two 1- to 2-hour interviews over a 2½ year period and gathered a wealth of qualitative data on a topic that should interest counselors, social workers, psychologists, educators, school administrators, and many other professionals. The team had something unique—longitudinal quantitative and qualitative data on individuals' career development from adolescence to adulthood. Even more exciting was the diversity of the individuals whose stories were obtained: whites, blacks, Asians, and Hispanics; persons in a wide range of careers, including waitresses and surgeons; immigrants and native-born Americans. The team gathered together the dreams, fears, triumphs, and frustrations of individuals who grew up on farms and in the inner city, amidst wealth as well as in poverty.

The respondents have been given pseudonyms to ensure confidentiality. Their words provide much for the reader to ponder and learn from. Their stories allow insights into women's career development, the career development of people of color, gender differences in the pursuit of science careers, the effects of socioeconomic status on career and family issues, career development in rural areas, the balance of work and family roles, the experiences of immigrants, and more.

Chapter 1 outlines the social learning theoretical framework underlying the longitudinal study on which the book is based. This chapter also describes the procedures used in the study as well as the participants and the interview protocol.

Other than the two beginning and the two ending chapters, the chapters in the body of the book (Chapters 2-13) follow a similar outline. Each of these chapters is based on a subset of the interviews conducted with 57 women and 48 men. The chapters differ in the focus or lens they bring to these life stories. Each author has selected the participants' stories that match her purpose. Each chapter opens with a general introduction summarizing research relevant to its focus. Each author states her personal views and experiences as they affect the interpretations she makes. Third, the author presents an overview of the themes identified from the interviews and then illustrates these themes with representative quotes. The closing section of each of these chapters relates the themes to the social learning theoretical framework used throughout the book.

Chapter 2 is based on the stories of the women interviewed who had wanted a career in science or technology when they were in high school and who, 10 years later, had entered one of these careers. In contrast, Chapter 3 discusses the women who also had wanted a career in science or technology when they were in high school but, 10 years later, had entered a career in a different field. Chapter 4 takes a subset of the women interviewed, those who had wanted a career in high school in engineering or computer science, and compares their career choice process with that of men with similar career goals. Chapter 5 focuses on the life stories of women who were high achievers both in school and in their careers, regardless of the career field they chose. Chapter 6 explores gender differences in the life stories of these men and women. Chapter 7 reports on the ways in which ethnic discrimination affected the career development of persons of color. Chapter 8 illustrates how some persons of color were able to find satisfying careers in spite of discrimination and, often, a lack of resources, even though it took them longer to do so. Chapter 9 examines the stories of children of immigrants, including those who immigrated with their parents and those who are first-generation Americans. Chapter 10 focuses on the experiences of participants who made a significant occupational increase in socioeconomic status compared with their parents. Chapter 11 explores the career development of participants from two rural high schools. Chapter 12 focuses on the past influences of family on the career development of participants. Chapter 13 explores the ways participants who were just beginning to combine work and family roles were coping with multiple roles. The closing two chapters focus on career counseling for young people today and in the coming decade as well as on research needs with respect to women's optimal career development.

This book provides an opportunity to learn about career development from a variety of perspectives. The reader may begin to get to know the participants across the chapters, as many of them are quoted in several places; the participants are multifaceted individuals whose career development is as unique as they are. The authors of this book hope to stimulate the reader to act on the information presented here—to encourage, support, challenge, and assist others seeking to achieve their career goals, whether adolescents or adults, and to join with others to tear down the barriers to success that so many face today.

This book is an excellent resource for anyone involved or interested in issues related to the career development of women, women in science, and women and achievement. Persons interested in issues of diversity and ethnicity, and of family impact on career development, will also find this book of interest. The stories and findings in the book would be useful reading for career and guidance counselors, social workers, psychologists, high school teachers, college professors involved in research and teaching on career development, undergraduate students who are in the process of making career decisions, and graduate students who are in training to become career counselors. Outside of academic settings, human resource development professionals and people in positions of managing diverse staffs will also find this book a useful resource.

Acknowledgments

Because this book is based on a longitudinal study encompassing nearly two decades, there are numerous individuals and agencies that deserve acknowledgment for their contributions. In 1977, the National Institute of Education (NIE) funded the first wave of data collection. A pilot study was conducted in 1979 to test the measures; it involved nine high schools and several thousand students. This was followed by data collected with revised measures from six high schools in 1980. In 1990, the National Science Foundation (NSF) funded a follow-up study with the 1980 participants that included data collection and interviews. During the years between, the University of Illinois Research Board and Center for Advanced Study provided funding and support for various aspects of the study. To all these agencies and their staffs, I owe a great debt of gratitude.

I am indebted to many persons who provided access to the participants when they were in high school: to Brenda Lerner, who randomly selected the participant schools and arranged data collection procedures with school personnel, and to school superintendents, principals, teachers, and counselors who provided access to their students and made the necessary arrangements for our visits to their schools. Similarly, the students who participated in this study in 1979, 1980, 1990, and 1991-1993 are gratefully acknowledged for their generosity in giving their time. Special thanks to the participants who were interviewed and who shared their life stories. I am also indebted to William Full and his colleagues at the Illinois State Department of Education, who gave willingly of their time to discuss ways to improve education in Illinois.

More than 30 graduate students participated in this project:

Janice Altman	Susanne Crabtree	Barbara Powell
Mary Z. Anderson	Frank Fugita	Kirsten Peterson
Shahin Ardebelli-Naftchi	Leslie Fyans	Jana Reddin
Karla Brock-Fugita	Susan Giurleo	Rhonda Risinger
Amy Carter	Cindy Glidden	Gail Rooney
Ya-Mei Chen	Dee Horn	Katelyn Swan
Kathy Croce	Anne Isenberg	Lenore Tipping
Barry Y. Chung	Jerri Keane	Walter Vispoel
JoAnn Cohn	Fu-Lin Lee	Melissa Whalen
Rebecca Conrad	Veronica Lugris	Elizabeth Weiss
Lorena Covington	Susanne Mazzeo	Leonora Yang

Without them, the measures and data would not have been as reliable or valid, and many of the insights reported would have been missed. Most recently, nine of these students participated in the preparation of this book. In addition, several undergraduate students assisted with aspects of the quantitative data analyses.

In the first phase of the study, faculty colleagues Lenore Harmon, Bob Linn, Martin Maehr, and Klaus Witz were actively involved in providing helpful feedback and suggestions on the measures, design, analyses, and interpretation of the study findings. In phase two, Jim Wardrop ensured that our statistical analyses were sound, and Carole Ames, Carolyn Anderson, and Lenore Harmon provided important input especially with respect to the measures and analyses. In the interview phase, Alan Peshkin provided the essential guidance needed for the design of the interview and analyses of the transcripts.

Special thanks to Sage Acquisitions Editor Jim Nageotte for believing in this book, and to the Sage Women's Mental Health and Development Series Editor, Barbara Okun, for her helpful reviews and feedback. Thanks, too, to the reviewers of draft versions of this book whose contributions improved the clarity and readability of the finished product.

Throughout this project, secretarial support was generously provided by the University of Illinois, College of Education staff and the Department of Educational Psychology staff for preparation of measures, proposals, address lists, correspondence, reports, interview transcripts, computer-based interview data, and the book itself. Most recently, such support was provided by the college word processing staff, directed first by June Chambliss and later by Lana Bates. In our department, Audrey Thompson, Beverly Jackson, and Pam Stynchula provided invaluable assistance with various aspects of the study over a period of years.

Finally, the first author's husband's love, encouragement, support, and patience during the conduct of this study and the writing of this book were immeasurable.

Part I

Introduction

Theoretical Overview: The Longitudinal Study

The counseling needs of women have been a focus for career development theorists interested in optimizing the career development of women since the 1960s. At that time, it was clear that classical career development theory (Super, 1957) did not provide adequate guidance for counselors who wanted to help women reach their career potential (Astin, 1967; Harmon, 1970; Farmer & Bohn, 1970; Osipow, 1966; Psathas, 1968). Several theories of women's career development and/or career choice have emerged in the intervening years (Astin, 1984; Betz & Fitzgerald, 1987; Betz & Hackett, 1983; Farmer, 1978, 1985; Gottfredson, 1981). Some of these are reviewed in Brown, Brooks, and Associates (1996) and Osipow and Fitzgerald (1996).

Recently, Savickas and Lent (1994) reported on findings from a conference on convergence in career development theories. These authors pointed to the continuing seminal influence and value of Super's (1957, 1990) and Holland's (1966, 1985) theories of career development and choice. I concur with this evaluation. However, I also agree with Savickas and Lent's conclusion that promise for a more comprehensive theory, relevant for the diversity of persons in the U.S. population today in terms of ethnicity, gender, and sexual orientation, will likely come from the emerging theories based on social learning theory such as those of Mitchell and Krumboltz (1996) and Lent, Brown, and Hackett (1996).

Donald Super's Career Development Theory

Super's developmental stage theory and related research has been found to fit the experiences of middle-class white boys/men but is less suited to the experiences of persons from poor families, persons of color, or women (Osipow, 1966). Women, for example, have been found to experience more complexity in making their career plans and choices because of the continuing societal expectation that they will take primary responsibility for homemaking and child rearing (Harmon, 1970). Also, sex role socialization experiences affect many young girls in their early years when they learn what roles are appropriate for girls and what roles are not (Gottfredson, 1981). Gottfredson noted how these experiences led girls to constrict their career choices and to compromise their career potential. Chapter 8 in this book focuses on how Super's career development stages are not helpful for persons of color in the United States today because of discrimination in their communities and at school as well as in the workplace. These persons do not satisfactorily navigate even the first career development growth stage (ages 4–14), and because they do not develop adequately at this stage, they are ill prepared to navigate the subsequent exploratory and establishment stages described by Super (1957, 1990).

John Holland's Person-Environment Fit Theory

The other major "classical" career choice theory is that of John Holland (1966, 1985). Holland's theory differs from Super's in that it focuses on making satisfying career choices, ones that match a person's interests with the activities required in a particular occupation. Extensive research on Holland's theory has demonstrated that Holland's "congruence" theory of person-environment fit significantly predicts satisfaction in a career (Spokane, 1996). Holland does not, however, focus on how interests develop; rather, he assumes that interests are like personality attributes and are relatively stable by adolescence, and that the task a person confronts is to learn more about what occupations would match her or his interests. The Self Directed Search (SDS; Holland, Fritzsche, & Powell, 1994) developed by Holland in the 1960s and revised several times since then is widely used by counselors to assist persons with their career decision making. For many persons, including myself, the SDS interest scores may be helpful, either confirming a previous interest as they did for me, or suggesting a fit with an occupation that is appealing but is new to the person. Sometimes the SDS provides information that is consistent with a person's interests, but at the same time the obstacles the person faces related to implementing that choice seem insurmountable, for example, obstacles related to financial resources or to discrimination in that career field because of the color of her or his skin. The number of persons who find the SDS results puzzling or unsatisfying is not insignificant, and it is for this reason that we need to find other ways to help such persons plan their career choices. Also, women tend to obtain significantly higher scores on

Holland's "Social" interests related to occupations in the helping fields, whereas men tend to obtain significantly higher scores on "Realistic" interests related to occupations in the technical fields such as engineering (Holland, Fritzsche, & Powell, 1994). These differences may be due to lack of experience or to relatively stable personality attributes. Holland argues the latter (Spokane, 1996), reinforcing the status quo rather than encouraging adolescent girls to explore interest in activities that they previously may have avoided based on their socialization.

Social Learning Theory Applied to Career Development and Choice

The theoretical framework for the study reported in this book is based on social learning theory. Before I describe how this theory informs our study, I would like to point out how my adaptation of the theory differs from that of Krumboltz (Mitchell & Krumboltz, 1996) and of Lent et al. (1996) referred to previously.

Krumboltz's career development and choice theory is based on Bandura's (1969, 1978, 1986) social learning theory. Krumboltz and his associates have outlined a series of concepts affecting career development related to learning. Such concepts include associational learning, instrumental learning, the influence of genetic endowment on learning, and self-observation learning. Krumboltz has operationalized his theory for model testing and for assisting career counselors by developing several measures. The Career Beliefs Inventory (Krumboltz, 1991) assesses a person's negative and positive beliefs about him- or herself and the environment, which are thought to influence his or her career development processes.

Lent et al. (1996) also draw on Bandura's social learning theory, and have focused on the relevance of Bandura's self-efficacy and related concepts such as causal antecedents and outcomes (i.e., outcome expectations and goals) in their explanatory model for predicting career choice. The model for our study also includes the concept of self-efficacy, but this concept is not central to our theoretical conception whereas it is central in the Lent et al. model.

My theoretical framework, based in social learning theory, is focused on sex role socialization processes as these affect beliefs, attitudes, and self-concepts, which in turn affect motivation, choices, and behaviors, especially for women. My hope is that this theoretical framework will complement the current theoretical models based on social learning theory and contribute to testable ways to capture the negative and sometimes positive effects of sex role socialization and gender on career development and choice.

There are two aspects of Bandura's social learning theory that are central to the theories outlined by Mitchell and Krumboltz, by Lent et al., and by Farmer (1985). First, these models incorporate Bandura's broad emphasis on the triadic determinants of learning and behavior resulting from the recipro-cal interaction of the person with the environment. Second, Bandura's con-cept of personal "agency"—the capability within each individual that gives a person a shaping influence over his or her attitudes and feelings, as well as the ability to anticipate outcomes, and to plan ahead—is embedded in each of these three approaches. This aspect of the theories emphasizes an optimism for change for the better that is within a person's control. This contrasts with theories that view personality as relatively stable by adolescence.

The Theoretical Framework Underlying the Longitudinal Study

I completed a book with Tom Backer in 1977 on women's career develop-ment (Farmer & Backer, 1977), and at that time I was trying to understand what inhibits career and achievement motivation in women—why women achieve less than men in the arts, sciences, and humanities (Commission on the Status of Women, 1970). In spite of the fact that they represented over 40% of the professional labor force at that time and have represented at least 30% of professionals since 1890, fewer women, proportionally, rise to the top of their professions. For example, only 20% of managers were women in 1974. Today, women have made some gains: 43% of women were in top management positions in 1995 (Worton, 1996). Yet in many fields, particu-larly in the physical sciences (25%) and engineering (11%), women remain underrepresented (National Science Foundation, 1994).

I followed the 1977 book with an article outlining an explanatory model for women's career motivation (Farmer, 1978). Figure 1.1 presents this model in a simple but conceptually useful way. The crucial elements in the model are (a) the idea that both personal and situational factors influence women's achievement motivation and career commitment and (b) that some of these factors facilitate while others inhibit optimal career motivation. I knew based on my experience and based on research (Maccoby & Jacklin, 1974) that women are as intelligent as men. I also knew that when their

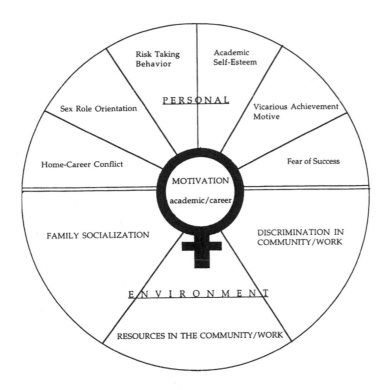

Figure 1.1. A Conceptual Model for Understanding Inhibited Academic/
Career Motivation in Women
SOURCE: Adapted from Farmer (1978).

achievements, in terms of higher education degrees, salary, and recognition, were considered, women lagged behind men (Commission on the Status of Women, 1970). Yet in high school, the measured achievement motivation of women was as high as that of men (Maccoby & Jacklin, 1974). What was happening to cause this gap between women's strivings and their achievements? What were the environmental and internal sources of this achievement gap? These were the primary questions guiding the design of the longitudinal study funded in 1978. Of concern was the waste of human potential both for our society as a whole and for individual women. Underlying this concern was a desire to help women realize their career potential more fully. The next two paragraphs describe the variables listed in Figure 1.1.

The Variables in the 1978 Model

Personal variables. The personal or self-concept variables included in Figure 1.1 were primarily variables related to sex role socialization (Bem, 1981) and other self-concepts found in the literature to affect women's achievement and career motivation in ways that differed from the way they affected men. For example, the literature on gender differences in achievement motivation had identified the inhibiting effect on achievement of women's fear of success (Horner, 1978), lower risk taking behavior (Rubovits, 1975), lower academic self-esteem (Maccoby & Jacklin, 1974), higher vicarious achievement motivation (Lipman-Blumen & Leavitt, 1976), and higher home-career role conflict (Farmer & Bohn, 1970).

Environment variables. The environment or context variables presented in Figure 1.1 (Farmer, 1978) included socialization experiences in the family, such as parental expectations and support or lack of support for girls'/women's career strivings, and socialization experiences in the school and community (Crandall & Battle, 1970; Rubovits, 1975). These latter variables were experiences with teachers and school counselors either providing or not providing support for girls'/women's achievement and career development. Perceptions of economic conditions in the workplace that might encourage or discourage women's achievement and career motivation were also included (U.S. Department of Labor, 1972).

I hoped that by understanding how women came to be where they were in a career, I would be better able to help women optimize their career potential. The theoretical propositions embedded in Figure 1.1 are not new. Personality and learning theorists have reflected similar views as far back as Murray (1938). The work of Endler and Magnusson (1976) was a forceful reminder to educators and psychologists in the 1970s of the importance of explaining learning and behavior as the outcomes of personal and situational factors. The shift away from radical behaviorism (Skinner, 1953), which largely discounted input from the individual, was timely because it returned a sense of power to women that was within themselves and under their control, at least to some degree. Bandura was in the forefront of this theoretical shift from a focus on situational learning. Many of Bandura's concepts related to social learning theory echo Murray's and Endler and Magnusson's emphasis on learning as an interactive process between the person and her or his environment (Bandura, 1969, 1978, 1986). Bandura's broad theoretical framework

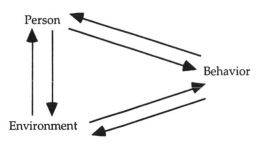

Figure 1.2. A Model of Reciprocal Transactions
SOURCE: Based on Bandura (1986).

is presented in Figure 1.2. He noted that

> explanations of human behavior have generally favored unidirectional causal
> models emphasizing either environmental or internal determinants of behav-
> ior. In social learning theory, causal processes are conceptualized in terms of
> reciprocal determinism. Viewed from this perspective, psychological func-
> tioning involves a continuous reciprocal interaction between behavioral, cog-
> nitive, and environmental influences. (Bandura, 1978, p. 344)

This theoretical orientation guided the selection of measures assessed in
1980 and in 1990 as well as the design of the interview protocol for our longitudinal study. Figure 1.3 presents the conceptual model we used to investigate
the behaviors, self-concepts, and experiences that influenced our participants' achievement motivation and career choices. The model assumes that
over time a broad range of interacting influences shape interest in and selection of a career.

Social learning theory is optimistic in that it allows for behaviors to
change over time as a result of new experiences, new ideas, and self-
perceptions and plans. Astin (1984) refers to this potential for change as the
"structure of opportunity." Prior sex role socialization may enhance or limit a
woman's view of the opportunity structure but new possibilities exist
throughout life. The role of the person as agent in her or his learning—and
choosing—and behaving is an important aspect of social learning theory. The
fact that persons are capable of forethought, learning from observing others,
self-reflection, and setting internal standards for their own behavior and
choices points to the potential for self-determination. This is relevant to understanding women's career development. Operating within many realistic
constraints, women still may have much to say about their destinies.

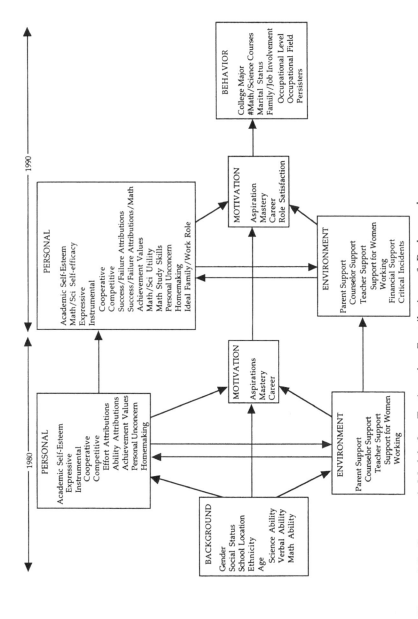

Figure 1.3. Conceptual Model for Testing the Contribution of Background, Personal, Environment, and Motivation Factors to Occupational Choice (Behavior)

The evidence presented in this book related to social learning theory is provided primarily by the stories participants told us in the interviews we conducted. Two aspects of social learning theory—how the personalities of individuals affect their learning and choices, and how the experiences people have in their families, schools, and communities affect their learning and choices—are illustrated by various participants. Throughout the book, the stories of two participants are told in greater detail to illustrate these two themes. The first theme, how personality affects choices, is illustrated by the story of Gena. Later, in Chapter 4, the story of Norma is told to illustrate the second theme. Gena exemplifies a person who takes charge of her own life. She is a Native American woman who grew up in the inner city. She said:

We grew up in a neighborhood, it was a brand new housing development. My parents bought a house and we had like thirty kids on the block. So there was always competitions, games going on and things like that. So I grew up there with a bunch of kids and all the games I played involved competition of some type or another. And it was fun, fun winning, I mean. I didn't mind losing to the extent where I was a sore loser, you know; some kids hated losing. They'd take the ball away and go home. I just liked to play.

Gena is now a mechanical engineer and planning on earning a master's degree. When we asked her if the guidance counselor at Metro High School had helped her plan for her college major, she said,

We had a guidance counselor that was supposed to help us with choosing colleges and stuff. She was this old lady who I thought was half crazy. Basically we went and did our own research up in the guidance office. I mean, we went through the files ourselves, and that's how I found out about engineering and stuff. I think if it was up to her she'd have us being nuns or something. We went up there and asked her questions. We used to go and talk to her all the time but she really never gave us any helpful information. She let us look through the files, do our own little research. But she never told us about scholarships and this and that. We used to go up to the library and fool around, so then we started to go into the guidance department. It was probably just by accident that we thought, maybe we should look through these files.

We asked Gena how she came to pick engineering. She said,

When I was in high school, if I hadn't gone out and sought out engineering on my own, no one would have ever recommended that to me. It was like for the men, you know! Even though my best subjects were math and science. My junior year in high school I had physics. And I started with the upper math classes. And I really liked physics and that's when I started going to the guidance office all the time looking through the books and things like that. I found things in engineering and started reading up about it. And that's basically how I found out about it. And then I started contacting the schools. Well, they send you everything so I looked at their curriculums and what classes are involved and then I went and visited some colleges and talked to their people. So that's really how I learned about it. Like math and science were my best subjects, and my favorites. So I was looking in the fields that involved math and science that would also be lucrative. I started looking into engineering and it really sounded like it would fit my particular skills and it sounded interesting to me, solving problems. And the fact that there were very few women in it was another inspiration to me. Well I made it through the first semester in college. I don't know how—I realized from talking to people that some of their high schools were a lot more advanced. They did college prep courses which our school didn't offer. I didn't even realize that I could of gone to a much better high school. But, I did as well as I could. Someone once told me that—I always remember this—the world is run by C students. Grades are important but that's not the end of the world because a lot of students get a B or a C. This person said, the world's run by C students, think about that and don't get so stressed out about grades. I had to struggle that first semester at college to catch up with everybody else. I just always wanted to be best in the class. And when I was in grammar school I was at the top. When I was in high school it was a little bit tougher. And when I got to college, forget it. I was in the middle of the pack. Which was the hardest thing about the first semester in college. It was a rude awakening. But I made it!

Gena's ability to get the information she needed, and to stick with her goal even when she encountered obstacles, served her well. The person who is able to exercise some control over her choices is a person who has a kind of self-assurance that she can succeed, no matter what. In spite of sexism in her high school, and lack of career guidance, she found a way to choose a career that suited her interests and personality, and she found a way to finance it, in spite of a lack of family financial resources.

In my own early years, I was not planful, and by the time I finally got to study for a Ph.D. in my mid-30s, I realized that if I had been more planful I wouldn't have wasted so many years floundering. I became convinced at that time, and remain convinced, that persons who lack planfulness can be taught the relevant skills (Farmer, 1976a) as early as grade school. At that time I adopted a cognitive-behavioral theoretical approach to counseling based on information processing models (Miller, Galanter, & Pribram, 1960). The goal of such counseling is to empower a client who lacks the initiative demonstrated by Gena by teaching the client problem-solving and decision-making skills.

More of Gena's story is told in Chapters 3 and 4. Gena was pregnant when we interviewed her and her plans for combining work and family are discussed in Chapters 6 and 9 as well.

The measures assessed in 1980 and 1990 for our longitudinal study are briefly described next. Details on these measures—their item content, their reliability and validity—are contained in Farmer (1985) and Farmer, Wardrop, Anderson, and Risinger (1995). These variables and related measures will be referred to later in the book; some readers may wish to refer back later to the section that follows, which describes the variables in Figure 1.3. However, a detailed knowledge of these variables is not essential to understanding the main themes in the book.

Measures in the Phase 1 (1980) Model

Some of the variables in the 1978 model were retained for the model of women's career and achievement motivation tested in the 1980 study, or Phase 1 of the longitudinal study reported in this book. The proposal to obtain funding for this study was written in 1977. Figure 1.3 presents the model and the variables assessed in 1980. Several of the measures used to assess these variables were borrowed or adapted from existing measures based on my belief that measure development is a time-consuming process and that it is better to use a measure already in existence, given that there is adequate reliability and validity evidence to support it.

Background measures. The model included several background variables based on prior theory and research, especially the status attainment literature (Sewell & Hauser, 1975). Socioeconomic status, gender, ethnicity, and geographic location (rural, urban, inner city) were included. Also, age was included as a variable based on Super's (1957) career development stage theory. Age turned out not to be a useful variable in our study because the age span of the 1980 participants who were 9th and 12th graders was three to five years (13-18) and fit within Super's "exploration stage" of career development. The only age difference found in the 1980 data was for parent support for career plans, with younger students scoring higher on this measure (Farmer, 1985).

Ability was included in the background variable set based on the relationship of ability to achievement motivation found in the literature (Atkinson, 1978) as well as to career aspiration (Sewell & Hauser, 1975). We had to be content to collect achievement data to represent ability rather than IQ data.

Personal measures. The research team developed some of the personal measures for the 1980 study: cooperative achievement style, success/failure attributions, and achievement values. Others were adapted from existing measures. The personal measures for academic self-esteem (Coopersmith, 1980), sex role orientation (measured by Expressive and Instrumental scales derived from factor analyses of Bem's Sex Role Inventory, 1981), and fear of success (measured by Spence & Helmreich's, 1978, Personal Unconcern measure) were consistent with the 1978 model. The measures of cooperative (Farmer, 1985) and competitive achievement style (Spence & Helmreich, 1978) replaced the vicarious achievement motive variable from the earlier model (Figure 1.1) based on findings on achievement motivation by researchers such as Alper (1974) and Bardwick (1971). The risk-taking behavior variable was replaced by measures assessing success/failure attributions on the four dimensions identified by Weiner (1974): ability, effort, luck, and task difficulty. These attributions differ significantly for gender with girls/women exhibiting an achievement-inhibiting pattern significantly more than boys/men (Frieze, Whiteley, Hanusa, & McHugh, 1982). Instead of the home-career conflict, a measure of home role salience was included in the 1980 model (Figure 1.3) derived from Super and Cuhla's (1976) Work Salience Inventory. A measure assessing achievement values was developed for this study based on Super's (1970) research demonstrating the important role of values in career development and choice.

Environment measures. The environment measures used in 1980 were similar to variables in the earlier model (Figure 1.1) and were developed by the research team for parent support, teacher support, counselor support, and support for women working (the latter adapted from a series of "myths" published by the U.S. Department of Labor, Women's Bureau, 1972).

Motivation measures. The motivation variables, the dependent or outcome variables in the model (Figure 1.3), were expanded from two (i.e., career motivation and achievement motivation) to three. The motivation variable added was career aspiration/education level. The motivation variables were measured using Spence and Helmreich's (1978) measure of "mastery" for achievement motivation. The choice of this measure was based on the view that achievement motivation may be expressed by achievements in a broad range of contexts encompassing personal, leisure, and social contexts as well as work and school contexts, and that this approach would more accurately gauge girls'/women's achievement motivation. The mastery measure assesses short-range mastery motivation to achieve and persist on challenging tasks. Career motivation was measured using Super and Cuhla's (1976) Career Salience scale from their Role Salience Inventory. The Career Salience scale assesses long-range commitment to a career role. The measure for aspiration motivation was a combination of (a) the prestige level of the occupation/career realistically aspired to and (b) the educational level aspired to, and was based on the theory and research of the status attainment theorists (Sewell & Hauser, 1975).

Measures in the Phase 2 (1990) Model

Most of the variables measured in 1980 were assessed again with the same students when they were 10 years older in 1990. Some additional variables were assessed based on the developmental stage of our participants in 1990 when they were 23–28 years old. Other variables were added that were found in the literature to be related to women's career development and choice during the intervening decade. A third reason for adding variables in 1990 was that the study had been narrowed from a focus on "why women don't contribute as much to the arts, humanities, and sciences" to a focus on science, especially the factors related to women's persistence in a science career if they had expressed interest in such a career when they were in high school. The reason for this focus was the greater lag in women's participation rates in the natural sciences and in engineering compared with the arts and humanities.

Among new variables assessed in 1990, three were adapted for the new focus on science: The achievement values measure was adapted for math/science and named "math/science utility" (Eccles, Adler, & Meece, 1984). The attribution measure was adapted to assess success/failure experiences specifically in math. A new math self-efficacy measure was added, based on the research of Betz and Hackett (1983). This measure assessed participants' confidence in their math ability at various time periods in their education. An additional measure, math study skills (Ames & Archer, 1988), was also added, consistent with the focus on math as a critical filter for entry into challenging science careers (Sells, 1975).

Personal measures. In the personal set, the variables from 1980 were all repeated in 1990: academic self-esteem, expressive and instrumental self-concepts, cooperative and competitive achievement styles, personal uncon-cern, home role salience, achievement values, and success/failure attribu-tions. As noted above, we added math self-efficacy, math/science utility, and math study skills based on the literature on gender differences in math and sci-ence (Ames & Archer, 1988; Betz & Hackett, 1983; Eccles et al., 1984). For math/science self-efficacy, we assessed, in addition to the math self-efficacy measure noted above, participants' confidence in their ability to handle vari-ous courses they had taken in math and science in high school and in college (Betz & Hackett, 1983). We asked, "How confident do you feel about your math/science ability in this type of math/science course?" Given the missing data, because respondents had not taken the same courses, we were unable to use much of this information in our statistical analyses.

Environment measures. In the environment variable set, the measures from 1980 were all repeated in 1990: parent, teacher, counselor support for girls'/women's school achievements and career plans, and a measure of sup-port for women working. We added a measure assessing financial support re-ceived for a college education. We also assessed whether or not financial aid for college was a necessary condition for college attendance.

Behavior measures. We added a behavior set that included assessment of the number of semesters of high school and college math and science each participant had taken. We assessed their college majors, college degrees com-pleted, and current occupations. In addition, we assessed marital status, number of children, and percentage of time devoted to work and family.

Some Assumptions Underlying Our Interpretations

Some important assumptions underlie our study, especially related to what good career planning and choices are. For women and for men, I believe that career planning must take place within a life planning framework, and that such plans must take into account other life roles such as spouse or part-ner and parent as well as other personal roles (Farmer & Backer, 1977). This is especially true for women. This assumption is consistent with the life span developmental framework elaborated by Donald Super, whose published work on this topic spans more than five decades (Super, 1990).

A second assumption is that choice of a career field should be consistent with a woman's or a man's abilities, aptitudes, values, and interests, and should be realistic in light of societal opportunities and constraints. Often a woman's socialization has instilled values in her that limit the choices she considers. Women are prone to the home-career conflict, which has a dampening effect on their career choices (Farmer & Bohn, 1970; Farmer, 1984; Tipping & Farmer, 1991). Women need help to disentangle those values that are personally important to them from others they have been taught that may be less important. For example, the values a woman learns related to her role as mother and wife may conflict with her values for a career, and she may need help to think through what is really important to her. This aspect of women's career development is not adequately addressed in Super's (1990) or Holland's (1985) theories.

A third assumption is that women are not using their full potential in the workforce for many reasons, among them their experiences leading them to believe that their family, friends, and society in general don't care whether they work or not (Betz & Hackett, 1983). Betz and Hackett refer to the "null environment" that women experience with respect to their careers, an environment that appears indifferent to their interest in a career and their preparation for a career. Girls get messages to "do what you want to do" and "be happy," whereas boys get the message, "Get good grades so you can get into the best schools and be successful in a career."

Subjectivity

It is my belief that all interpretations of data—of science—are biased in some ways. Interpretation of qualitative interview data is especially vulnerable to the personal biases of the researcher. Glesne and Peshkin (1992) encourage the qualitative researcher to identify her or his subjectivity and make it explicit to the reader. These authors also believe that early personal experiences often determine these subjective biases. So I will tell you some things about my early experiences that I think are relevant to how I have interpreted the data.

I was born in a rural part of Ontario, Canada, and grew up working in the fields and interacting with women who were strong, intelligent, and well educated. In fact, the women in my part of the world were better educated than the men. As a result, I have an abiding belief in women's intelligence, strength, and potential for contributing to society through their careers as well as through their families. These experiences have made me more optimistic about the potential and future for women than are some writers on this topic.

Second, I have a strong commitment to helping the "underdog." A contributing factor was my shyness as a child, which frequently led to a feeling of being left out. My own wanting to be included has led me to want to help others to feel included. I was also somewhat dyslexic in my early school years. This expressed itself in my spelling and inability to grasp the rules of grammar. I recall one day in high school when my geography teacher was returning exams to us. He held up a paper and said, "This person had 54 spelling mistakes." Then he handed the paper to me.

Another aspect of my subjectivity is derived from the early work of Karen Horney (1945), who believed that women are human beings first; that is, the common ground between men and women is larger than their biological differences. This view is one I adopted from Horney when I was in graduate school in the 1950s, and have found it to be a powerful attitude for counseling others as well as counseling myself. This distinction is related to the concepts of the emic and etic aspects of peoples and cultures (Kluckhohn, 1956). *Emic* refers to universal phenomena across cultures, whereas *etic* refers to those characteristics that are unique to a particular culture. Some authors prefer to view women as existing primarily within an etic world, one separate from men (for example, Bernard, 1981; Gilligan, 1982). I do not take this view. I am convinced, however, that a person's outlook on life and the human condition affects the way she or he behaves, and that this outlook may differ from mine. Persons who have experienced discrimination and other forms of disadvantage in our society may well exist within "two worlds." We included a theme in our interview analyses that we call "World View" (see Appendix E, "Analysis Themes"). This theme was an attempt reduce the effect of my subjectivity and to capture the participants' perspective on life and how it affected their behavior.

This is my second book about women and careers. The first was written 20 years ago in the heyday of "sex equity" fervor (Farmer & Backer, 1977). I recall how at that time some of my friends, after spending a few hours in the library reading the research on women and work, said how depressing they found this experience. I, on the contrary, found such reading stimulating. I was riding a crest of optimism about the future and equity in the workplace for women. Twenty years later, my optimism has been toned down, not lost. There have been important gains for women during those decades, but we are still a long way from sex equity in the workplace and in our society as a whole. The goal of equality, justice for all, and parity in the workplace for women eludes us. We are in a decade where *affirmative action* and *feminist* are dirty words to many, rather than ideals that beckon.

It is a dream of mine to place the theory of women's career development and choice within the broader context of time, social change, and history. Humankind has evolved through many stages and no doubt will continue to evolve. Yet there is a constancy within these changes that relates to living, loving, procreating, and nurturing. It is within this larger context that we present this book, a book that maps the present better than the future. The book provides snapshots that contain pointers for change—change that could improve the quality of life for both women and men in the coming decades.

The next section describes the procedures used in the study, the participants, and the interview.

The Longitudinal Study

In this section, I describe the longitudinal study on which the findings in this book are based. The participants, their high schools, and the interview are all described briefly. Some supplemental information is provided in the appendixes, and requests for copies of the measures may be addressed to me at the University of Illinois. The study took place during three time periods: 1980, 1990, 1991-1993. The first two periods involved collection of questionnaire data. The third involved interviews, and it is these latter data that are a primary source for this book. Information in this chapter is organized around the phases. Table 1.1 provides some information on the samples in each of the three time periods.

Phase 1 (1980)

The focus of the study in 1980 was the career motivation patterns of high schools students, both women and men. Several colleagues helped to design this phase of the study, and several graduate students assisted in the data collection and analyses (see the Acknowledgments). We began our study with support from the National Institute of Education. At that time, we collected information and questionnaire data from all 9th and 12th grade students in six randomly selected high schools in the Midwest. The sample included two schools each from rural, suburban, and inner-city school districts. These schools were selected to be representative of the U.S. population, and met

Table 1.1 Descriptive Information for the Three Research Phases

| | Male | Female | 1980/1990 Science | | 1980/1990 Nonscience | | Total |
			New to Science (female, male)	Science Persisters (female, male)	Science Nonpersisters (female, male)	Other Careers (female, male)	
Phase 1: 1980	1055	1027					2082[b]
Phase 2: 1980/1990[a]							
1980 science aspirants	77	96		70 (35, 35)	103 (61, 42)		173[c]
1990 science versus nonscience	192	267	43 (26, 17)	70 (35, 35)	103 (61, 42)	243 (145, 98)	459[d]
Phase 3: Interviews	48	57	6 (6, 0)	46 (21, 25)	47 (25, 21)	7 (5, 2)	105

a. Research in Phase 2 involved matched samples so that participants who completed and returned questionnaires in 1980 and 1990 were used.
b. Research based on complete data for this sample appeared in Farmer (1985; n = 1,863).
c. Research based on these data appeared in Farmer, Wardrop, Anderson, and Risinger (1995; n = 173).
d. Research based on these data was presented at the American Psychological Association annual meeting 1995, and at a National Science Foundation conference, December 1995 (n = 459).

that criterion with the possible exception of the deep South (D. Sudman, Survey Research Laboratory, University of Illinois, personal communication, 1978). More detail on these schools is provided later in this chapter and also in Appendixes A and B. The measures included those listed in Figure 1.3. Several graduate students and I went to each school twice and collected the data in two administrations of one hour each. At that time, we told the high school students that we wanted to follow up with them in a few years and that we would be contacting them by letter at the time of the follow-up. We obtained questionnaires from 2,082 students; however, after we checked for missing data, we had a usable sample of 1,863. Findings from this phase of the study are reported in Farmer (1983, 1985) and elsewhere.

Participant Schools

In 1980, I visited with the principals and then either with some of the teachers or with the counselor at the six participant schools. All the data were collected at that time by women who were doctoral-level counseling psychology students.

The schools had somewhat different personalities. The suburban schools were the largest, and the buildings' inside environments were busy and noisy. The rural schools were the smallest, with an atmosphere of friendly bustle. The inner-city schools were parochial and were the quietest and cleanest. Difficulty in obtaining access to public schools in the inner city led us to use parochial schools to achieve ethnic representativeness.

The six participant schools have been given pseudonyms for purposes of protecting their anonymity. The rural schools are Farmerville and Country. The suburban schools are Garden City and Suburban. The inner-city schools are Metro and City. Table 1.2 and Figure 1.4 provide the socioeconomic and educational range of the parents of our participants in 1980 as well as the ethnic and gender composition. Data on education and occupation levels, broken down by school, are provided in Appendixes A and B. It will be clear from a perusal of these data that our participant schools were not very affluent, and although randomly drawn, these schools tended to have proportionately more parents in the lower half of the socioeconomic and educational distributions. The fact that only 14% of the fathers and 7% of the mothers had a four-year or higher college degree indicates that for many of our participants, mentoring for career planning and college was less available. In the school descriptions

Table 1.2 Some Participant High School Background Characteristics: Fathers' and
Mothers' Education and Occupational Prestige, Phase 1 ($n = 1,863$)[a]

Characteristic	%[b]
Father's educational level	
less than high school	24
H.S. diploma	46
Jr. college degree	12
B.A.	9
M.A.	4
Ph.D. or professional	1
Mother's educational level	
less than high school	18
H.S. diploma	56
Jr. college degree	11
R.N. (nurse)	6
B.A.	5
M.A.	2
Ph.D. or professional	0
Father's occupational level[c]	
76-100 quartile	13
51-75 quartile	23
26-50 quartile	36
0-25 quartile	28
Mother's educational level	
76-100 quartile	5
51-75 quartile	27
26-50 quartile	22
0-25 quartile	16
Mother not working	30

a. Mean parent occupational level in Phase 2 was similar (i.e., 48 on the Duncan SEI scale) to that for the Phase 1 larger sample; 1,863 represents usable data.
b. Percentage may not add up to 100% because of incomplete responses on some questions.
c. Occupational level was based on assessment of parent occupation using the Duncan Socioeconomic Index, revised (Stevens & Cho, 1985).

that follow, the full 1980 data set is used as it better represents the student characteristics in these schools as a whole.

Rural schools. Farmerville and Country high schools had the smallest enrollments, representing 18% of our 1980 sample, and were relatively ethnically homogeneous. Farmerville was 89% white; Country was 94% white. The percentage of fathers and mothers who had earned a four-year college degree or better was relatively similar to the average for our six schools (Table 1.2; Figure 1.4). The number of employed mothers was also similar to the average for the six schools (i.e., 70%). Competitive sports were important at

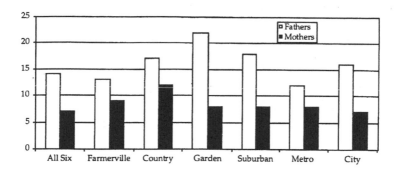

Figure 1.4. Parents Who Have A Four-year College Degree Or Higher In Participant Schools: Phase One, 1980

both schools. Both schools had a vocational curriculum and a college prep curriculum. These were not formal "tracks"; however, students planning a vocational technical career could choose to work half days in the community during their junior and senior years and attend school the rest of the day. Both schools had counselors and held "career days" to introduce students to a variety of career options. Science teachers brought scientists in from various fields to describe their work to students. Both boys and girls participated in science clubs as well as in regional science competitions. It was possible to take math and science courses throughout the four years of high school; however, advanced courses (i.e., calculus) in math and science (i.e., microbiology) were not offered.

Suburban schools. The Garden City and Suburban schools had the largest enrollments, representing 46% of the 1980 sample, and also were relatively ethnically homogeneous. Garden City was 92% white and Suburban was 90% white. At Garden City school, 21% of fathers had earned a four-year college degree, which is somewhat higher than the average of 14% for our six schools. The proportion of mothers who had earned a four-year college degree or higher was comparable to the average for the six schools. At Garden City, 80% of the mothers were employed, compared with the average of 70% (Table 1.2). At Suburban school, the proportion of fathers and mothers who had earned a four-year college degree or higher was close to the average for the six schools (Table 1.2). The percentage of mothers that were employed at Suburban High School was also similar to that for the six schools. Our two suburban high schools emphasized competitive sports. Band was also an important. Both schools had a vocational option for their students; persons choosing this option attended a local community college for half of the school day. A college prep curriculum was also in place. Both schools had a school counselor and held a career day once a year to introduce students to a range of different careers.

Inner-city schools. Metro and City schools had moderate enrollments, representing 36% of our sample, and were ethnically diverse. Metro was 15% African American, 14% Hispanic, 3% Asian and Native American, and 68% white. City school was 36% African American, 37% Hispanic, 12% Asian and Native American, and 15% white. The proportion of fathers and mothers who had earned a four-year college degree or higher was about average (14%) at City High School. At Metro, the proportion of fathers who had earned a four-year college degree or higher was 11%, compared with the average of 14% for the six schools. The proportion of mothers who had earned a four-year college degree or higher at Metro was similar to that for all six schools. At Metro, 65% of the mothers were employed; at City, 73% were. Many of the parents of Metro students worked or had worked in the failing steel industry in the south end of the city. Several had been laid off in the years our participants were growing up. The public schools in this metropolitan area were difficult for researchers to gain access to. Our inner-city schools were parochial private schools for which parents paid tuition. These parents were not affluent and had to sacrifice to send their children these schools. A few of our student participants were on athletic scholarships. Competitive sports were important at both schools, but especially so at Metro. Band appeared to be more important at City. Both schools had vocational and college prep curricula. The vocational programs used a work-study approach that had these students work half a day at a relevant work site and then spend the other half of the day at school. Students who graduated from these schools and went on to college to major in engineering found that they were poorly prepared for college calculus. Both schools had counselors and both held annual college recruiting days. On these occasions, representatives from various colleges and from the U.S. Army, Navy and Air Force presented their programs to students.

There were several special programs available to students in these inner-city schools sponsored by either government or local agencies. Prominent among these was the INROADS project designed to introduce promising minority students to preengineering curricula on weekends and in the summer. Another project, sponsored by a local newspaper, gave promising minority

Table 1.3　Longitudinal Sample Characteristics: Phase 1 (1980) and Phase 2 (1990)

	Phase 1[a]		Phase 2[b]	
	Sample: 2,082 (1980)		Sample: 459 (1990)	
	#	%	#	%
Gender				
Men	1,055	50.7	192	41.6
Women	1,027	49.3	267	58.4
Ethnicity				
American Indian	107	5.1	2	.4
Asian			4	.9
Black	152	7.3	22	4.8
Hispanic[c]	175	8.4	38	8.3
White	1,428	68.6	393	85.6
Mixed[d]	220	10.5		
High school location				
rural	345	16.6	123	26.8
suburban	948	45.5	203	44.2
inner city	789	37.9	133	29.0
High school math grades				
A	298	14.3	93	20.3
B	439	25.9	141	30.7
C	582	28.0	127	27.7
D	429	20.6	86	18.7
missing	234	11.2	12	2.6
High school English grades				
A	345	17.0	130	28.3
B	623	29.9	149	32.5
C	685	32.9	140	30.5
D	247	11.9	33	7.2
missing	173	8.3	7	1.5

a. The *n* for this sample represents the number of returned questionnaires (1,863 of these were complete).
b. The *n* for this sample represents the number of completed questionnaires.
c. Two participants listed under Hispanic were biracial, Asian-Hispanic.
d. Persons who checked this category in 1980 were classified in 1990 into an ethnic minority group if they said either parent belonged to that group (i.e., Native American father, Irish mother = minority). Others who wrote that their parents were European were classified as white.

students experiences in journalism. Local hospitals had programs for students interested in working in a hospital setting.

Phase 2 (1990)

In preparation for collecting data in 1990, we revisited the six schools to obtain the most current addresses in their files for our 1980 participants. In addition, we met with some of our 1980 participants over dinner in a location near their former high school to discuss various ways for updating our address lists. These alums were very enthusiastic about our research and extremely helpful to us; we were able to provide them with our final address lists for their use in planning their tenth-year reunions.

The Matched 1980-1990 Sample

In 1990, we collected data from the 1980 participants, this time with financial support from the National Science Foundation and the University of Illinois Research Board. We obtained mailing addresses for about 1,500 of the 1,863 members of the 1980 sample, and 459 of these returned usable data. The low return rate was likely due to (a) undelivered mail and (b) the length of the questionnaire (54 pages). The revised measure is described in Farmer, Wardrop, Anderson, and Risinger (1995), and copies are available from the author. The 1990 questionnaire included a question asking participants if they would be willing to be interviewed, thus setting the stage for Phase 3.

We expected that participants completing the questionnaires in 1990 would be biased in some ways (i.e., brighter, more successful) compared with the larger 1980 sample. We compared the two samples on gender, ethnicity, ability, socioeconomic status (SES), and school location to determine whether there was sample bias on these dimensions. These comparisons are presented in Table 1.3 except for SES. Women represented 49% of the sample in 1980 and 58% in 1990; majority white participants were less represented in 1980 than in 1990. A more detailed review for ethnicity indicated that the proportions of Hispanics in 1980 and 1990 were similar (i.e., 8%), whereas for African Americans the proportion in 1980 was 7% and in 1990, 5%. SES was similar, with means of 49 and 48 for the 1980 and 1990 samples, respectively, based on the Duncan Socioeconomic Index (Stevens & Cho, 1985). In terms of school location, proportionately more rural participants but fewer inner-city participants responded in 1990 compared with 1980. The proportion for suburban students remained similar for the two time periods. In terms of ability, the 1990 sample had more students who had A- and B-level math GPAs (51%) in high school compared with the 1980 sample (40%), and 59% either had completed a four-year college degree or higher or were enrolled in school. In 1992, the National Center for Education Statistics (1995) reported that 26% of men and 22% of women age 25-34 had completed four-year college degrees. From these data, we can infer that our 1990 sample was biased in terms of the number of participants who had completed college.

Both in 1980 and in 1990, 9th and 12th graders had similar proportions in our sample.

The Science Persister/Nonpersister Subsample

In Phase 2, we identified the participants who aspired to a science or technology career in 1980 when they were in high school ($n = 173$; see Table 1.1). Then we further refined this subsample into those who persisted in a science or technology career in 1990 and those who did not. We used some fairly complicated criteria for determining whether a career was in a science or technology field. A combination of the U.S. Department of Labor (1991) classification system and John Holland's (1985; Gottfredson & Holland, 1989) occupational classification system was used. (See Appendix E.) We classified 70 as persisters and 103 as nonpersisters; of these, 144 were white and 29 were of minority ethnicity. Findings related to this subsample are reported in Farmer, Wardrop, Anderson, and Risinger (1995).

The Science/Nonscience Subsample

A second set of subsamples was formed from the matched 1980-1990 participants comparing those who were in a science or technology career in 1990 with whose who were in other fields. As you might expect, there were some participants who, although they had not expressed interest in a science career in 1980, were now in a science or technology career ($n = 43$). The combination of the 70 science persisters and the others in a science or technology career provided a subsample of 113 persons (see Table 1.1). The remainder of the 1980-1990 matched sample ($n = 346$) was compared on the dimensions of the theoretical model (Figure 1.3) with the science sample. Findings from this comparison are reported in Farmer, Wardrop, and Crabtree (1995) and in Crabtree, Farmer, Anderson, and Wardrop (1995). Throughout the book, these findings are presented in summary form when relevant to the discussion of interview data.

The quantitative data and related tables are helpful for an overview of the more generalizable findings from this longitudinal study. The focus in this book, however, is the qualitative data, which are not intended to be generalizable; rather, they are intended to help explain the complexity of the career development and choice process experienced by the young people we interviewed.

Phase 3 (1991–1993)

We focused the interview portion of the study on women and men who had expressed an interest in a science or technology career in 1980 when they were still in high school. As noted above, by 1990 the focus of our longitudinal study had shifted from a broad one on women in the arts, sciences, and humanities to women's participation in the sciences. Although, in the 20 or more years since affirmative action legislation was enacted, women had increased their participation in some of the career fields where they were previously underrepresented, they continued to be underrepresented in the sciences, especially in the natural sciences such as physics and chemistry and in technical fields such as mechanical and aeronautical engineering (National Science Foundation, 1994).

After we had analyzed our data from Phase 2, it became clear that our questionnaire data had provided some important clues to understanding women's career choice process, but these data had also raised some puzzling issues that could only be answered by talking directly to some of our participants. For example, we found that the women who had changed their aspirations from a science or technology field to some other field had, on average, significantly higher long-range career commitment (Farmer, Wardrop, Anderson, & Risinger, 1995). We also found that less than half of the students aspiring to a science or technology career in high school had persisted in one of these careers 10 years later (see Table 1.1). Why was this so?

Peshkin (1988) has distinguished qualitative research from quantitative research: Quantitative research seeks generalizations and representativeness and tends to mask unique and nonlinear aspects of a phenomena. Qualitative research, however, is capable of explaining and describing the complexity of a phenomena. For example, through observation of the interaction of high school students and parents in an interracial school for a period of several months, Peshkin found that ethnic stereotypes of African American adolescent behavior often did not hold up under close examination, particularly when these behaviors were observed in various contexts such as school and family. In school, there was much more ethnic mixing in friendship groups than was acceptable within the family. Using qualitative processes, we hoped to clarify the complexity of the career development and choice process for women in the interview phase of our study. This phase of the study was supported by the National Science Foundation.

Selection of the Interview Subsample

For the interview subsample, we selected those who had, in 1990, agreed to be interviewed from among those we identified as persons who had aspired to a career in science or technology in 1980. We chose this sample to help us better understand what had occurred during the intervening 10-year period that sustained some of these persons in their science choice and discouraged others. There were 173 persons in the science and technology subsample (see Table 1.1) and 153 of these had agreed to be interviewed. Among this subsample were 47 persons who now lived more than 200 miles from the researcher's home base, with some as far away as Germany, South America, and Alaska. We could not afford to travel to interview them. We did, however, compare these 47 persons with the rest of the science and technology volunteer subsample on gender and ethnicity. We found that the gender distribution was similar, but ethnicity was different: 91% were white compared with 79% in the nondistant, remaining group, and 9% were minority compared with 21% in the remaining group. We concluded that fewer minority persons had moved away from their home states compared with white participants. However, this allowed us to interview proportionally more minority persons. It may be interesting to note that 61% of the interview participants had earned a four-year college degree or higher, indicating that the interview sample was biased even more than the 1980-1990 quantitative sample toward college graduates.

At the time we identified the interview sample in 1990, we had not perfected our procedure for identifying participants in science and technology. We interviewed 13 persons (11 women and 2 men) who were classified incorrectly. Six of the women were in a science or technology career by 1990, but had not aspired to these career fields in 1980. Seven interviewees had never aspired to a science or technology career. Holland's classification for Investigative (Gottfredson & Holland, 1989) includes such occupations as sculptors and dancers. When we discovered this, we added the U.S. Department of Labor (1991) science classification procedure and were thus able to exclude persons interested in careers such as dancing.

The final count for the interview subsample was 105. Of these, 57 were women, 27 of whom were in science careers (21 persisters and 6 new to science); 25 were in other career fields; and 5, as noted above, were included who previously had not seriously considered a science or technology career. Of the 48 men, 25 were science persisters, 21 were nonpersisters, and 2 had never considered a science or technology career. Table 1.4 provides frequencies for interview participants for gender, ethnicity, school location, grade in 1980, and whether or not they were immigrants to America or children of immigrants.

We resisted the temptation to compare these 105 interview participants with the larger science subsample of 173 from Phase 2 because such a comparison could mislead the reader into thinking in terms of generalizations, a quantitative mind-set. Instead, the life stories of the interview participants are told primarily to uncover anomalies in the quantitative findings and to provide a better understanding of the complexities of the career development and choice process.

The Interview Protocol

The interview protocol included questions to elicit information on early experiences leading up to each participant's present situation (see Appendix C). Also, because women are typically socialized to take primary responsibility for homemaking (Farmer, 1985; Gilbert, 1985, 1994b), many women planning for a career consider trade-offs between career and family roles in making their choices. The interview questions were designed to obtain information on how these women and men thought about the intersection between home and work roles. We invited participants to identify what, if any, experiences, during which time periods, were most influential in their career and life choices. We wanted to identify both personal and environmental influences, and both positives and negatives, consistent with social learning theory. Environmental influences included experiences and feelings in the family, school, and community as well as important persons in the participant's life, including parents, siblings, teachers, friends, relatives, counselors, and neighbors. Personal questions involved behaviors, coping style, values, interests, abilities, goals, needs, feelings, attitudes, and beliefs.

The overarching goal was to obtain a more complete picture of the individual's life story, but each interview also covered general areas specific to our purpose. The order for covering these areas was not rigidly held to because the interviewee might spontaneously discuss something early in the interview and the interviewer could then follow the interviewee's lead, provided it was consistent with the general overall purpose.

The general areas for the first interview included (a) a clear description of the participant's current work or career activities; (b) a clear description of the work environment in which the participant worked; (c) the participant's view of the relationship of her or his work/career role to other life

Table 1.4 Phase 3 Interviewee Frequencies by School, Gender, Grade in School, and Ethnicity (*n* = 105)

			Grade				
School	*Women*	*Men*	*9th*	*12th*	*Minority*[a]	*Majority*	*Immigrant*[b]
Rural							
Farmerville	10	5	9	6	1	14	2
Country	9	7	8	8	2	14	1
Suburban							
Garden	7	7	10	4	1	13	1
Suburban	12	8	13	7	0	20	2
Inner city							
Metro	11	17	16	12	8	20	5
City	8	4	10	2	10	2	4
Total	57	48	66	39	22	83	15

a. These persons are the focus of Chapters 7 and 8.
b. These persons were either immigrants as children or first-generation children of immigrants. Details on this group are the focus of Chapter 9.

roles, especially family and leisure; (d) the earliest memories of how the interest in their present career/work situation began; and (e) exploration of other career fields considered by the participant.

The audiotapes of the first interview were then reviewed by the interviewer, who identified areas she would like to explore further. At weekly meetings with the interviewers, plans for the second interview were discussed. The purpose of the second interview was to understand what factors had motivated the person to choose and persist in her or his career. The second interview consisted of two parts. The first focused on two general factors: (a) positive and negative personal factors that affected career choice, including personality and physical attributes, and (b) positive and negative environmental factors, including significant other, programs, and experiences.

The second part of the second interview explored the underlying values that motivated the person to pursue her or his particular career. Also included were questions exploring other possible factors such as (a) the extent of career planning support available at the high school from counselors, teachers, and peers; (b) the participant's aspiration (if she or he could change the current situation and be or do anything); (c) what the participant would say to local high school students today in a talk on careers; and (d) why the participant agreed to be interviewed.

A pilot study was conducted with a draft interview protocol with three persons who represented the same age cohort as the interviewees, two women and one man. On the basis of this pilot, we determined that two interviews lasting about one hour each were best for establishing rapport and obtaining in-depth information from participants. A third interview did not yield enough additional data to warrant it. On the other hand, a single interview was not sufficient to obtain in-depth information. Only unusual circumstances led us to conduct three interviews, such as when a second interview was cut short by some unforseen interruption (i.e., a sick child).

Interview Procedures

Graduate women who were in a doctoral-level counseling psychology program were trained to conduct the interviews. Their counseling experience was considered useful because of their ease in establishing rapport with and eliciting information and feelings from interviewees. Three of these interviewers have written chapters in this book. The interviews took place over a two-year period beginning in spring 1991 and continuing through summer 1993. Training involved trial interviews with other interviewers. Interviewers were also trained in the use of audio equipment. A letter was mailed to each participant explaining the interview purpose and procedures. Confidentiality was assured at that time, and written consent was obtained from each interviewee. This was followed by a telephone call to set up an interview time.

Analyses of Interview Transcripts

Analyses of the interview transcripts was a long, complicated process. First, the audiotapes were transcribed. Then I met with the interviewers over a period of one year, during which time we identified salient themes from the three pilot sample transcripts. Alan Peshkin (Glesne & Peshkin, 1991) guided our approach to analyses of the interview transcripts. We also used grounded theory methods described by Lincoln and Guba (1985). The major themes are presented in Table 1.5 (see Appendix E for the subthemes). An analysis manual was developed with definitions for each theme and examples of what each subtheme was and was not. The five clusters among the themes are family, education, work, self, and experiences.

Table 1.5 Phase 3: Major Analyses Themes for Interviews

Family	Self
Parents	Decisions
	Motivation
Early education	Significant others
Education: high school	Role models
College/university	Transitions
Counseling/guidance	Worldview
Work	Experiences
Work/home	Obstacles
	Critical Events

The labor-intensive process of analyzing each of the 105 transcripts continued over a two-year period. Then, for each respondent, the researchers wrote a 5- to 10-page summary, organized around the themes, with potential quotes noted. Finally, the transcript files were transferred to a HyperQual format (Padilla, 1991), which allowed us to print the transcript sections for each theme together.

The authors of this book other than myself then engaged in further theme analyses for their chapters based on the more focused purpose they had in mind. Throughout the book, attempts are made to answer such questions as the following: Why is what our participants told us important? Why is it important for that person? Why is it important for society as a whole?

We sought to integrate across themes to identify how themes related to each other both for the individual and for society. We also probed participants' answers for relationships with social learning theory. In quantitative research, themes are identified inductively (Lincoln & Guba, 1985) from the interview transcripts. Only later are relationships to known research and theory drawn. This latter step is important and each author ends their chapter with a paragraph or two pointing out the relationship of the themes to theory and prior research. Most identified themes could be related to social learning theory; however, some themes clearly fit within the older career choice theories, particularly those of Holland (1985) and Super (1990).

Career Aspirations of Women: Their Life Stories Compared With Those of Men

Women Who Persisted in Their High School Aspirations for Careers in Science or Technology

This chapter focuses on the women we interviewed in 1991–1993 who had aspired to a science or technology career in 1980 when they were in high school, and who in 1990 were still pursuing a career in these fields. As we noted in Chapter 1, women are less well represented in science and technology careers, and many of these fields offer better salary opportunities for women (National Science Foundation, 1994). Women are very underrepresented in the natural sciences, in particular in physics and chemistry. In 1994, the National Science Foundation published data indicating that women represent 15% of the B.A. degrees in physics and 9% of the Ph.D.s.

Of the 57 women interviewed between 1991 and 1993, 21 were employed in or completing training for a science-related career. Of these 57 women, 6 who had not expressed an interest in science in 1980 were now in science or technology careers. The focus of this chapter is on the 21 women who persisted in a science career. These women, age 23–28 at the time of the interviews, had achieved their goal of entering a science-related career or were currently finishing up their education for that career.

Before we explore the stories of these women, I will describe the context in which this study was first conceived in the 1970s. This was a time of optimism because of the Presidential Executive Order 11426 requiring affirmative action (in the 1960s) and because of revisions in equity legislation (in 1972). What follows is a brief history of affirmative action and some of the gains made during the past two decades.

Affirmative Action: 1970 and 1990

There is currently a negative backlash against affirmative action and both the former Senate Majority Leader, Bob Dole, and Jesse Helms, member of the House of Representatives, introduced legislation in 1995 to severely curtail affirmative action (Sala, Ashton, & Fitzpatrick, 1995). At the state level, there are some initiatives to greatly reduce affirmative action, and one of these was passed in California in 1996.

Several social scientists have conducted national surveys to determine the basis of the negative sentiment toward affirmative action (DeAngelis, 1995). DeAngelis reported that most of the negative feelings toward Executive Order 11246 are related to monetary grants to minority-owned businesses, race-based school scholarships, and the use of quotas in admissions and hiring, even though the latter is clearly forbidden by the executive order. These negative feelings are enhanced in the current period in the United States because real salaries at the skilled and unskilled levels have not increased in the last 20 years (Cassidy, 1995).

Affirmative action plans are intended to "level the playing field" for persons of color, persons with disability, and women in employment, access to education, education, and pursuit of business endeavors. Affirmative action legislation dates back to the 1960s when President Johnson passed Executive Order 11426 . This order was revised by President Nixon in 1969. It requires all government contractors receiving $50,000 or more from the government and having at least 50 employees to report the ethnic and sex composition of their workforce. In 1973, affirmative action requirements were extended to include persons with disabilities. Affirmative action plans must be developed by each applicable contractor responsive to any discrimination in the labor force identified by the Office of Federal Contract Compliance (OFCC). Goals and a timetable must then be developed and affirmative action be taken to achieve these goals. In higher education, these goals apply to both employees and students. Most educational institutions receive sufficient federal funding to require them to conform to affirmative action guidelines. This includes about 80% of the colleges and universities in the United States. Thus admissions policies, scholarship and fellowship programs, and special training programs come under the scrutiny of the OFCC.

The Supreme Court has been involved in a number of rulings related to the interpretation of affirmative action guidelines in educational institutions. In the 1978 Supreme Court ruling in the case of *Bakke v. the Regents of the University of California,* the Court acknowledged that the university could consider race as part of its admissions policy, but that the use of quotas was not acceptable (see Sala et al., 1995). More recently, in 1994, in *Podberesky v. Kirwan,* Podberesky, a Hispanic student, charged that a scholarship program administered by the University of Maryland was unfairly limited to African Americans. The Supreme Court refused to review the case and in effect supported a lower court ruling that concluded the program was "not narrowly tailored" to reduce the underrepresentation of African American students. This ruling is related to the Court's recent emphasis on the need for "strict scrutiny" of all affirmative action plans (see Sala et al., 1995). In 1995, in *Adarand Constructors Inc. v. Pena,* an all-white Colorado firm claimed discrimination. In June 1995, the Supreme Court did not strike down the minority contractor program in contention in Adarand; rather, the lower court was ordered to reconsider this program under "strict scrutiny." The purpose of strict scrutiny is to distinguish legitimate from illegitimate uses of race and gender in affirmative action decision making and to differentiate between permissible and impermissible uses of race and gender (Sala et al., 1995, p. 74). Supreme Court members differ in their interpretation of the effects of strict scrutiny. Some view it as fatal to affirmative action. Others, such as Justice O'Connor, state that "the persistence of both the practice and lingering effects of racial discrimination in this country today will in some cases justify a narrowly tailored race-based remedy" and may withstand a reverse discrimination challenge (Sala et al., 1995, p. S-9).

Mend It, Don't End It

Because there is a current national debate concerning the future of affirmative action, President Clinton's remarks in support of it are relevant. On July 19, 1995, President Clinton said,

> The job is not done. We should reaffirm the principle of affirmative action and fix the practices: . . . mend it, but don't end it. Affirmative action is an effort to develop a systematic approach to open the doors of education, employment and business development opportunities to qualified individuals who happen to be members of groups that have experienced longstanding and persistent discrimination. . . . In every instance, we will seek reasonable ways to achieve the objectives of inclusion and antidiscrimination without specific reliance on group membership. But where our legitimate objectives cannot be achieved through such means, the federal government will continue to support lawful consideration of race, ethnicity and gender under programs that are flexible, realistic, subject to reevaluation, and fair.[1]

Affirmative Action Gains: Women and Science

There is evidence that women have made gains in their levels of participation in science and technology fields where they were previously underrepre-

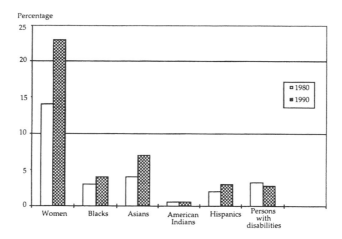

Figure 2.1. Women, Minorities, and Persons With Disabilities in the Science and Engineering Labor Force: 1980 and 1990

SOURCE: Adapted from the National Science Foundation (1994, p. 91).

NOTE: Individuals belonging to more than one group (e.g., Asian women) are included in both categories (e.g., women and Asian).

sented. In 1974, women represented less than 1% of engineers (Farmer & Backer, 1977). In 1981, women earned 11% of the B.A. degrees in engineering, and in 1991, 14% (NSF, 1994). Overall, in science and engineering, women earned 38% of the B.A. degrees in 1981 and 44% in 1991. These overall gains include the social sciences, and the gains for women within the field of psychology have been particularly large. For example, current data indicate that women earn a majority of the Ph.D.s in psychology (NSF, 1994), a phenomena referred to as the "feminization" of the field. Figure 2.1 provides some data on women, minorities, and persons with disabilities in the science and engineering labor force for 1980 and 1990. As a whole, women have increased their representation in these fields from approximately 13% to 23%. Figure 2.2 shows the percentage of women earning Ph.D.s in science and engineering fields.

The number of women earning master's degrees in science and engineering increased 7% in the decade 1981-1991, from 29% to 36% (NSF, 1994). The number of women earning Ph.D.s in science and engineering has increased about 5% in the decade 1982-1992—from 23% to 28%. The percentage of women earning Ph.D.s in all fields (science and humanities and so on)was 13% in 1970, 30% in 1981, and 37% in 1991. However, the increases in science and engineering at the Ph.D. level are greatest in psychology and the

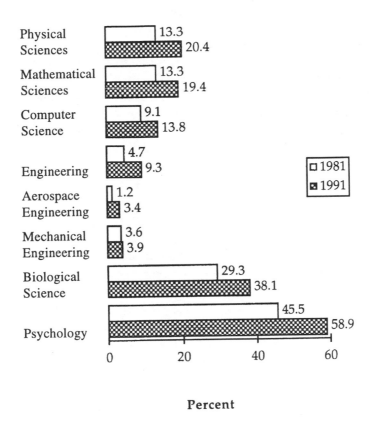

Figure 2.2. Percentage of Women Ph.D.s in Science and Engineering: 1981 and 1991
SOURCE: National Science Foundation (1994).

biological sciences (Figure 2.2) and are not reflected in other areas. The smallest gains were in engineering, especially for specialties such as aerospace and mechanical engineering.

As noted earlier, the science sample in our longitudinal study was identified using Gottfredson and Holland's (1989) *Dictionary of Holland Occupational Codes*. This dictionary assigned three Holland codes to each occupation to represent the three areas of occupational interests most frequently endorsed by persons in these occupations. Holland (1985) has classified occupational interests into six clusters representing Investigative (I), Realistic (R), Artistic (A), Social (S), Enterprising (E), and Conventional (C). The interested reader is referred to Holland (1985) for a description of this theory.

Gottfredson and Holland reported that 96% of occupations with Investigative (I) or Realistic (R) in their three-letter code are in science occupations. All the women in Table 2.1 have occupational codes with an I or an R in them. An examination of the third Holland code letter for these women indicates that 48 had a Social code; 28, Artistic; 15, Enterprising; and 10, Conventional. There is considerable research evidence that more women obtain "Social" codes compared with men (Holland, Powell, & Fritzsche, 1994), and this fact is sometimes used by counselors to discourage women from considering science careers. The occupational codes of the 61 women in science presented here would suggest otherwise. There are several science careers that include "Social" interests, such as mechanical engineer and physician, occupations where women are underrepresented.

In our longitudinal study, the 61 women who were in a science major or employed in a science career in 1990 (Phase 2) were in a wide range of science-related careers. Table 2.1 presents the occupations, prestige level, and Holland occupational code for these women. Many of them (16) were in the nursing area and several others (13) were health-related technicians or therapists. The prestige of these nursing and health technician occupations ranged from 46 to 67 on a scale from 04 to 96. Some (22) were in occupations with higher prestige, but the number in engineering (2) and medicine (physician, 2) was small. None was in physics, and one woman was a chemist. When we compared the prestige levels of these 61 women in science careers with the levels for the 52 men in the Phase 2 sample in science careers, we found that prestige was significantly lower for the women. There is more on gender differences for these two groups in Chapter 6.

Women in Science: Interviewees

We had expected more 9th-grade women compared with 12th-grade women we interviewed to choose and persist in science and technology fields based on our expectations that sex equity legislation, such as Title IX of the Education Amendments in 1972 and the Affirmative Action Executive Order 11246, amended in 1968 to include sex, would facilitate this movement because the 9th-grade women would have had longer exposure to these sex equity initiatives. This expectation was not supported. Perhaps the time span, a three-year difference in age for these two cohorts, was too short for large differences to have occurred. Although several of our participants were employed

Table 2.1 Phase 2: Occupations Majored/Employed in Currently by Women in Science Sample ($n = 61$)

Occupation	Frequency	Prestige Level	Holland Code
Accountants	8	78	CRS
Architect	2	90	AIR
Chemist	1	79	IRE
Computer systems analyst	3	62	IER
Computer programmer	5	62	IRE
Dental hygienist	1	48	SAI
Economics professor	1	84	IAS
Electronics draftsperson	1	67	IRE
Engineer biomedical	1	86	IRE
Engineer mechanical	1	82	RIS
Market research analyst	1	85	ISC
Nurse, R.N.	15	46	SIA
Nurse supervisor	1	66	SEI
Optometrist	1	79	ISR
Pharmacist	1	82	IES
Physician	1	92	ISA
Physician, surgeon	1	92	IRA
Psychologist	3	81	SIA
Research worker (scientific)	1	65	IRS
Therapist (occupational)	1	67	SRE
Therapist (physical)	1	58	SIE
Therapist (respiratory)	1	58	SIR
Tech (animal lab)	1	62	IRS
Tech (surgical)	1	48	ISR
Technician (health)	4	48	ISA
Tech (radiological)	1	48	RSI
Technician (lab)	1	48	RIE
Technician (emergency medical)	1	48	ESI

at the time of our interviews, our focus in this chapter is on the experiences the science women we interviewed had had in their families and early schooling.

Table 2.2 provides some information on these women including their pseudonyms and their science or technology career. Most of these 21 women were married, and 9 of them had one or more children. (Chapter 13, by Lenore Tipping, focuses on the relation between work and family roles for some of these women.)

(text continues on p. 46)

Table 2.2 *Phase 3: Women We Interviewed Who Persisted in a Science Career (1980/1990) or Were New to a Science Career in 1990 (n = 27)*

High School / Name	Degree	Occupation	Father	Mother	Children	Married
			Education			
Garden City High School						
Christine	B.S.	Nurse	2	2		x
Letitia	B.S.	Nurse	1	1	2	x
Sally	B.S.	Physical therapist	2	1		x
Darlene	M.S.	Microbiologist	2	2		
Samantha[c]	M.A.	Accountant	2	2		
Suburban High School						
Ethel	B.S.	Computer programmer	3	3		x
Natalie	B.A.	Accountant	1	1		
Dorothy	A.A.	Nurse	4	2		
Doreen	B.S.	Biology teacher	2	4		x
Zena[c]	M.A.	Accountant	2	2		
Metro High School						
Leonora	A.A.	Medical tech	2	1	1	
Laura	B.S.	Nurse	2	3		x
Gena[b]	B.S.	Mechanical engineer	4	5	1	x
Ophelia[c]	B.A.	Accountant	2	2		
Noreen[c]	B.A.	Computer programmer				
Susan[b,c]	B.A.	Psychology	2	2	2	x

NOTE: Parent education: 1 = less than high school diploma; 2 = high school diploma; 3 = some college; 4 = two-year college degree (A.A.); 5 = four-year college degree (B.A./B.S.); 6 = master's degree; and 7 = Ph.D. or professional degree (i.e., M.D.).
a. Completing degree.
b. First-generation Italian: Beatrice.
c. Women of color: Tina and Vicky, African American; Vanessa and Wendy, Hispanic.

Table 2.2 (continued)

High School / Name	Degree	Occupation	Father	Mother	Children	Married
			Education			
City High School						
Margaret[b]	B.S.	Medical therapist	2	2	4	x
Jackie[b]	B.A.[d]	Accountant	2	2	2	x
Polly	B.S.[d]	Nurse	1	1	x	
Kimberly[b]	B.S.	Lab tech	5	3		x
Juanita[b]	A.A.	Nurse	1	1	1	x
Tehila[c]	B.A.[d]	Accountant	1	1		
Farmerville High School						
Sophie	A.A.	Nurse	2	3	2	x
Joyce	B.S.	Computer programmer	1	1		x
Esther	B.S.	Respiratory therapist	2	2	3	x
Country High School						
Linda[b]	M.D.	Surgeon	7	2		x
Nona	B.S.	Biology lab tech	2	5	1	x

NOTE: Parent education: 1 = less than high school diploma; 2 = high school diploma; 3 = some college; 4 = two-year college degree (A.A.); 5 = four-year college degree (B.A./B.S.); 6 = master's degree; and 7 = Ph.D. or professional degree (i.e., M.D.).
a. Completing degree.
b. First-generation Italian: Beatrice.
c. Women of color: Tina and Vicky, African American; Vanessa and Wendy, Hispanic.

Of the 21 women who persisted, 12 had earned B.A./B.S. degrees at the time of the interview, and several of these women were working on master's degrees. Four of the women had two-year A.A. degrees and were working on B.A./B.S. degrees. Two women were finishing up their B.A./B.S. degrees. Two had M.A.s, one of these women planned to earn a Ph.D., and another had an M.D. Most of our women science persisters had parents who did not have a college education. Five of them had parents with less than a high school degree; seven had high school degrees. Of the nine remaining, three had parents with some college, five had one parent with a college degree, and one had a father with an M.D. None of these families was affluent. Clearly, these women had achieved a level of education well above that of their parents. As noted in Chapter 1, in recent years, of women age 24-34 throughout the United States, 22% graduate with a four-year degree (National Center for Education Statistics, 1995). The science women we interviewed were more highly educated than the U.S. population as a whole for their age group and gender.

When we focused on the specializations chosen by these women within science and technology, an overwhelming majority had chosen specialties that were traditional for women. For example, 7 of the 21 persisters were nurses and 7 more were medical technicians, medical therapists, or biologists. The remaining seven women were in less traditional science and engineering fields—two were in computer science, three were in accounting, one was a surgeon, and one was a mechanical engineer.

To better understand why these 21 women persisted in a science-related career, I will share some of the stories they told us when we interviewed them and let you draw your own conclusions. I believe these stories illustrate what motivated these women to persist. First, I will describe, using their own words, some aspects of their school cultures and their experience with teachers. Then I will present some of their answers to what we have come to call the "magic wand" question, which I will describe later. Finally, I will share their thoughts about what they would want to tell high school students in their respective alma maters today.

I will be quoting from the interviews of 13 of these 21 women. As Table 2.1 indicates, these women went to different high schools and had different resources available to them. Among the 21 women, 9 attended suburban schools: 4, Garden City school, and 5, Suburban school. Eight attended inner-city schools: 5, City school, and 5, Metro school. Four attended rural schools: 2, Farmerville school, and 2, Country school.

School Culture and Experiences Related to Science/Math

In our analysis of the questionnaire data from 1980 and 1990, the most important predictor of persistence in a science-related career for women was the number of elective science courses they had taken in high school (Farmer, Wardrop, Anderson, & Risinger, 1995). In fact, compared with the other women in the interview study, the 21 women who persisted had collectively taken more than double the number of elective science courses. Means were 1.45 and 3.0, respectively. Means for elective science for the larger Phase 2 sample of women who had persisted in Science ($n = 35$) compared with women who had not persisted ($n = 61$) were also significantly different ($p < .001$).

Because taking elective science courses in high school has been found to be an important predictor that a person will enter a science major in college (National Science Foundation, 1994), and because we found this in our study, I wanted to examine what science courses the women had taken to see if there was any particular science chosen more frequently than others. Chemistry and physics were the most popular choices. Microbiology, anatomy, and environmental science were taken less frequently. In fact, these latter courses typically may be offered less frequently by high schools. We did request information on this from our high school principals in 1990, but their records were not accessible for the 1980–1983 period when our participants were in their schools and their recollections were somewhat vague. In 1990, Phase 2 of our study, the questionnaire we used included a measure on why respondents had taken more elective science courses in high school. Participants responded to two statements: first, "I WANTED to take more science than required"; second, "I was EXPECTED to take more science than required." The 21 women persisters endorsed the first question more than the second. Means on a 5-point scale, from 5 = "strongly agree" to 1 = strongly disagree, were 3.9 versus 3.1. We can tentatively conclude from these scores that the women who chose science or technology careers were more intrinsically motivated to learn science. Their mean scores on the questions for elective math courses, however, were not much different (3.5 versus 3.1), which suggests that these women took extra math courses both for intrinsic reasons and because they were expected to by others. Differences in their high school grades in the natural sciences were not large when comparing the women in science with those in other career fields (2.8 versus 2.5). These differences as well as gender differences are discussed in more detail in Chapters 3, 4, and 6.

Some Liked Science But Not Math

Some of the school experiences of these women are described next. These women's stories indicated that you didn't have to like math to like science, although some liked both science and math. And a third group, straight-A students, thought of scientists as "nerds" (i.e., unpopular).

An example of the first type, a woman who liked science but didn't like math, is Ethel. She had attended Suburban High School and was a computer programmer working toward an M.B.A. When the interviewer asked Ethel about science and math classes, she said,

> I was not very good in math because I only got up to college algebra. I took trig and I failed in college. Well I dropped it before I failed it . . . you don't really need a lot of math to do technical science.

Nona had attended Country High School. She is now a biology lab technologist with a bachelor's degree. Nona said,

> I only took one math class and I did not like math so I didn't take anymore math. I probably should have but I didn't. I took two years of biology and then I took chemistry and that probably was an elective and, in fact, when I started trying to figure out what I might do in science, what I really wanted to be, I said, well I'll just major in science.

For some time, the research on women in science has linked math and science as basic foundations to future success in these fields (Eccles, 1994; Klein, 1985). Math has been labeled a "critical filter" (Sells, 1975) for entry into science fields. Yet, on reflection, it is possible to successfully engage in computer science and some of the medical technology fields without a strong math background. Perhaps the idea that persons who like math also like science, and vice versa, needs to be reexamined.

Others Liked Science and Math

Some of these women did like both math and science, for example, Darlene, who attended Garden City High School. She had a master's degree in molecular biochemistry and wanted to earn her Ph.D. Darlene said,

> In grade school math and science were the easiest classes. I got good grades in everything, but I had more fun and enjoyed myself a lot more with the work in the math and science classes. By sixth grade, I must have been watching like a Jacques Cousteau or some nature program that had to do with

studying the ocean and marine life, I was really into dolphins, really up on dolphins, and that's where I was pinpointing my career goals. So getting through grade school and into high school I took the college prep and loaded down more with math and science. I never really deviated from that goal.

Gena, the mechanical engineer described in Chapter 1, also enjoyed both science and math, even though she had a biology teacher who put women down and called them dumb. But Gena was exceptionally inner directed, as noted earlier, and was not put off by this kind of sexism.

Only Nerds Take Advanced Science and Math

Sally, who also attended Garden City High School and is now a physical therapist with a bachelor's degree, experienced the pull between being popular and taking advanced, elective science and math courses. She indicated that she took elective science and math courses because she was expected to by the teachers in her school, not because she wanted to. Sally said,

You know what, in high school the smart people are the nerdy people. So in the honors classes (I hated the honors classes because they weren't fun) my friends weren't in them. I didn't like being in the advanced classes because they were usually the kids that you didn't want to hang out with. The kids that didn't have a social life, when I always did.

Sally had some comments to make about the physics courses in her high school:

The physics class is for the eggheads. Well I took it and I did fine in it and I liked it. So even though you have a negative attitude about who takes these classes, I took them and did all right. So maybe that's why I transferred into science.

Among our women science persisters, none majored in physics in college. As Table 2.2 indicates, several women did take physics classes. But they didn't get turned on enough to pursue this field in college. When I reviewed the science occupations entered by the women who had returned questionnaires in 1990 (Table 2.1), I found that they had entered a broader range of science and technology fields than the women we interviewed.

In summary, for the 21 women interviewed who persisted in a science-related career, some enjoyed and did well in both science and math; others did not do well in or like math but enjoyed and did well in science. Another aspect of school culture was also noted, namely, a tendency to view the students who took chemistry and physics as "nerds" or "eggheads"; for the popular, socially minded student who was also bright, this presented a conflict.

We had expected to find that teachers and counselors had played a significant and important role in these women's career development. However, when we asked participants in the interviews about significant teachers, very few indicated that was so. On the other hand, it was very clear to us in the stories most participants told that their families had had a significant influence on their career paths. Chapter 12 by Janice Altman describes this aspect of their lives. A few of our science women spoke of the impact of one or more of their teachers. These included Linda, the surgeon, who had had a good experience with her biology teacher at Country High School. She said that this teacher was not well liked by other students, but that he challenged her and she learned a lot from him. Gena, the mechanical engineer, also mentioned her physics teacher as one who had positively influenced her at Metro High School. Doreen, now a science teacher, attended Suburban High School. She spoke highly of one of her biology teachers as well. But these three women were exceptions. Most of the women did not view their teachers as having had a significant impact on their career motivation and choices.

An understanding of what motivated these women seemed illusive. There was another part of our interview that probed their motivation, and we turn to that now.

The Magic Wand

There is some evidence that if women feel free to do whatever they want, unrestricted by the realistic constraints of multiple roles, lack of finances, or discrimination in the workplace, they will choose more prestigious and challenging careers (Farmer & Bohn, 1970). In the Farmer and Bohn study, women were given the Strong Interest Inventory and then two weeks later they were given the inventory again, this time following a fantasy experimental "set" suggesting that raising a family well is very possible for a career woman, that men and women are promoted equally in business and the professions, and that men like intelligent women. Their Strong Interest Inventory scores from the second administration were significantly increased on careers such as doctor, psychologist, and lawyer—all careers in which women were highly underrepresented in the 1960s. Following this line of reasoning, in 1980 our participants first were asked to write in what career they expected to end up. Then they were asked to "daydream" and list three or more careers they had ever dreamed about. We expected the "daydream" careers to be higher in prestige and to be ones that were more nontraditional for women. This expectation was not supported (Farmer et al., 1981). In spite of the lack of support for our hypothesis in 1980, we pursued this idea in more depth when we interviewed our participants in the 1990s.

Toward the end of the second interview, the interviewer would say something like the following:

OK, now we're going to try something different and I am going to give you a magic wand, and the magic wand allows you to change things so that you can do anything that you want. It also gives you special powers so that you are not confined by any previous experiences or any current kind of circumstances. It lets you decide when you want to begin to use the wand as well. So with this magic wand how would you use it?

Responses to this invitation to dream varied widely. Some wanted to continue doing what they were doing at present, with some possible upgrading. These women were highly committed to their careers. Others shifted the focus from career to family and making things better for their families. For these women, career was not as important as family life. A third group of these women wished for a different kind of life, including travel or changing their personalities. These women were dissatisfied with their current lives. A surprise was that their "magic wand" did not place them in some other career. Instead, these women were interested in more self-indulgent wish fulfillment.

We begin by describing the stories of some of the women who wanted to continue what they were doing.

One Dream Was to Continue What They Were Doing

Among those wanting to continue what they were currently doing, Darlene said,

Oh my-ooh, magic wand to do anything I wanted huh? Probably the only thing that I would change is the three letters after my name, add three letters after my name [i.e., Ph.D.]. Yeah cause otherwise I'm pretty satisfied with the way things are.

Nona, a biology lab technician with a B.S. and planning to earn an M.B.A., said,

Oh, I have no idea, I have a hard time doing things that I don't already know how to do. It would probably be, you know, some kind of public relations person in a lab. Like I said, I just feel there needs to be a lot more communication going on between the doctors and the administrators and the lab.

Jackie, a woman of Puerto Rican descent who was a tax accountant, said,

I would really like to be a CPA, and work downtown in a very nice firm in the Chicago loop. I would go downtown every day and have a beautiful office that had a great view. I would see 15 or 20 clients each day, and do a quality, ethical, honest, and competent job for each one of them and then come home and relax.

Dream Related More to Family

Some women responded to the magic wand question by shifting their focus to family. Laura, a nurse with a B.S. degree, said,

Personally thinking, you know, a nice home, nice family, a nice area to live, somewhere in Chicago close to here, close to home, where family is—still being a nurse.

Margaret, an African American medical therapist, pregnant when she was interviewed, said,

I would have delivered already! That's the only thing that I'm really wishing because you know, I don't like waiting. So is there anything that I would change? a bigger house? a better car? things like that? someone to clean my house? the only thing I would really want for myself is for the baby to go full term because my last two pregnancies were premature.

Dream Related to Radical Change

A third group of these women demonstrated a desire to change their lives quite radically.

Polly, currently in training to become a nurse, said,

I'd probably be rich and travel around the world, rich enough to travel all over the place, that's what I'd want to do, is just travel, see the world, stay as long as I wanted to, pick up and leave when I wanted to, yes that's probably exactly what I want to do.

Letitia, who had wanted to be a doctor when she was in high school and is now a nurse aiming to become a nurse practitioner with a master's degree, said,

I don't know, I would probably want to go through steps and be a number of different things. I would probably like to be a physician for a while, and then maybe a malpractice lawyer, and then be able to lead the life of leisure for a while and travel all over the world.

The women who had these latter dreams were either still struggling to achieve their goals or had given up on their original goals. These are just a sample of the dreams these women had, some consistent with their present life, others very different. The "magic wand" stories told us that not all women had fantasy careers that were more challenging than their present career choices. This finding may help explain the lack of difference found by Farmer et al. (1981) between realistic and fantasy career aspirations.

In Chapter 1, I noted one of the puzzling findings from the quantitative analyses (Farmer, Wardrop, Anderson, & Risinger, 1995) was that the women who persisted in a science or technology career were less career committed than the women who switched to another career field. This quantitative finding was counterintuitive. However, when we reviewed the mean scores for these two groups on the Career Commitment measure, there was no significant difference. As we studied the model further, we realized that the relationship of career commitment to persistence in a science career should be interpreted in light of the relationships of other variables in the model to career commitment. These include (a) an effect for age, with 9th graders being higher on both career commitment and on math/science utility (i.e., valuing math and science for their relation to career goals); (b) an effect for the Society Support measure assessing the women's perception of support or lack of support for their careers in the workplace; and (c) an effect for the math/science utility variable. With these multiple relationships, it is very difficult to make any meaningful interpretations from the model concerning career commitment. But the magic wand stories, with their wide variety, suggest that not all the women who persisted in science were strongly career committed. Some were and others were not.

Still trying to understand what motivated these 21 women, we asked yet another question in the interview—what kind of advice they would want to give high school students today.

School Guidance Stories

A surprise, at least to me, was that the role of the school counselor was not very prominent in these women's stories. Most of them didn't remember talking with a counselor. Those who did recalled their counselor contact as not being very helpful. Counselors, they said, were good when it came to personal problems, but as far as career guidance was concerned, they offered limited help. The 1980 questionnaire had three questions related to high school counselors to assess whether or not students perceived their counselors as interested in their career plans and as encouraging them to take math and science courses. On a 5-point scale, with 5 being strongly agree, the mean score for 14 of these 21 women was 3.0, or in the "not sure" response range. The other 7 women left this question blank. For all the women responding in Phase 2 of the study, the mean score was 3.2, with a standard deviation of .85. There were no differences between means for women in science versus women in other career fields.

If counselors were not perceived as very helpful to these women, we wondered what kind of career guidance they would consider beneficial for young people in high school today. We asked the following question toward the end of the second interview:

Let's say that the local junior high or your old high school invited you to talk to their classes about careers, how would you want to present that—what would you want to be sure to get across to those kids?

Their answers usually reflected the woman's values and insights about career choice and achievement. A prominent theme was to tell students to choose something they liked. Some of the women added to this advice by suggesting that students gather information about a lot of different careers before making a choice. Another group encouraged women to set goals and to stick with them. One group encouraged women to choose careers that would guarantee their ability to be economically independent. A fifth group of women, those who had had to overcome obstacles such as racial discrimination, sexism, and poverty, encouraged students to persist no matter what and to have a positive attitude.

Pick a Career You Will Enjoy

Examples of the first type of response include Darlene's:

I think the main point I'd want to get across to them is to enter a field which they like, that they enjoy, that they wake up in the morning not dreading to go to work, actually enjoying it, being excited about it. . . . I think an important part of anything that you do is to have fun . . . life's too short.

Sally, a physical therapist, said,

Think about what you like to do in your free time and then take that and turn it into a job. Think of your interests. If you're in the middle of a class and hate the class, what do you dream of, what do you daydream of, what would you rather be doing, what is it? and then take that and see if a job can fit that.

Leonora, a medical technician, said,

Pick a career that you want to do and no matter what anyone tells you, if you feel you can do it I think you should just go ahead and do it, no matter what they tell you, even if they tell you you can't do it you should go ahead. Whether you fail or succeed you know you gave it your best shot. If you succeed, then you're better off for it.

This advice is consistent with the best career development and choice theories exemplified by the work of Donald Super (1990) and John Holland (1985). Holland found that persons who enter careers that interest them are more likely to be satisfied with their work. Consistent with this, the stories emphasizing this theme seemed to come from women happy in their careers.

Super and Holland also encourage young people, especially adolescents, to explore a wide range of career options, do volunteer work, take courses, interview persons in different careers, so when they choose careers they have some knowledge of how they will like it and how well they will do. Some of our women science persisters wanted to give that advice to young people today.

Explore a Lot of Different Careers

Recall what Gena said in Chapter 1. She is the Native American mechanical engineer who had attended Metro High School. She described how she and a classmate had gone to the counselor's office and spent time studying the college catalogs and career materials they found there. Gena felt that she had to take the initiative to do this, and she had found this exploration very helpful for planning for college. Gena's response to the school guidance question:

Tell them to investigate career choices, see what they're good at in school, what they like, what they dislike. Talk to people in jobs that involve those skills. Actually go out and visit people at work, see what they do, really just do research, start looking, talking to people, don't wait for it to come to you because you'll be sitting there for a long time in most cases . . . start writing down things, see what jobs involve things that you like to do.

Nona, who had attended Country High School and was a biology lab technician with a B.S. degree, said,

I think you have to start somewhere, but you really should look at different types of jobs, talk to different people, try and find something that might interest you and then look into it.

The guidance stories that emphasized the need to explore several kinds of careers before making a choice came from women happy in their careers, but, not a surprise, women who also were from homes in which their mothers had four-year college degrees (Table 2.1). As noted before, Chapter 12 will describe the influence of family on career development in more depth.

Set Goals

Given this sound advice from some women, we wondered if there was something in addition they wanted to say. We found that there was, regarding goal setting, which has been found to be positively motivating by researchers studying outcome expectations in career development (Lent, Brown, & Hackett, 1995).

Christine, a nurse with a B.S. degree, said:

I guess just to set goals, set goals for yourself and set them higher . . . if you set them higher, don't worry, you probably still can reach them because I didn't think I could be a nurse, I mean just because I knew I was scared. I mean I guess I knew I could do it, but I knew I was scared and if I could just overcome that, you know, I could do it.

Jackie, a Puerto Rican tax accountant who had attended City High School, said,

I would tell kids to focus on who they are and what they want and then let nothing get in their way. If they're presented with obstacles, kids need to be taught that those are just obstacles that you need to work around or go through, and to not give up their dreams. It is just very important to stay focused on what it is that you want, and then just go after it.

Economic Independence

Divorce in the family seemed to reinforce a different kind of motivation. Women who had experienced divorce, either of their parents or of a close relative, were committed to obtaining a career to ensure their financial independence. They saw what happened to women who were divorced and had to support not only themselves but also their children, and this experience left an indelible mark on them. Many of these women went into nursing because it offered job security and flexibility in terms of hours. Dorothy, a nurse, said,

I was thinking I wanted something where I could depend on myself. Because my mom and her sisters, they're all supported by their husbands. They had the babies and they quit working. That was it. In today's society, it doesn't work that way. And I was covering myself. I want to have a family and all that kind of stuff. But if I need to go back to work afterward I won't have to worry. My aunt's a nurse. She had a beautiful marriage and then they got divorced. It's like, well, if it could happen to them it could happen to anybody. I said, it is nice she still has her three kids. She is raising them. No problem. She picked up her bags and moved to a different state and went back into nursing. Then there's my skating coach, his wife works part-time to help out as a bagger at minimum wage. I was thinking, forget it—no way. I want to be in control and nursing has got wonderful opportunities. It is fabulous.

Hang in There When the Going Gets Tough

We had asked our participants to share with us any difficulties they had experienced in their lives. Some of these were critical incidents with long-lasting effects on their career choices and plans. Others described obstacles to achievement of career plans. Critical incidents included death of a parent or sibling, divorce in the family, child abuse, and various kinds of sex and racial discrimination. Chapters 7 and 8 focus on the discrimination experienced by women and by men of color.

The fifth type of "guidance" story emphasized persisting even when faced with serious challenges. These stories were typically from women who had experienced various kinds of obstacles in their career planning.

Polly, in training to be a nurse and the first member of her family to earn a college degree, said,

I'd tell them to stay in school. If they want to join the air force, or the army do it, that's the main thing, just do it. If you want to and you think you can, try it, don't give up. That's the main thing I would tell them is just don't give up, don't be a quitter you know, don't give up things easily just because it's easy to quit, don't do it .

Margaret, an African American who had attended City High School and was a medical therapist with a B.S. degree, said,

Talk about choice? as far as saying something to keep them in school, yes, most definitely I would, I would try to encourage that, to stay in school. People say, yes, I have the smarts to do it, but what is an education going to get me? You hear that from a lot of black students, am I going to get a job? 'Cause a woman sees so much of this still, the higher up you get, a lot of blacks go to school but still have problems with jobs, you have to give all you can. Just don't blow it off just because other educated black people who don't have jobs . . . I would encourage you to continue to push yourself and don't allow so many other things to bring you down, be up for the fight, be more determined, and that's it, what more can you say.

This fifth type of guidance story, the one emphasizing "hanging in there" whatever the difficulties, came from women who were either of an ethnic minority race and/or from relatively poor families in which both parents had high school educations but no college experience. How does career development theory relate to these "don't give up" stories? Social cognitive learning theory (Bandura, 1986) guided our investigation from the beginning. It focuses not only on personal cognitive determinants but also on environmental, experiential determinants of career choice. As he evolved his theory over the years, Bandura also emphasized the role of the person as an agent in her or his own destiny. That is, a woman learns new things as a result of her experiences with others and with the environment, and through reflection on the consequences of these experiences and behaviors, she changes. (Chapter 1 discusses Bandura's theory in more detail.)

The women we interviewed who advocated "hanging in there" had developed a coping strategy. This interpretation would be consistent with Mitchell and Krumboltz's (1990) adaptation of Bandura's social learning theory to the career choice process, which helps us understand individual differences in their career development. The experiences that people have, and how they cope with these experiences, are powerful influences on the life course.

Coping With Obstacles

To illustrate how one woman handled difficulty, here is Darlene's story about a deep disappointment she had at the point when she was planning her college training. As readers may recall, Darlene is a microbiologist with an M.S. degree whose "magic wand" story indicated she wanted a Ph.D. Darlene's parents both graduated from high school. She is a middle child of 11 children. Here is some of her story about the obstacles she faced and overcame to achieve her current status. When she was in high school, she very much wanted to be an oceanographer:

I enjoyed studying and school stuff. My parents never really forced direction on any of us. We had to go to grade school, we had to go to high school and it wasn't that we were forced to graduate high school or anything like that. They just kind of put it, "Well if you don't want to go and finish high school then you're going to be on your own." So, for the most part when I was growing up my parents were really supportive for school. We had books. My mom would sit us down in the summer and tell us we had to do our writing lessons and our reading things and math before we could go out and play during the summer, stuff like that. So they were very education conscious. They knew what it would take to get out into the world.

When we asked Darlene how her parents felt about college, she said,

If we wanted to go, "great" and they emotionally supported us. There was no way they could financially support all of us to go to college. So they didn't force us, . . . "do what you want to do and we will support you . . . we will be behind you 100%." So they were very helpful. Yeah in high school I wanted to be an oceanographer, and when I was a senior I applied to the Coast Guard academy and I had gotten through everything up to the point where the physical part was and I had had knee surgery my sophomore year in high school and my doctor, who did the surgery told them, the people there at the academy, that any sudden movement and the knee could go, which I didn't appreciate considering that at the time (two years after the injury) I was playing all the sports, basketball, and softball, and I was running, I was doing everything and it was like, I mean that was more or less the turning point. Because, as far as oceanography, it kind of put it more on the back burner and I had to go around in a roundabout way because with the Coast Guard academy they would send you to school and basically oceanography was a program they had. So that would have been like just walking in the door and it would have been perfect! And then all I would have to do is four years. But I kind of got waylaid by a doctor who really didn't know what he was talking about. And then the doctors at the academy took him for his word instead of even giving me a physical, or an equivalent to tryout. They would have seen that once I put my mind to something I am going to do it. And that's another reason why I ended up going to community college the first year because unfortunately I had put all my concentration and direction into going to the academy. I had never anticipated being turned down. And when I was it was past the deadlines for a lot of colleges, especially for scholarships and all that. So now if I had to do it over again I'd send out everything no matter what and then be able to pick and choose when the offers came in. I'm trying to forget about the academy—except I went by the recruiting office yesterday and I was about ready to bomb it, no I'm only teasing. I'm pretty happy with where I am. After my master's degree I gave myself about five years to work and pay off some of my loans before I would go back for my doctorate. So that is what I'm planning. I want to get my doctorate in neurobiology.

Darlene and a few other persisters in science were very determined to get what they wanted, and obstacles were challenges to them that they figured out how to get around. More of Darlene's story is told in Chapter 5, and she is featured in Chapters 12 and 14. In 1980, we had given these women Bem's Sex Role Inventory (BSRI; 1981) to measure of their self-concept. We factor analyzed data on this measure and extracted a factor we called Independent, with 12 items. Other factor analyses performed with data from the BSRI have extracted a similar factor and named it Instrumental (Moreland, Gulanick, Montague, & Harren, 1978). Persons who score high on this measure view themselves as assertive, aggressive, independent, with a strong personality, who defend their own beliefs, make decisions easily, are willing to take risks, are self-reliant, have leadership abilities, act as a leader, are willing to take a stand, and are individualistic. Darlene's score on this measure was very high, more than one standard deviation above the mean. Gena, the mechanical engineer whom we introduced previously, had a similarly high score on this measure; in fact, five of the women in this group of 21 had very high scores on Independent. The other three were Kimberly, Linda, and Natalie. On the other hand, the mean score on Independent for the 21 women persisters was in the average range. The women who advocated patience and "hanging in there" were highly instrumental, and this characteristic was likely very useful to them in achieving their goals.

I have not specifically tried to answer the question of "why" some women persisted in a science career and others did not. Instead, I have provided some descriptions of the persisters' motivation and experiences. At the very least, I learned that simplistic answers to the question of "why" would not do, and that quantitative findings are only of limited help in understanding the persistence of these women.

We know that these women were bright and that they had achieved more than their parents in terms of education and career. We also know that when they faced serious obstacles, because of racial or sexual discrimination or because of lack of finances or trouble at home, they didn't give up. They were persistent and had come to believe it was important not only for themselves but also for young people today to hear this message. We also need to understand why almost as many of the women who aspired to a science career in high school did not persist. The next chapter takes up this theme.

Note

1. This quotation from Sala et al. was reprinted with permission from the *Labor Relations Reporter,* Special Supplement, "Affirmative Action After Adarand," 1995, Vol. 68, No. 6, pp. S-3, 45. Published by the Bureau of National Affairs, Inc.

3

Why Women Don't Persist in Their High School Science Career Aspirations

Of the 57 women we interviewed, 25 had changed from their 1980 aspiration for a science-related career to another career field. The women who changed are referred to as "career changers" rather than "nonpersisters," because many of them entered career fields more suited to their interests and talents. We wanted to understand better why these women had changed their career aspirations. Four basic reasons emerged from the interviews. Some of these women had changed simply because they had chosen a popular career in high school and likely had put down something off the top of their heads without really thinking about it. A second group had chosen a career field in 1980 that did not suit their interests or personality and they had found a better fit by the 1990s. A third group also found a better fit but had to overcome many obstacles to achieve their career goals. Others had been derailed from their 1980 aspiration by some critical external event or series of events that changed their plans. It is this fourth group that is a concern for counselors who want to help women optimize their potential. I describe all four groups in this chapter but give most attention to the fourth group.

Table 3.1 presents the names of the 25 women who changed their career field as well as their college degree, their current occupation, marital status, and parents' education. Nine of these women graduated from high school and took a few college courses but did not pursue a college degree. Three had earned A.A. degrees, eight had earned B.A. degrees, four had earned M.A. degrees, and one was a lawyer.

I began the review of the interview transcripts from these 25 women by comparing their stories with those of the women persisters in response to the "magic wand" question and the "school guidance" question as well as what they told us about their school environment. The answer to the "magic wand" question clustered around the same themes that were present in the stories the women persisters in science had told us (Chapter 2). Tonya, who is an urban planner, had a dream about serving in the Peace Corps overseas and of delaying marriage. This dream seemed consistent with her interests and her present career, just a bit more in tune with her idealism. Other dreams were not as related to present circumstances but involved getting away, traveling, and moving to another state, and reflected less contentment with present circumstances. Some women thought of their families first and would help them. Answers to some of our questions revealed the hopes and regrets of these women in a powerful way.

We asked them to tell us what they would want to be sure to say if they were invited to give a talk at their former high school. Their answers, again, were very similar to the answers the women in science had given us (see Chapter 2). A majority of these women believed strongly that people should choose careers that interest them, and that this was more important than the money they might earn or the prestige of the career. They would encourage young people today to be proactive, to explore, try out different jobs part-time in the summer or after school. Some also encouraged goal setting and earning a college degree for "security," similar to the science women. Similar too were their stories encouraging young people to "hang in there" no matter what.

The women career changers' experiences with teachers in high school appeared neither more positive nor more negative than those described by the women who remained in a science career. However, there were differences in the way these women chose their careers and the reasons the women gave us for changing career fields.

Choosing the Popular Career Field in High School

It seems natural that some women who aspired to a science career when they were in the ninth grade would change their minds later and choose a career in another field. This is so because in ninth grade many students do not know what they want to be when they grow up (Super, 1990). In their midtwenties, when we interviewed these women, many said they just put down something "for the sake of answering the question." These were typical careers such as computer programmer and engineer that were touted as the "wave of the future for women" by the media and by some teachers and high school counselors. An example of a woman like this is Wanda, who said she wanted to be a doctor in 1980 when she was in the ninth grade. She attended

Table 3.1 *Women Career Changers: Education; Parent Education; Marital Status (n = 25)*

High School / Name	Degree	Occupation	Father	Mother	Children	Married
			Education			
Garden City High School						
Quinn	A.A.[a]	Youth counselor	2	2		
Becky	B.A.	Sales	5	3		
Suburban High School						
Ginny	B.A.	Teacher, elementary	—	2		x
Lorna	H.S.	Secretary	2	2		x
Lenore	H.S.	Waitress	3	2	2	
Eunice	H.S.	Manager	1	1	2	
Ileen	A.A.	Secretary	2	2		x
Metro High School						
Tonya	M.A.	Urban planner	2	6	1	x
Beatrice[b]	M.A.	Counselor	2	2	1	x
Tina[c]	M.A.	College administrator	2	5		x
Kathy	M.S.	Manager	2	3		x
Erica	H.S.	Legal secretary	—	—	1	

NOTE: Parent education: 1 = less than high school diploma; 2 = high school diploma; 3 = some college; 4 = two-year college degree (A.A.); 5 = four-year college degree (B.A./B.S.); 6 = master's degree; and 7 = Ph.D. or professional degree (i.e., M.D.).
a. Completing degree.
b. First-generation Italian: Beatrice.
c. Women of color: Tina and Vicky, African American; Vanessa and Wendy, Hispanic.

Table 3.1 (continued)

High School / Name	Degree	Occupation	Father	Mother	Children	Married
			Education			
City High School						
Vicky^c	B.A.	Community developer	2	4		x
Vanessa^c	H.S.	Secretary		1	—	2
Farmerville High School						
Sandra	H.S.	Credit manager	1	2		
Terry	A.A.	Industrial design	2	2	3	x
Opal	B.A.	Marketing	2	1		x
Erin	L.L.D.*	Lawyer	6	5		
Wanda	B.A.	Sales manager	6	3		x
Norma	H.S.	Forms design analyst	6	3		x
Wendy^c	B.A.	Journalist	7	2		
Elaine	H.S.	UPS Supervisor	5	3		x
Country High School						
Rachel	H.S.	Secretary	1	2		x
Cindy	B.A.	Teacher, junior high, language				x
Theresa	B.A.	Sales				

NOTE: Parent education: 1 = less than high school diploma; 2 = high school diploma; 3 = some college; 4 = two-year college degree (A.A.); 5 = four-year college degree (B.A./B.S.); 6 = master's degree; and 7 = Ph.D. or professional degree (i.e., M.D.).
a. Completing degree.
b. First-generation Italian: Beatrice.
c. Women of color: Tina and Vicky, African American; Vanessa and Wendy, Hispanic.

65

Farmerville High School. When she was reminded of what she had written down, she said,

I wanted to be a doctor? I don't know where that came from. That's the year that I was living on my own, and my brother who is four years older, was there living with me, and my dad was wherever. I don't know why I would put a doctor. I thought for a long time when I was a child that I wanted to be a nurse, maybe I had progressed and set my sights higher and wanted to be a doctor. I have no desire to do that at this point. I would not want to be in school for 12 years and I don't think I'd want to live the lifestyle of a doctor either.

Norma, who had also attended Farmerville, had put down psychologist in 1980 when she was a ninth grader, and she said,

Yeah, you know after you left I don't know if we discussed I'd been thinking about a psychology career. It kind of hit me. The latest I can remember I was in junior high, it must have been seventh or eighth grade, and I had always wanted to be a psychologist and so we had some, like career day, and they showed films on what you wanted to do, and they gave you handouts about how long it would take you to get through school on certain things, and what you needed to do and it showed me some statistics then on becoming a psychologist and I decided after that I wouldn't want to do it, because I didn't want to spend my whole life in school, that's how I felt then. I felt by the time I'm 30 I'm still going to be in school if I go for a Ph.D.

So even though Norma had put down "psychologist," she really didn't want that career in 1980. Researchers assessing career aspiration for ninth-grade students should not put much reliance on the field of choice a student makes at that age. In Chapter 4, Susan Giurleo will present more details on the women who made early choices of computer science and engineering and then changed their minds. In addition to engineering being a popular choice, it was often one that students who chose it knew little about. Tina, an African American who was in the ninth grade at Metro High School in 1980, and, at the time of the interview was a college student adviser, noted,

And a lot of them, said, oh they want to major in engineering. But they didn't even know what engineers did. So I would tell those student they need to make sure they understand what the job entailed and what that particular person in the field would do every day! What would a typical day be like? So then these students, thinking they wanted to major in engineering, would take classes and "Ooh it's not what I thought" and they would get upset with failure in math courses and just too many courses. And they'd say, "Well I really thought I knew what I wanted to do. And after being in this field for so many months, now I know I don't want to do this, and I'm upset because I don't know what I want to do now."

Eventually, most of the women who felt misplaced found a better fit for their interests and talents, but it took longer to graduate. Are special high school programs aimed at increasing the participation of women in science and engineering misplaced efforts? The answer should be no, but to correct for misplaced interest, these programs could be provided along with other programs that give adolescent girls exposure to role models and experiences that cover a full range of occupational fields.

Career Interests: 1980 Compared With 1990

Holland's (1985) theory of career types may be useful here and, in fact, has been applied in some school districts as an organizing principle for career education in high school. Basically, Holland has simplified the number of career options by identifying six primary clusters of occupational interests that have a predominant set of activities and traits related to each: Realistic (technical), Investigative (science), Artistic (creative), Social (helping), Enterprising (persuasion), and Conventional (detail). For most people, three of these career interest areas are dominant over the other three interest areas. Holland has classified several thousand occupations with the three interest areas that are highest for those persons employed in the occupation (Gottfredson & Holland, 1989). Se Holland (1985) for an explanation.

We had hypothesized that the general field of an occupational choice, when it is defined broadly within Holland's (1985) theory, may be relatively stable by ninth grade, whereas the choice of a particular occupation may be unrealistic at that time (Super, 1990). Holland's Self Directed Search (Holland, Powell, & Fritzsche, 1994), the instrument he developed to assess career interests, begins with a section asking respondents to list up to eight occupations, including those from their earliest memories. Holland (1985) reported that these "daydreams" elicited from high school and college students "tend to belong to the same category" (p.128). That is, from the earliest years, the occupations that a person considers or daydreams about tend to have the same Holland codes, albeit arranged in a different order, but the same three are likely to appear in most of these daydreams for any one individual.

Holland's three-letter occupational codes were used to classify the occupational aspirations of these women in both 1980 and the 1990s. For 1990, we used the occupation from the interview data if it differed from that reported in the 1990 questionnaire.

The 25 women who had dropped their interest in a science career all had either Investigative (I) or Realistic (R) Holland codes in their occupational aspiration in 1980 because it was on this basis that they were identified as having a science-related career aspiration. All but three of these women had Investigative in their 1980 occupational code (Table 3.2), but only one had Investigative in her 1990 three-letter interest code (Table 3.2). Of these 25 women, 14 had the Realistic letter in their occupational code in 1980 but only 2 had the Realistic code in their 1990 three-letter occupational code. All 25 women had some Holland code that remained present from 1980 to 1990, as Holland's theory would predict. The stable codes were mostly Social (S) and/or Enterprising (E). All 25 women had both Social and Enterprising occupational codes in their 1990 three-letter codes. These S and E codes had been combined with I and R career interest codes in 1980 for these women, and 10 years later the I and R had largely dropped out of their primary career interests. They changed their minds as they gained more experience and information about themselves and about science and other career options; better informed, they chose a career field that they liked better and that suited them better. Based on these 25 women, the support for Holland's theory is somewhat mixed. Some Holland codes did indeed remain constant from 1980 to 1990 (i.e., Social and Enterprising career interests). However, their earlier career interest in Realistic and Investigative activities were no longer dominant.

Occupational Prestige Level:
1980 Compared With 1990 Choices

The prestige level of careers chosen is one indication of the motivation and commitment a woman has to a career as an important life role. Aspired to occupational prestige level may be assessed more validly at an earlier age, at 9–12 years according to Gottfredson (1981), than career interests, which tend to crystallize during high school (Gottfredson, 1981; Super, 1990). We assessed the prestige level of the occupational aspirations of these 25 women in 1980 and again in 1990 (Table 3.2). On average, the prestige level had remained

Table 3.2 Career Changer Women: Occupations Aspired to in 1980 and in the 1990s: Prestige and Holland Code (n = 25)

Name	1980			1990		
	Code	Occupation	Prestige	Code	Occupation	Prestige
Kathy	CRS	Accountant	78	ESR	Manager	84
Ileen	CRS	Accountant	78	CSE	Secretary	61
Lorna	CRS	Accountant	78	CSE	Secretary	61
Wendy	IRE	Chemist	79	ESI	Journalist	82
Becky	IRE	Computer programmer	62	ESA	Sales	70
Vanessa	IRE	Computer programmer	62	CSE	Secretary	61
Terry	IRE	Computer programmer	62	AES	Interior Designer	62
Lenore	EIS	Computer programmer	62	CES	Waitress	16
Vicky	RIE	Controller	56	AES	Community developer	82
Theresa	SIA	Airplane pilot	79	ESA	Sales	70
Erica	SIA	Nurse	46	CSE	Secretary	61
Tina	SIA	Nurse	46	SEA	College administrator	72
Elaine	SIA	Nurse	46	CSE	Supervisor (UPS)	44
Opal	SIA	Nurse	46	ESC	Marketing	72
Wanda	ISA	Physician	92	ESA	Sales manager	70
Tonya	SEI	Political scientist	81	SEA	Urban planner	54
Norma	SIA	Psychologist	81	CSE	Forms design analyst	61
Bernadette	SIA	Psychologist	81	SEC	Youth counselor	44
Sandra	SIA	Psychologist	81	ESC	Credit manager	74
Cindy	IES	Sociologist	81	SAE	Teacher	72
Quin	RSI	Radiologist	48	SAE	Counselor	72
Rachael	SIR	Health therapist	58	CSE	Secretary	61
Erin	SRE	Occupational therapist	67	ESA	Lawyer	93
Ginny	IRS	Veterinarian	78	SAE	Teacher	72
Eunice	IRS	Veterinarian	78	ESR	Manager	80

relatively similar (63.3 and 66.0, respectively). Of interest is the finding that, in 1990, the women in our interview study who were still in a science-related occupation had an average occupational prestige level of 62.0. It may be seen from these figures that the women who changed from a science field to other fields, on average, did not enter lower-prestige occupations when compared with those women who stayed in science-related fields.

Finding a Better Career Fit

In the United States, women are far below parity in the sciences and the technical fields, although the biological sciences are an exception (National Science Foundation, 1994). It was hoped, following affirmative action legislation, that more women would enter the underrepresented science fields. However, the opportunity to earn more money, in a higher-prestige occupation, is not as important as some other factors for many of the women we interviewed. For the most part, both those in science (see Chapter 2) and those eventually choosing other fields indicated that a career should be one that you like, that you enjoy, rather than one in which you might earn a lot of money but be unhappy. Middle-class Americans have considerable freedom to choose an occupation to a large extent based on interest, provided that they have the requisite ability and their emotional energy is not directed elsewhere. Lower-middle-class Americans experience a variety of constraints on their freedom to choose, including lack of resources and discrimination. So, even when schoolteachers and counselors encourage bright women to consider computer programming and engineering, some of those who began a major in college in these fields changed their fields because they did not enjoy that type of work.

Many of the women we interviewed who had wanted a science-related career in high school eventually found a better fit for their interests and abilities in another career field. Some of them, who were ninth graders in 1980, had shifted their career goals by the time they entered college and did not waste any time studying for the wrong career.

Tina had been interested in computer programming in 1980, but when she entered college she found the courses related to this major not to her liking. She liked working more with people, and she switched to a major in educational administration. She was completing her master's degree when we interviewed her and she was feeling very good about her career future. Similarly, Tonya, who had chosen political science in 1980 and was dreaming about the

Peace Corps, ended up majoring in urban planning. Her early political experiences helping her uncle and later her stepfather to get elected had influenced her earlier choice. But she found she had a strong interest in helping community groups improve their living conditions and she found a major that fit this interest better.

Finding a Better Career Fit Despite a Series of Obstacles

Vicky is a woman we interviewed who found a better fit, but she did this only by overcoming a series of obstacles. She is an African American woman from City High School. Her mother had an A.A. degree and wanted her daughter to be a doctor. In 1980, she put down controller/accountant as her career aspiration. She was in ninth grade. Now she is a successful community developer and enjoys making museum-quality historical dolls on the side. How did she change her career choice? A high school program helped. In her inner-city high school, a program was introduced to involve interested young people in working on a local newspaper. Vicky was selected to participate. She found she loved journalism and she was good at it. She wanted a job where she could help people and she thought journalism would allow her voice to be heard, so she majored in journalism in college. It was only later when she became disillusioned with the commercialism and politics of journalism that she switched to community development as a better way to help people in trouble. She is married to a supportive spouse and is very happy with her life and work today. More of Vicky's story is told in Chapters 7 and 8.

Few of the "changers" who aspired to a science career became discouraged because of ethnic discrimination in school or at work. Those women who experienced discrimination from classmates, teachers, and employers proved very resilient and found careers that satisfied them in spite of discrimination. For example, Vicky was placed in an ethnically diverse, racially integrated inner-city high school by her mother. When she went to a state university that was not racially integrated, she said,

I just didn't like it. I went from this place where everybody is different and you're celebrating people's differences. It's a small world after all. Then you go to a place where people, 17-year-olds who had never met a black person in their life. My very first roommate had never met a black person. And there was this suddenly culture shock and I hated it, because there were all these misconceptions. One day I came back to my room and found a hate blacks message pinned to the door. Classes toward the sophomore year got smaller and smaller. I found myself seeing fewer and fewer black people. You kind of get sick of being a role model. You just want to be left alone. After two years I came home and went to a college in the city.

Vicky completed her B.A. degree in journalism and then changed her career to community developer, a career that suited her ideals better. Vicky doesn't remember much about her high school counselor. She was not a positive or a negative influence for her. Vicky noted that if a teacher seemed to enjoy teaching and was nice to her, she really liked that teacher, and a few of her teachers were like that. She received recognition for her creative writing at school and for her work on the newspaper, and these positive experiences helped her when she encountered obstacles. The school environment was difficult for Vicky because she was overweight and not attractive in her own eyes. As a result, she endured insults from classmates and, in an attempt to be accepted by them, tried to steal something from a local store and got caught. Then she attempted suicide. The school provided counseling at this point to both Vicky and her mother and that got her through the difficult period. Vicky is a woman who showed determination.

Wendy also showed resolve. She is Hispanic and has three brothers and one sister. She attended Farmerville High School. Her father is a successful physician, and he wanted all his children to be doctors. Wendy put down chemist in 1980 when we first asked her what she wanted to be. She thought that the occupation of chemist was related to medicine. She was a very good student and enjoyed her science and math classes, but her interests also led her to join the high school newspaper staff. She won several prizes for her writing and ended up as the newspaper editor in her senior year in high school. When she went to college, she majored in journalism, despite her father's unwillingness to help pay her college expenses. She is now a successful reporter for a metropolitan newspaper.

Several years later, after Wendy was successful in her journalism career, she said,

My father said, "You know, I was wrong" and now he is one of my biggest supporters.

Wendy had a difficult time in the all-white Country High School because of her Hispanic ethnicity. She had an accent in a rural environment, and the kids were often cruel. However, she had some good experiences with some of her teachers and with her counselor, and she excelled in English and on the school newspaper. The positive experiences seemed to keep her going when she experienced difficulties. She too showed her determination. But some of the women who changed their aspirations were not able to "hang in there"; they were derailed by circumstances seemingly beyond their control. These women's stories are described next.

Derailed by Circumstances Beyond Their Ability to Cope

Sex Role Socialization

Some of the women we interviewed changed their aspirations not because of dysfunctional family experiences but because of their sex role socialization in their family. These women learned from their parents that the most important thing they could do in life was marry and raise a family. Norma, a straight-A student in high school who wanted to be a psychologist in 1980 when she was in ninth grade, commented,

My mom always encouraged me, just like he [her father] did. She stayed home and raised three kids before she ever went to work. I loved having her home and I wouldn't have had it any other way. I think looking to the future when I have my own kids, that was a big influence. All through high school I was thinking I don' t really want to go to college for four years, get a career, and then decide to stay home and raise my children. So she was a big role model in that part of it, as far as raising children. Staying home and taking care of them. To me it was an either/or situation. I could either have a career or stay home to raise my children and have the career later.

Norma made some other comments during the interview that indicated she was somewhat conflicted about her role as a woman:

My mother never worked until I was in high school. She stayed home with us. I remember thinking as a kid, look at her life, she had given up her own life to take care of us. I remember thinking, I'm never going to do that, she was just . . . I felt bad because I thought she had ruined her life to do that, but I enjoyed having her home, and I wouldn't have that any other way. I thought that was great. But I remember thinking if I have kids there is no way that I'm going to give up the rest of my life just to take care of those kids. But as you get older you realize, there's things in life you want and you make sacrifices.

Norma married soon after she finished high school, then she went to college for two years and studied computer programming. She didn't graduate, perhaps because she moved with her husband to a distant city where he had been offered a good position. After several brief jobs in various locations, the couple returned to their home town. There she obtained a position as a computer forms design analyst. She said,

> Yeah, I remember being confused as to what I wanted to do, what I was going to do. I really didn't have a plan, and everyone, you know seeing questionnaires come in like this and it made you stop and make up a plan. So I don't know, there were points in my life where I thought, I'm just going to get married and have kids, and yeah I remember being confused as to what I wanted to do, that I would stay home and take care of them anyway, why would I need to go through school, get a career and then have to stop what I'm doing to take care of the kids. And then on the other hand I was thinking, I'm never going to get married and have kids, I'm just going to go out, go to school and have a career forever. At that time too, if I remember, my parents didn't have a lot of money. They had just sent my older brother away to college. Living at home you hear about that. They were real quiet about that kind of stuff, but I always knew. And I felt since I didn't really have a definite plan of what I wanted to do, if I was just going to go to college to take stuff, it wouldn't be worth my time or their money.

You may recall that Norma had ruled out psychology as a career when she learned that it would take about 12 years of college and graduate school to qualify. But it seems that Norma's experiences in her family were influential in that decision. Why else would 12 years seem too long to invest in a career? She had already internalized the idea that her role as a woman was to be married and have children, and that having children meant staying home to care for them, not going off to work. But she also enjoyed school and academic challenges and thought her mother had wasted her life. Norma had also learned, it seems, that a man's role is to be the breadwinner, and therefore investing in a college education for sons is more important than doing the same for daughters. Ironically, in Norma's case, her brothers' grades were not as good as Norma's in elementary and high school, but they were the ones who went on to college and both earned graduate degrees. Norma recalls,

> My brothers and I were real close in age. We were all just a year apart, and there was a lot of competition as far as the grades and who did better on what. And at the time I was learning to write I remember, who writes better than who, and all of that type of stuff. But I was bored and I remember wishing that I could just go on with this class and go up to the next grade. I don't know why I was thinking that in first grade, but then my brothers, one being a

year ahead of me I knew that would create a lot of problems. I don't think I ever suggested to anybody, a teacher or parent, that that happen. I have no idea if I ever said anything, but I don't remember telling them. And I don't know if it would be considered back then when I was in grade school at such a small school, you just didn't see kids skipping grades. You saw them being held back a lot, but not skipping grades. I just know that if they would have put me into his class it would have probably caused a lot more problems. My brothers were more of just a pain. And I think we're a little too close for the age growing up. Three kids that age in a small house got a little hectic at times. My older brother liked to beat up everybody so I had to learn to fight at a young age. And they really never were big in school, they made good enough grades, but they were more like class clowns, and didn't take school that seriously. They surprised me when they both went to college and graduated, that really surprised me because they did better in college than they did in high school.

Norma appears to illustrate Gottfredson's (1981) point. According to Gottfredson, occupational sex role stereotypes are learned early in life and are prepotent over achievement strivings and career interests, both of which mature later.

Critical Events

Vanessa, a Hispanic woman who attended City High School, had wanted to be a computer programmer when she was in the 12th grade. She had a series of difficult experiences. Her mother died of cancer when Vanessa was 13. Her father, an immigrant from Mexico, only held menial jobs and there wasn't much money. Her grades were all As and Bs before her mother died, but then they fell off to Cs and Ds. She became pregnant at age 16 and her high school wouldn't take her back after she had the baby. She had to go to City High School to finish her degree. She said,

In high school my plans were to go to college and get a career. Which those plans didn't work out. I only went to college like half a year and I dropped out. The reason was I had a child, first I had to worry about her. And then I was working while I did go to college so it was tough for me so I decided college is not for me.

She was not able to achieve her goals. She was attending the top state university, an institution that only accepts the top 10% of graduating high school students. Her grades had picked up again by the time she graduated from high school. But the combined effort to go to college, work half time, and care for her infant daughter were too much for Vanessa. She regrets her situation. When she was asked what she would want to be sure to tell young people today, she said, "Go to college, have a definite plan and stick to it." Vanessa is determined that her daughters will go to college. She had a second child 2 months old at the time of the interview. Her first child is now 14 years old.

An outstanding characteristic of the stories some of these women told about their career development was that it was taking them longer to figure out what they wanted to do. Wanda said, "If I knew what I wanted to do, I would do it." Terry said, "I want to know what my special thing is." Why this uncertainty? In listening to their stories, it became clear that the external events affecting their career development were complex and often involved their family situation as well as their experiences in school.

One of the pervasive external influences on the career development of some of these women was growing up in an alcoholic, abusive family or a family with a mentally ill parent. Wanda, for example, had parents who divorced in her freshman year at Farmerville High School. She said, "Things were just kind of distorted then." Her mother had moved to another town before the divorce and then her father took up with another woman and he moved out. Wanda didn't want to leave her high school friends, so she was allowed to stay in her home with her older, 18-year-old brother. For the next six months, she went wild, partying, drinking, using drugs. Eventually she was removed from the cheerleader team and then asked to leave school. She had several narcotics arrests during this period as well. She moved in with her father and his new wife and kids for a while, but that didn't work out. She got in trouble in school again. Then she moved back with her mom and eventually finished high school and college. Wanda said,

My dad, he's really different. I mean he's a very volatile person, when he blows up, when he's like living in a hormonal cycle thing, every so often he just lost his mind and just would scream and wildly break things, never hurt anyone, but words are sometimes more sharp than objects. So it was a kind of tense childhood sometimes, in regard to parents arguing. He would just go crazy, nobody argued with him. . . . One occasion where the potatoes were too soupy he broke every piece of fine china we had into the potatoes on the table. This was at a family dinner, that's just an example of how nutty he would be, and it's like, what is your problem, you know—about twice a week.

Wanda continued,

Before the divorce my brother and my sister had a lot of opportunities. They had cars bought for them, college educations offered and homes bought for them when they married. Then when they divorced that kind of, just poof, was gone and there were no opportunities for me.

In spite of these circumstances, Wanda earned money to put herself through college and has a bachelor's degree in psychology. She had put down doctor in 1980 when she was in ninth grade. But, as noted earlier in this chapter, she couldn't remember why. She works now in a sales management position and was thinking about moving into real estate when we interviewed her. She found that her strengths lie in sales.

Terry is another of our participants who was derailed by circumstances seemingly beyond her control from pursuing a career in a science-related field. Yet she persevered and eventually earned her college degree. She said she wanted to be a computer programmer when she was in high school:

I had a very rough childhood, not knowing who my father was until I was 10. My mother lived with a man and then married him a year later. It changed my mother drastically, they are both alcoholics now. I grew up with, "Come on have your friends over and we'll have a party." I wanted so bad to get away from that. I thought maybe I could go into something that I could work with, I think engineering or architecture or some type of design work, because I see things in three dimensions, rather than working with figures on a flat piece of paper. . . . I did not have family support in order to go into different areas. I started working two weeks after my sixteenth birthday and I continued to work through high school.

An early marriage, and the birth of three children, have interrupted her career plans. When we interviewed her, she was thinking about going back to school or to work. She said,

If there was just some type of guidance—even if it wasn't sit down and hold my hand, but someone to take those two things, what you like and what you are good at and put them together and say "try this" you know. I wish I could find out what that is that I am good at. I'm still trying to find that.

Since our interview, Terry has completed an A.A. degree in interior design. She is working in this career field and loves it.

School Experiences

Other reasons for "derailment" from their original career goals included experiences in school. What were the schools like that educated these women? What were math and science classes like? Did the students have counselors they could go to for help with planning their careers? Beatrice, who had aspired to be a psychologist when she was in ninth grade at Metro High School, lowered her sights and chose to earn a master's degree instead of a Ph.D. because she was afraid of taking the statistics courses that would be required by the latter. She said,

The Cs in math. It was just, it started out that math wasn't my strong point, and then as I got older I just became phobic about it, which didn't help very much. Math and I, that's always been a negative. Then in biology the teacher was an idiot. The most sexist person, I remember him saying there's only one thing on earth stupider than horses, and it's women. And now when I think back, I think, I should've reported him. But when you're a freshman you don't. I just hated him first of all, and then I had no interest in biology. I remember the final, he had Fs, and then he had super Fs. I got a super F. Yeah boys are smarter maybe in science. I still don't think its because they're naturally smarter, but the teachers get geared towards the men and science so I always thought that they had it easier. So when I went to college I wanted to go into psychology, but I found that you had to take a lot of math in psychology, a lot of stats and stuff like that, and I just hate math so I switched.

The experiences of Beatrice and of Norma related to their sex role socialization appear to have seriously constricted these women's achievement in a career. One of my female graduate students who is also a sixth-grade science teacher had been doing science experiments with her pupils and encouraging the girls to consider science for their future careers. When she asked her students to "draw a scientist," her results were discouraging to her. Girls were more likely to draw a nerdy man than a female scientist (Figure 3.1). The results this teacher obtained suggest that by the sixth grade, many girls have internalized the societal view that scientists are male and nerdy, and this view deters them from seriously considering a science career for themselves.

Eunice had such a bad experience in her English writing classes at Suburban High School that she decided she couldn't earn a college degree. She took a job directly out of high school and today is the manager in a business. She said,

Figure 3.1. A Sixth-Grade Girl's Drawing of "a Scientist"

I have a phobia about college—really scary. It started in junior high. I had a real strict teacher and I believe it was sixth grade. She was real strict as far as English goes and she wasn't one just to work with you on something. She would kind of raise her voice and I don't handle that well. I felt the teacher was putting so much pressure on getting it right that I was blocking out getting it right.

In high school, she was interested in being both a veterinarian and an architect, but because of her English phobia she was afraid to go to college. She continues to enjoy animals, and she also enjoys designing houses. She is currently building her own house, which she helped design. She seems "hung up" on her English skills, which has affected her ability to think clearly about what she wants to do with her life. She said,

I never really picked anything definite. It wasn't anything, in fact I've taken several career courses to try and help figure this out. And the one question that they ask the first night was what would be your dream job? As though it's out of reach or you think it's out of reach. My thinking is if I knew what that was I'd be it. Nothing would be in my way. I'd go for it. It's just a matter of determining what it is.

Summary and Conclusions

In trying to understand why some of the women we interviewed had changed their career aspirations from a science-related career to something else, we discovered that for many of them high school was too early to ask them what they wanted to be when they grew up. Many of them ended up in satisfying careers, which, on average, were as high in prestige level as the science careers they had indicated an interest in in 1980. Theoretical explanations for this can be found in the classical theories of Super (1990) and Holland (1985).

The women who overcame obstacles to achieve their goals deserve our awe and admiration. But other women were derailed by external circumstances beyond their ability to cope and did not find a satisfying career. Some of these women are still hoping for something better. The women who were A students in high school and ended their education with high school graduation are working and achieving well below their potential (i.e., Lenore, Norma, and Elaine). Better theoretical explanations for these women can be found in the theories designed especially for women described in Chapter 1 (Astin, 1984; Betz & Fitzgerald, 1987; Betz & Hackett, 1983; Farmer, 1978, 1985). These theories take into account the influence of context and socialization and their potential for positive or negative impact on career development. Betz and Hackett and Farmer have grounded their theories for women's career development in the broader cognitive learning theory of Albert Bandura (1989). We will turn to these theories again in Chapter 14 when we discuss how counselors might help these women.

There are important implications from these women's experiences for counselors, teachers, and parents. Especially important in this regard are the women who were derailed by circumstances seemingly beyond their ability to cope. In Norma's case, her family sex role socialization kept this talented woman from investing in a college education. What kind of intervention could have changed this outcome? For Vanessa, the death of her mother when she was 13, the birth of her child out of wedlock when she was 16, and lack of funds led her to give up on her college degree. What kind of intervention could have changed this outcome? Later in this book we address these questions, especially in Chapter 14 on counseling.

4

Persisters and Career Changers in Technical Careers

Are There Gender Differences?

SUSAN GIURLEO

For many years, there have been biases against women in the sciences, especially in engineering and technical careers (Fitzpatrick & Silverman, 1989; Hackett, Betz, Casas, & Rocha-Singh, 1992; McIlwee & Robinson, 1992; Morgan, 1992). Academic and professional discrimination have been widely studied (Hackett et al., 1992; McDade, 1988; McIlwee & Robinson, 1992) as well as the barriers that exist to women's choosing and succeeding in engineering training programs and professional careers (Fitzpatrick & Silverman, 1989; McDade, 1988; McIlwee & Robinson, 1992; Morgan, 1992).

It has been found that women and men often believe that women are less prepared and less competent in the study of hard science and engineering (McDade, 1988; McIlwee & Robinson, 1992). In their extensive study of women in engineering, McIlwee and Robinson (1992) found that many women felt that they were not as prepared or socialized to feel comfortable in an engineering work climate. They stated that boys were encouraged from an early age to explore and work with mechanical things such as cars, but girls did not receive that type of experience while growing up. Women therefore felt uncomfortable designing and experimenting and were generally underprepared compared with their male classmates. This discomfort often led to their own questioning of their engineering abilities. McDade (1988) also found that women who dropped out of mathematics and chemistry majors questioned their abilities and competence. On the other hand, men who left these majors cited better opportunities in other majors and did not cite lack of ability as a reason to change majors.

Given the abundance of quantitative research on the topic of women's experiences in science and engineering (Betz, 1990; Betz & Hackett, 1983; Brush, 1991; Ethington & Wolfle, 1988; Fitzpatrick & Silverman, 1989; Hackett et al., 1992; Jagacinski, 1987; Lane, 1990; McDade, 1988; McDonald,

Clarke, & Dobson, 1990; Morgan, 1992; Ware & Lee, 1988), I chose to investigate these issues qualitatively. I am interested in how women's experiences in these fields are different than men's and how the training and work environment can be improved for women. I felt it would be interesting to compare women who persisted in technical careers and women who changed careers with men who persisted and who changed careers.

To better understand my perspective when analyzing this data, I gave careful consideration to my subjectivity. First and foremost, my subjectivity is based on being a woman examining the experiences of women and men in male-dominated careers. I am similar to my female subjects in our shared sex and possible experiences in working with men. However, I have never worked in a field that is nontraditional. My subjectivity in this research is similar to that of my previous research with women in engineering. Based on my limited experiences at my brother's undergraduate engineering campus, I believe that the engineering environment is often hostile to women. This environment could explain why fewer women pursue technical careers in the first place, and why those who do choose such a career early on often pursue other interests later in their career development. I feel that there exists some form of discrimination against women in technical education and jobs. I also feel that engineering and computer science are not "people-oriented" fields, and that women and men who like to work with people will seek other areas in which to work regardless of their aptitude for technical careers. These perspectives may have colored my understanding and interpretation of the stories of the men and women presented here. For example, I may have been especially sensitive to evidence that women find the engineering climate more hostile and discriminatory than do men. Several of my findings do support my subjective beliefs about the educational and occupational engineering climates for women. However, some of my results run counter to what I believed. This was especially true in my analyses of the stories of the women who persisted in technical careers.

I analyzed the data with my subjectivity in mind. Of the 105 interviews conducted for this study, there were a total of 22 persisters and career changers in technical careers, specifically engineering and computer science. However, only 5 of these were women. To have approximate gender balance, I narrowed my participant pool to 11 including 3 male and 3 female science persisters, 3 male career changers, and 2 female career changers. Although the information and themes proposed in this chapter are based on all 11 interviewees' experiences, the experiences and quotations presented here are from 6 interviewees. All themes are fairly representative of other participants' experiences.

This chapter will first explore themes and results from the career changers and then explain the findings for those who pursued a science-related career. There are some similarities for the men and women who switched careers, and those findings will be presented first. As might be expected, women experienced some unique barriers and difficulties in pursuing technical careers and these results will be presented next, followed by the themes related to the male career changers. Because the types of obstacles faced by the female career changers are similar to those experienced by the women who chose to pursue a technical career, the themes related to female persisters will then be presented. Finally, it appears that the men and women who pursue technical careers have many experiences and traits in common. These similarities and themes will be explored. The implications of these findings on career development research will be proposed, along with suggestions for further research.

Men and Women Who Changed Careers

In reading the interviews of those who made a career change, it appears that individuals who work in technical careers, but also enjoy working with people, often switch their career focus. It also seems that those who switched their focus found that they did not enjoy the training involved in their college classes, and they generally did not like the technical work required for an engineering or computer science career.

Several career changers actually did begin college in engineering or computer science but kept looking for ways to work with people on a more human level. One man even worked as a computer programmer for a year until he became frustrated and made a risky career change so that he could work with people on a regular basis. This theme is persistent through both men and women career changers' stories.

Kevin, an African American male participant who attended Metro High School, had a realistic understanding of engineering work and concepts but kept searching for an engineering discipline where he could work with people. He set his sights on industrial engineering but found that unfulfilling and eventually decided to pursue a business degree. He worked as an accountant for a while, but at the time of his interview was recruiting students for a college and giving motivational speeches to high school students. Kevin had this to say about his desire to work with people and his attempt to find an engineering field that would allow him to have more social contact:

Let me think about mechanical engineering as my college major. Since I was taking some machine drawing classes in high school it seemed logical. However, it was very technical oriented. Very self oriented, meaning you're by yourself doing . . . and I very quickly realized that that wasn't for me. When I got into college during my freshman year I took a few engineering classes. I liked industrial engineering. And I said "Wow, industrial engineering." They tend to be more people oriented but it was still more technical than what I thought, or what I wanted What else is there out there? And that's when I turned to business.

A related theme concerns the idea that career changers did not like the technical work required in the engineering and computer fields. Several of these individuals did not actually know what type of work engineers and computer programmers did before they chose these careers as goals in high school. Lenore is a Caucasian woman who attended Suburban High School. She aspired to be a computer scientist in high school but had never even worked on a computer during her high school years. It seems that several of these individuals, including Lenore, were either told or heard in the popular media that computers and technology were the careers of the future where one could make money in a secure job. Because most of these people were quite bright and successful in school, they felt they could pursue any career and naturally wanted to go into a stable, lucrative career. In explaining her career choice as a high school student, Lenore said,

My career goal was to be a computer science major. I enjoyed math and I just thought that that would be the business of the future. Which it is. And . . . that I would get so far in life with that career. . . . I guess I picked that career with just dollar signs in my eyes. I just thought that that would be the most up-coming thing for me.

Similarly, Dorian, a male Caucasian career changer who attended Metro High School, worked as a computer programmer for the Navy and switched to a career as a Navy recruiter. He had this to say:

I guess what I initially had an interest in was computers, the idea behind that was to be successful whether it was in computers, electrical engineering, or mechanical engineering. I wanted to make the bucks and I wanted something that was modern, up-and-coming. You know computer science was the happening thing at that time. Every one said, "Man, when you become a computer programmer, you're going to make money." So, money was a motivator and still is. More so, saying I wanted to do that route because that's where the money's at and that's where the careers are, without even knowing what computers were about. I had the opportunity with the Navy to work with computers and I realized that when you lock me in with this computer in a room with no windows, I was ready to throw the computer out. Me and the computer were not going to get along.

Others did have a better understanding of what type of work engineers did, and were good at math and science in high school, but they did not enjoy their engineering or computer classes once they got to college. Some felt that the college classes were much harder than what they learned in high school and, consequently, felt underprepared and discouraged. Lenore experienced this difficulty and said,

I took the computer science classes [at college], and I could not catch on for the life of me. I even would ask friends to tutor me, to help me so I could grasp it, but I got so discouraged, I just thought, "Well, how come I could do so well in high school and I just can't grasp this?" . . . It was just terrible. So I figured, "Oh, well." I left. I left there and I took business courses at a little college. . . . I just had no interest in school anymore.

Although male and female career changers did present some common themes, female changers compared with male changers had some different experiences that may have led them to abandon their original career goals.

The Women Who Changed Careers

In our sample, there were not many women who indicated in high school that they would like to pursue technical careers. I identified two female career changers—a woman who originally wanted to be a computer scientist, Lenore, and one who wanted to become a commercial pilot, Theresa.

Both of these women experienced some form of sexual discrimination in the pursuit of their goals. Lenore, who attended Suburban High School, also experienced a great deal of sexual harassment in her high school years from science teachers, which may have restricted her career pursuits. She explains the experience in this way:

My chemistry teacher was just really bizarre and, I felt really almost inhibited with him because I would ask questions, I'd bring up my lab book and he'd brush against my breast, you know. And then I thought OK, this was an accident. So the next time . . . I'd have questions and we'd be doing labs, and he'd come by and he you know, it was always the touching. . . . And then I kind of went into myself and I just didn't ask questions anymore, and I think that's when my concentration went down to hell. . . . So I just stayed away from him in my class . . . I just withdrew, I did. And so I know I didn't want to go into the sciences because I couldn't handle chemistry.

Although an excellent student in high school, Lenore did not find much success in college. She attributed this to being unprepared both academically and socially for the college experience. In 1992, she was working as a waitress and bartender and enjoyed her work very much. She emphasized that her job was enjoyable because of the people she worked with and the customers she came to know and care about.

After graduating from County High School, Theresa went on to complete her aviation degree in college. Her goal was to become a commercial pilot, but she found it very difficult to get work after graduating. She stated that more white men were being hired than women or minorities and it seems that this may have limited her job opportunities. In college, she felt that there was no discrimination against the women, even though they were a significant minority. She explained that she originally thought that being a woman would be an advantage to her career, but it did not turn out that way:

It was strange there [were] only 10 of us [women] in a 120. There [were] 10 women and only 5 of us made it, only 5 of us graduated. And I thought all along that would be an advantage. Which until about two years ago, it was. And then they started the reverse discrimination things where they went back to hiring more white males and less females. . . . I mean for a long time I thought it would be an advantage but it didn't work out that way.

To support herself financially, she began working at a cosmetics counter and seemed satisfied with the work. She felt there were opportunities to advance into management in the company if she wanted to. Although disappointed that she was not flying or using her degree in her work, she appeared optimistic about the future in the cosmetics company. However, because she did not keep up with her flying, it will be difficult for her to get a job as a pilot. At the time of the interview, she had a tentative offer to be a pilot, but it was a long shot and it did not appear that she would pursue a career as a pilot. She did have the intention to pursue flying as a hobby, however.

Unfortunately, it seems that these women were derailed early from their original career interests. This premature interruption of career exploration did not allow them to determine a definite career path. They seem to have found work that satisfied their immediate needs of financial support and comfort in working with people. However, they have not had the opportunity to delve into a more complex career development process. It would appear that the external influences of sexual discrimination and/or harassment hurt their internal career exploration processes.

The male nonpersisters did not specify discrimination, harassment, or feeling out of place in technical careers as reasons for their switching to other careers. It seems that the men went through a more uninterrupted career development than the women and ultimately decided that engineering or computer science wasn't for them. Because they did not have to struggle with their comfort level or proving themselves competent, it is possible that they could concentrate more on their likes, dislikes, and achievement needs in their careers as opposed to having to focus only on their survival needs.

The Men Who Changed Careers

Of interest, the male nonpersisters had some initial success in achieving their career goals in technical areas. They did not find the course work difficult or have any problem finding work in their chosen fields. Unlike the women, they were allowed to come to a decision that these careers were not for them after experiencing the work for a time. The Navy recruiter, Dorian, worked as a computer programmer for a year before deciding to switch to his current career. He explains the process this way:

I worked with computers for the Navy for about a year. I quickly got fed up with the computer field, something I always thought I would *like*. I got locked up with a computer and there [were] no people skills involved. It was me and this computer. That's how I realized, "This is *not* me."

Kevin, who changed his career from engineering to business, took an even more complex route to discover his social career needs. Kevin decided to major in accounting in college and got a job auditing banks. While in that job, he took the Myers Briggs test, which confirmed his belief that he was more of a people-oriented individual. He explains this understanding well in this quote:

And after I took that test, it was like, See you don't belong in the auditing banks business! That is not your fit! You are not the technical type, you are more people oriented. You are kind of analytical . . . (because I get into analyzing). When I meet people I begin to analyze them, study them and read them etc. Why? Because I am trying to really find out where they are, where they are coming from, what needs do they have, that kind of thing.

These people appeared to switch careers for various reasons, some positive and others negative, but the male career changers seemed content in their newly chosen careers. The women who changed careers did not complain about their current work, but they seemed to be not fully satisfied. Both Lenore and Theresa stated that they would quit or change their jobs if they had the chance and the financial means. They also both said that young people should be sure not to waste time and money in a college program that will not be useful in the long run. Neither of the male career changers had such feelings. The men appeared satisfied with their current line of work and were looking forward to developing their chosen careers in the future.

The men in this sample were fortunate to be able to examine their work interests and personality styles and find career paths that fit them well. The concept of personality and interests influencing career choice has been proposed and supported by the work of Holland (1985). Holland's theory proposes that people possessing certain personality traits will seek and find occupational environments that "fit" their personality, interests, and skills, which he refers to as "person-environment fit" (Holland, 1985). These ideas are also supported qualitatively in this sample of female and male persisters in engineering and computer science. Both the men and the women who persisted in these careers have many traits in common. However, the women do experience these careers differently.

Women in Engineering and Computer Science Careers

Like the female nonpersisters, female persisters acknowledge sex discrimination in their chosen technical careers. However, these women do not seem to be negatively affected by such discrimination and do not let it negatively influence their career pursuits. In fact, they appear to enjoy their unique position as women in male-dominated professions.

Gena is a Native American woman who attended Metro High School with Kevin and Dorian. She received her bachelor's degree in mechanical engineering and explains what it is like to be a woman working in this career:

I'm the first woman engineer they've ever hired there too. . . . There's all men in the shop. There's four women at the company, three secretaries and myself. So I have to deal with men who have been working there forever. And now they have to take orders from a girl, who's their daughter's age and all. You know that was a little difficult at first. But they came around. . . . I just had to prove what I was doing basically.

Joyce is a Caucasian woman who attended Farmerville High School. At the time of her interview, she was working as a computer programmer for a large insurance company. She sees discrimination against women as a force that might prevent her from moving into a management position. She had this to say about the lack of support she receives from her boss:

My supervisor is not going to buck the system. He would not put me on a list for management because he would have to back me. There would be a lot of work for him to get me into management. He'd rather just stay low keyed and not have to defend or present me to his peers. . . . If he did promote me into management and then I didn't do well it would reflect on him.

And so it does appear that some form of sexual discrimination or harassment does exist for women who stay in their chosen engineering or computing careers. However, these women do not allow such a work climate to derail them from the work they enjoy. In fact, several of them indicate that they enjoy being unique as women in the field. It does not bother them that they are a minority in their careers, and they seem to be proud of succeeding in the face of being one of only a few women in their workplaces.

Joyce, the computer programmer, had this to say about the challenge of being a woman in a computer career:

I think I've always been challenged. . . . I'm that kind of person that if you tell me "you can't do something" then I'm that much more motivated to do it. . . . To prove to myself, even though I am a woman I can do this job!

When asked about her status as a woman in an engineering career, Gena stated that being in the minority as a woman is not a problem for her:

See, that . . . was something I really liked. It didn't intimidate me. . . . Some women it may have intimidated. . . . Most women who are in engineering, that wasn't a problem for them. It's the people that don't get into it because they're afraid of [it] that it's a problem for. . . . Because all the women I went to college with [it] never, never really seemed to bother. Most of them liked being the only [woman]. "Hey I'm the only girl in the class," you know. It was neat or something.

It is evident from Gena's and Joyce's stories that they are very motivated to succeed in an academic and occupational area that fits their personality and skills. Bandura's (1986) sociocognitive framework of career development seems to fit their experiences. Although they perceive their working environments as sometimes difficult, there is something about them as people, some internal motivation and drive, that keeps them pushing forward and doing work they intrinsically enjoy. The enjoyment of being unique and approaching challenging situations seems to have helped these women in sticking with sometimes difficult academic and work environments. Of interest, these qualities of enjoying uniqueness and challenge are evident in all the engineers and computer programmers interviewed for this study, both male and female. These are themes that arise again and again in their stories.

Similarities Between Men and Women Who Persisted in Engineering and Computer Science

From analysis of the interviews, it appears that male persisters and female persisters have similar traits and personality characteristics. A separate section on male persisters does not seem useful given that these similarities are evident. The themes most evident for both women and men who pursued engineering and computer science careers were a desire to be the best in all that they do, a strong tendency to be competitive, and an enjoyment in working on challenging tasks and problem solving.

One recurring theme for all of the persisters was a strong desire to be the best in their work. They feel that this drive has been a part of them since childhood, and some attribute their success in their careers to this desire to be good at everything they do. Gena, the female engineer, expresses her desire to be the best this way:

I always wanted to be the best in the class. And when [I was] in grammar [school], I was at the top. When I was in high school it was a little bit tougher. And I got to college, forget it. I was in the middle of the pack. Which that was the hardest thing about your first semester in college, was that when you came from the top of the school but so did all these other people. It was a rude awakening.

Edwin is the son of a German immigrant father and attended County High School. In high school, he was unsure of what he wanted to do for a future career and more or less majored in athletics. He chose to study engineering in his senior year because he wanted to be involved in inventing new things. Throughout his story, Edwin emphasized that he always had a desire to be the best at everything he did. This quote is representative of his personality style in this regard:

I've always wanted to be the best, which is a weakness. It's a ridiculous point of view. . . . It goes back to first grade or even before that, I always wanted to be the best, the fastest, the strongest. . . . I'm not this competitive idiot, but when it gets right down to competition I want to come out on top, and it's still that way, by the way.

Related to this desire to be the best is the theme of competitiveness. Most persisters admitted they enjoy competition, whether in the workplace or in their avocational pursuits. Again, this competitive tendency was also evident in their younger years. Russell is a Caucasian male engineer in the Air Force also attended County High School. When asked if he competed in sports in high school, he answered,

Yeah, I guess I did. I was on the baseball team up through junior year. I played golf all four years. Um, basketball—what else? . . . I guess I ran track one year. I didn't enjoy that too much. But, yeah I have tried to control my competitive nature as I've gotten older. Playing tennis you try not to throw as many fits as when you were younger and all that. But I'm still very competitive. You just try not to let it show as much as you used to.

And Gena had this to say about her competitive tendencies:

I like to compete and win. Or actually not even win. Just competing. Winning is the reward. But the competition itself I always enjoyed.

The final unique theme for male and female persisters is their enjoyment of tackling challenging tasks and problem solving. Joyce, the female computer programmer, summed up this idea well:

Problem solving does give me this thrill. When you're working on a program and . . . then when you get it to work, it's just like "aha!" . . . I know when we went to school, I'd be like, "Oh give me one more try, let me try this and see if it works." My husband would be like, "Let's go, let's go." When you'd get it, you'd just be so happy . . . you had conquered your challenge.

Similarly, when asked if he could go back and do something else with his career, Russell, the Air Force engineer, answered that he would have enjoyed pushing himself to more challenges:

I think I would go back and I would probably be in the medical field. And I would be a surgeon. And it would probably be something like, high stress; either open heart or brain surgery. And where you could do both surgery and do some research. You know, what little we know about the brain. I think there is still a lot to discover there. But I could, you know, there's hands on there working in an ER room. Fast pace to some extent.

Conclusions

In summary, it appears that these qualitative interviews support previous research that states that women experience unique difficulties in the pursuit of engineering and other technical careers (McDade, 1988; McIlwee & Robinson, 1992). Sexual discrimination and sometimes harassment were experienced by all of the female participants in this study. Some women were adversely affected by such difficulties and either did not finish college or completed their technical degree and then pursued other careers, either by choice or by necessity. Other women, however, took these difficulties as challenges to be overcome and succeeded despite the problems of being a female minority in a male-dominated career.

It also appears that women, compared with men, who do not persist in technical careers have fewer opportunities to explore their career options. The women seem to be derailed from their career pursuits early on, while the men have more opportunities to examine their likes, dislikes, strengths, and weaknesses before deciding to switch careers. Unfortunately, it appears that women career changers did not have such chances to explore, and moved on to other careers more out of necessity and frustration than out of a true desire to change their career direction.

Another interesting finding is that it appears people's personalities and interests, as well as their intellectual strengths, help determine their career choices. For instance, those people with a strong aptitude for engineering, but who preferred to work with people, seem to eventually gravitate toward more people-oriented careers. This finding supports Holland's (1985) person-environment fit model of career development.

Of particular interest are the findings that the engineers and computer programmers in this study, regardless of gender, had a strong need to be challenged in their work and a drive to be the best at whatever they tried to achieve. These characteristics serve these people well in fields that involve constant problem solving and a competitive environment in which companies rush to produce the newest, cutting edge technology.

It appears that women who possess a strong need for achievement and challenge do well in technical careers. In addition, the women described in this chapter had lower "fear of success" than the women who did change careers (Horner, 1972). On the questionnaire distributed to all participants, these women strongly disagreed with questions such as the following: "I worry because my success may cause others to dislike me." "I avoid discussing my accomplishments because other people might be jealous." "I sometimes work at less than my best because I feel that others may resent me for performing well." These responses could indicate that women who persist in engineering and computer science careers are less likely to be discouraged by sexual harassment and discrimination. Other people's opinions about them did not deter Gena or Lenore from the pursuit of their chosen careers. The sometimes difficult academic and working environment seemed to be perceived as a challenge to be overcome by these women. Because they admit they enjoy challenge and competition, this work environment is a good fit for them.

An interesting question presents itself. Could it be the environment or work climate of these technical fields that keep women in the minority? Bandura (1978) suggested that there is a "reciprocal interaction between behavioral, cognitive, and environmental influences" (p. 344) in how people learn and behave. Perhaps this reciprocal interaction could also be occurring in women's pursuit of technical careers. For example, some women who have math and science ability may have been given a message that engineering is difficult and not a good choice for women. These messages could influence a young woman's thoughts and behaviors concerning her career options and she may not consider engineering or computer science careers as viable for her. Further, there currently are many programs aimed at improving young women's math and science aptitudes in the hopes that more of these women will pursue careers in the sciences. However, if what our participant Gena said is true, that the women in her engineering classes liked being in the minority and the challenge that presented, it could be possible that highly qualified women who do not feel comfortable in that environment will not persist. In fact, most engineering and computer programming higher education is a competitive process, with the dreaded "weed out" math and science classes in the freshman year of college. Students, especially women, who are not academically prepared for such competition may conclude that they are not qualified for such a challenging discipline and switch to less competitive fields where they feel more comfortable (Astin & Astin, 1993; McIlwee & Robinson, 1992). One could continue to extrapolate about the socialization of women to be less competitive and more passive than men, and how this general socialization could lead to discomfort in the competitive technical climate.

These are questions to which there are no easy answers. Further research, both qualitative and quantitative, could help discern how much of the difficulty women have in technical careers is due to lack of academic preparation, hostile environments in education and industry, and/or the general atmosphere/competitive climate of these professions.

From a theoretical standpoint, these stories support aspects of Holland's (1985) and Bandura's (1986) conceptualizations of young adult development. Holland's person-environment fit model appears to support the career development of the men in this sample. Whether they persisted in a technical career or changed careers, the men seemed to have opportunities to make choices based on a fit among their personalities, interests, skills, and occupations. The women's career development does not easily fit into Holland's model. Bandura's (1986) social cognitive framework appears to fit these women's experiences. Both persisters and career changers seemed to take their personal qualities, interests, and skills in relationship to their environmental situations in progressing through career development. This process appears more complex to navigate than simply finding a career path that fits one's interests. Given the evidence from these women's stories, it may be that Holland's (1985) model may not adequately represent the reality of young women's career development and that Bandura's (1986) conceptualizations are more accurate.

5

High-Achieving Women

Career Development Patterns

JANA REDDIN

A study by Hollinger and Fleming (1992) compared gifted women's adolescent aspirations with their adult achievements and found that a substantial number of the gifted women in their sample had not realized their educational or occupational aspirations. Researchers question why this discrepancy between women's aspirations and achievements exists, and how the problem can be resolved. While researchers have relied largely on quantitative methods to study this problem, qualitative methods have been neglected.

Gifted and talented women are faced with unique challenges in the education and occupation arenas because of their intellectual potential and gender. They are caught in a conflict between sex role stereotypes and achievement expectations (Hollinger, 1991). This conflict begins in adolescence when girls are establishing their gender identity and discovering what society views as feminine. However, this feminine stereotype is juxtaposed with the expectation for the gifted to achieve and with occupational stereotypes that label high-status careers as masculine.

This conflict between sex role expectations and expectations of fulfilling one's academic and occupational potential is illustrated in the discrepant findings between gifted women's actual talent and performance ratings and self-perceptions of ability (Arnold, 1993; Hollinger, 1983). Given this conflict, it is not surprising that gifted and talented women are less likely than their male counterparts to have a professional career, and that those who choose a professional career often select occupations that have lower status, require less education, and are more compatible with family roles (Eccles, 1985).

Some researchers question the practice of measuring women's success based on this male standard. Hollinger and Fleming (1992) report that when they asked gifted women to identify their achievements since high school graduation, 55% identified relational achievements, such as establishing and maintaining a relationship with a spouse or significant other, and 21% identified personal achievements, such as political action, personal development, travel, or fitness. Therefore, Hollinger and Fleming (1992) noted that the sample's reported accomplishments in their study were a depressed estimate of their actual achievements. They noted that stereotypically feminine careers are usually assigned lower status, and the narrow definition of achievement excludes accomplishments in the personal and interpersonal spheres (Hollinger & Fleming, 1992). Therefore, to effectively address the problem of women's underachievement, it may be necessary to broaden our definition of achievement and rethink our conceptualization of one's realization of potential (Hollinger & Fleming, 1992).

This area is important to me personally because I am a woman pursuing nontraditional educational aspirations. To more fully understand my own situation, it seems natural to study women who are high achievers. However, because my educational and career goals are similar to these women's, it is possible that I might project my own feelings and experiences into these women's stories, rather than allowing their own stories to emerge. Therefore, in analyzing the interviews, it was necessary to be aware of the differences and similarities between my experiences and the experiences of the women interviewed.

In the present study, six women were selected based on their educational and occupational achievements. Each woman has demonstrated achievement by obtaining an advanced degree and/or through her career accomplishments. All six of the women were interviewed individually about their career development processes, life experiences, and personal values. Each woman's story offers a unique perspective that adds richness not found in quantitative research. Their stories illustrate the internal and external influences on their achievements. By examining their stories of success and listening to their voices, we view achievement through their eyes and come to understand the meanings they attach to success.

Darlene is a researcher at a pharmaceutical company and wants eventually to earn her Ph.D. Gena is a mechanical engineer who is expecting her first child. Kathy works in industrial relations and is considering how to balance her future roles. Linda is a physician who is completing a challenging residency in a specialized area of surgery. Tonya, also expecting her first child, is an urban planner who is politically active. And Wendy is an award winning media producer/reporter who recently has been divorced.

In this chapter, themes from the women's stories are identified and illustrated, and the significance of each is elaborated. The women's stories illustrate their personality characteristics of independence and curiosity as well as their goal-setting tendencies. Their stories also illustrate their attitudes toward women and their own self-doubts. Themes also arise that involve their career choice process and the value they place on work. Their stories present the context of their development and the environment in which they now live. The important influence of their families stands out in their stories as well as the role of high school counselors and teachers in their development. The obstacles these women encountered, and the role models they had or did not have, are also discussed. Finally, the women's future plans for work, home, and family are presented and discussed.

Independence

Several themes emerged from the women's stories that speak to their personalities and motivations—who they are. Many of these women emphasize their valuing of independence in their careers and their personal lives. Their independence is associated with their orientations toward their careers. Work is an essential part of their lives because it offers them independence. The careers they chose are also an expression of their independence. They have chosen careers that provide them not only with financial independence but with self-determination. Darlene explains the significance of work as it gives her independence: "I knew I always wanted to work. Work meant independence. . . . I wanted my independence I think since I was 6."

Gena, the mechanical engineer, explains her independence in terms of her career:

I like to work alone. I like to work unsupervised, and I can work independently, get things done. I'm not afraid to do things whether I'm sure of it or not. I'll go and learn and find answers on my own as opposed to having someone spoon feed me the information. Which in engineering, you really have to be able to work independently. You can't have someone over your shoulder all the time.

Gena's job allows her to delineate her time and prioritize her responsibilities, work independently, and express her self-motivating qualities. Her chosen career is an expression of her value of independence and her personal characteristics.

Linda, the surgeon, also expresses her independence through her profession. She explains, "I'm very independent. And I suppose that the people that go into surgery tend to be very independent and strong minded. You can't be indecisive and be in surgery." All three of these women chose careers that allow them to express their valuing of independence. They are in professions that require these characteristics, so their chosen fields are expressions of the women themselves.

Curiosity

Another theme that characterizes these high-achieving women's stories is their high achievement motivation. Several of the women describe aspects of their careers that motivate them. They are driven by a curiosity, a desire to search for answers. They find satisfaction in the search for solutions and in the solutions themselves; they are motivated to achieve. In Farmer's (1980) study of 10th-grade girls, high achievement motivation was a significant predictor of career motivation. Our women also demonstrate this relationship between achievement motivation and career motivation. Darlene describes her motivation to "dig" for answers:

I guess research to me means that you're delving into problems that you see. And you want to find an answer for. . . . I have always been that way. It is like if something is perplexing, I mean, I would want to find an answer, you know. I would just keep on digging and digging and digging until I found a response or an answer that I could accept.

Darlene's strong curiosity is expressed in her choice of careers as a researcher in a pharmaceutical company. She is on the cutting edge of technology, searching for a new medication that might prove to be the cure for a serious disease.

Wendy, the producer/reporter, also expresses her curiosity in her career. She searches for answers in the many people with whom she makes contact, and values the new knowledge she can acquire from others:

I learn so much about people. About how much I have to be thankful for. I just learn so much on this job. And it changes. . . . I really like to dig up stories. I broke a national story in January. And, it was the most incredible feeling. So, I really like following hunches and I *love* it when I am right! . . . I've always had like a really intense curiosity. And, so it's really the perfect job for me.

Wendy's career fulfills her curiosity because it gives her an opportunity to meet new people, ask questions, and "dig up stories." But there is also a sense of accomplishment in finding the answer. As Wendy said, "I *love* it when I am right!"

Gena also enjoys searching for answers and solving problems by creating a new product. She describes the satisfaction she receives when she solves a difficult problem. "You know, if you've figured out some particularly difficult problem where no one else could figure it out, . . . [it] makes you important. . . . Like you're contributing."

For many of these high-achieving women, one motivation in their careers is their curiosity to search for answers, to learn new things, to create a new product. They are driven by the process, the search, and they find great satisfaction and fulfillment when they reach the answer.

Goal Setting

Several of these six women also express a reliance on goal setting and planning to achieve success. Not only do they set goals, they use their goals to overcome obstacles. Goals provide another motivation in their careers. They are an important aspect to these women's successes because they provide a direction to move in, something to work toward. Using long-term and short-term goals, the women, step by step, realize their aims. Gaskill (1991) reports that career planning and goal setting are important factors in women's career success. These six women's stories illustrate Gaskill's (1991) quantitative finding.

Linda, the surgeon, explains that it is important to be goal oriented because it takes time to achieve in her profession.

Well, you learn to be patient in this profession. It takes a while to get there. Something my father always taught me was to be goal oriented. And that, you know, the really hard things, the really good things that you want in life are worth fighting for and persevering for. Probably the biggest thing here is that I've always known what I wanted; it's just that there have been people that have told me that I shouldn't do it along the way and my father has always encouraged me to do this anyway.

Despite a lack of support, Linda's goals gave her increased motivation to achieve. Her goals allowed her to ignore the lack of support she received from those around her because they provided a focus point, an end result—becoming a surgeon.

Wendy describes the role of goals when she was faced with obstacles. Not only must one define goals, one also must persist to make them a reality. Wendy explains, "I think that I have really learned over the years that just because someone may say no . . . it's not necessarily no always. And, if you persist that you can usually get what you want." Wendy has definitely achieved due to her persistence and goal-oriented behavior. Wendy chose journalism as a career against her father's wishes. As a result, her father refused to pay for her college education. So Wendy worked at numerous jobs while she was a full-time student, and persisted toward her goal. It was only in her last year of college that her father relented and assisted her financially. This experience lends greater understanding to her attitude of persisting even when some may tell you, "No."

Darlene, the researcher in a pharmaceutical company, also uses goal setting to pursue her career dreams. Not only does she keep in mind her end goal, she sets short-term goals to help her keep advancing. When asked if she sets goals for herself, Darlene responded,

Oh yeah. I do. Sometimes they're very unrealistic and I know that so it doesn't really bother me when I don't fulfill them. . . . [T]hen there's other times where I make short-term goals and succeed at them usually sooner than I think . . . and it just makes you feel good, you know, when you accomplish something, and so I try to do that too.

Achieving a short-term goal may reinforce one's long-term goal and provide the motivation to keep one working toward that end.

Most of these high-achieving women use goal setting as a way to persist through obstacles to fulfill their dreams. Rather than becoming paralyzed when faced with discrimination, financial barriers, or a lack of support, their goals give them a definite direction toward which to move. Their goal-setting behavior and persistence made their dreams realizable. At the time of our interviews, one woman, Kathy, who is in industrial relations, believed she was not a goal setter. Yet her behavior suggests she is. She explains that her career success simply "fell into place."

I'm not the kind of person that sits down and sets goals for myself, you know what I mean? I guess . . . things kind of just fall into place. . . . I'm a spontaneous person. . . . I don't really, I guess really have many career goals that I've set. . . . I think things, you know, things just happen.

Although Kathy tends not to take credit for her success, she described several incidents that have required her to plan or set goals. And, currently, she admits her goals are centered on her family and the ways she will negotiate the home and work spheres when she has a child.

Therefore, a common theme found in these women's stories of career success is their goal-directed behavior, their planfulness. These women did not allow circumstances to determine their futures, and they did not flounder when they did not know how to achieve their goals. Instead, they set goals and persisted toward them to realize success.

Attitude Toward Women

Much quantitative research focuses on gifted women's views of women's roles in society. This research has demonstrated that females generally believe in gender equality in the occupational and vocational spheres (Bakken, Hershey, & Miller, 1990; Dunnell & Bakken, 1991). However, Bakken et al. (1990) uncover the conflict experienced by many gifted women by reporting that, although less than 5% of the gifted women in their sample supported inequality in the educational and vocational arenas, 20% agreed with the traditional view of marriage in which the wife is primarily responsible for housework, and 35% agreed with the traditional view of dating, in which the male takes the initiative. It is obvious that women's attitudes regarding education and the workplace are changing, but their conceptualizations of their familial and social roles remain more steadfast, which creates conflict when considering the various interacting roles that constitute one's life.

The qualitative data from our high-achieving women's stories illustrate some liberating and some transitional attitudes toward their gender that reinforce their educational and occupational goals. Their experiences illustrate the conflict that results from the contradictory messages they receive about their ability as intelligent individuals and their roles as women. Although their ideas concerning women's roles in the educational and vocational spheres demonstrate an attitude of equality, their ideas concerning marriage and family are more transitional, that is, somewhere in the middle between nontraditional and traditional. Their various attitudes toward women are demonstrated by some different issues on which they choose to focus.

Darlene remembers getting her ideas of what women should be from seeing old movies and wanting things to be different. She is intolerant of the violence many women endure.

Yeah, women rather than men should have most responsibility for housekeeping, *no!* . . . But I don't know if anybody influenced me or not, like I said

the old movies you know, I look at them going, "smack 'em, smack 'em." . . .
I have definite views. You know like—battered women. . . . I mean it's like
haul off and wail on the son-of-a-gun. But I guess I'm not in that position so I
mean I probably would do the same thing in their position. Either that or not
find myself in that position at all, which I am not.

Despite their empowering attitudes toward women, the influences they experienced growing up were not always supportive of women. In fact, many
times they received confusing messages—expectations for them to achieve
but also negative attitudes suggesting that women could not achieve in the
work world. Linda's experience with her father illustrates these confusing
messages:

He taught all of us girls to be very, very independent, strong-minded
women. To make our own decisions, never to rely on somebody else. And yet
. . . he had a threatened lawsuit over some malpractice issue that was eventually dropped, but early on his lawyer was a woman and he came home from
the clinic one day and he goes, "Good grief, they sent a woman over here!"
. . . And I said, "Well Dad, are you saying that a woman lawyer can't be as
good as a man lawyer?" He goes, "Obviously not!"

Confusing messages and contradictory expectations seem to abound. As a
high-achieving individual, one is supposed to be assertive, independent,
self-motivated, intelligent, and career oriented, but as a woman, these characteristics seem less feminine. Rather than allowing the messages to stifle
their dreams, however, several of the women became proactive and tried to
change the stereotypes for women.

Gena, the engineer, worked with the Women in Science and Engineering
program during college. She helped introduce high school girls to women in
engineering, providing them with nontraditional role models. She describes
the results of her efforts. "Hopefully we helped a lot of high school girls. I
worked with the program for four years while I was in college. And every
year we had more of a percentage of girls entering engineering and science.
And like 90% of the girls that went through our program went to college."

Their attitudes toward women are also reflected in their relationships.
Four of these six women are married, one is divorced, and one is single. The
majority of these women espouse transitional ideas of the role of the woman
in a marriage and the power distribution in a relationship. Although they hold
nontraditional ideas about women in the workplace, some of the women are
more traditional in their attitudes concerning the home sphere.

Linda, the surgeon, explains that marriage was never a goal in her life. It seems her career and educational goals were her focus. "Marriage was not something that was a priority in my life. It took me a while to come around to thinking that I would get married. I actually thought that I would *never* get married.". Because Linda's parents' divorce was so traumatic for her, she was uncertain if marriage even had a place in her life. Marriage was not a central area of concern for her; her energies were devoted to career pursuits, which gave her more time and energy to achieve her career goals. However, Linda is now married and has a somewhat nontraditional relationship with her husband. She is in her medical residency and has limited mobility so her husband sacrificed his career to follow her. Yet, when she considers housework, Linda views it as her responsibility.

The women's relationships with their spouses are pictures of egalitarian values. They are free to be themselves in their relationships, and mutual support of activities, goals, and dreams flourish. Tonya, the urban planner, describes her relationship with her husband as one that allows her space to express herself and her interests. Although her husband may have different interests, he supports her choices of activities. In one example, she described her involvement in antiwar demonstrations during the Gulf War: "I was out every night downtown at the antiwar demonstrations while he sat at home. So, it doesn't bother him. . . . [I]t doesn't bother him and that's all that matters."

While other people in Tonya's life may not support her beliefs and actions, the support she gets from her husband allows her to express herself freely. This type of support is evident concerning the women's career plans, work activities, and negotiation of work and family roles. Kathy and her husband offer mutual support for each other's career goals. She explains, "There is definitely support . . . on both of our parts, I'm sure. You know, do whatever makes us happy or, you know, do whatever we feel is the right thing for us individually."

Gena, the engineer, also describes this type of relationship with her husband, except that in her story she focuses on the two being able to communicate with each other, being able to speak the same language. Because both Gena and her husband are in engineering fields, they can easily relate to each others' experiences:

That's one nice thing, we can talk about each other's work and we both understand exactly what we're talking about. . . . I can feel what he's going through at work if he's having problems and he can do the same thing for me.

Another aspect of this mutual support revolves around the very present conflict between home and career. To successfully combine the work and home spheres, as many high-achieving women wish, spousal support and flexibility are crucial given that societal institutions do little to assist women and families in reducing the stress associated with this conflict. The women who are married all participate in a dual-career lifestyle because their partners are also pursuing careers. The existing literature about dual-career couples demonstrates that mutual support, shared values, and coping strategies that focus on role redefinition, compromise, and commitment are central to a successful dual-career lifestyle (Gilbert & Rachlin, 1987). Kahn and Lichty (1987) refer to work conditions, family support, and personal attitudes as three influential factors affecting stress. And Steffy and Ashbaugh (1986) reported that dual-career planning, which involved joint discussions between both partners, was positively associated with spouse support and marital satisfaction and led to lower levels of role conflict.

The women's stories demonstrate the importance of spousal support. Kathy feels great tension between the home and work spheres even though she does not yet have children. She struggles with the positive and negative consequences of staying home or continuing to work once she does decide to have children. Kathy believes her husband would support any decision she makes to resolve this conflict, and would be flexible to assist in child care tasks.

I don't think he would really have a problem with it either way. I mean if I decided to stay at home, I think he'd be fine with it and if I decided to go to work, I think he'd be fine with that too. . . . I think he thinks its more or less my decision, you know, because I'd be the one giving something up, you know?"

Because Kathy believes she has support from her husband for any decision she makes concerning this issue, she is able to make a decision that will be best for herself and her family. However, Kathy doesn't consider any option with her husband as the primary caregiver. She naturally assumes it is her role to be the caregiver. Although she espouses nontraditional values for women in the workplace, she holds more traditional values in the home sphere.

On the other hand, lack of support for career and work-family plans may be detrimental to a woman, her career, and her relationships. Wendy, the producer/reporter who was recently divorced, commented on the factors that led to the breakdown in her marriage:

I knew that we weren't going to make it after our first year. . . . [I]t was just so hard because we were so different. And I knew I needed to do . . . other things. And he wanted me to stay home and have children . . . And it just didn't work.

Wendy's relationship with her husband constrained her choices concerning home and career conflicts and confined her so she wasn't able to freely express herself.

The examples drawn from the life stories of these high-achieving women create images of women who value independence, thrive on curiosity, plan for success, and hold empowering views about women. All of these characteristics are evident in their relationships with their spouses and family members. Their relationships must allow them freedom of expression and must be congruent with their ideas about women and how to negotiate home and career roles.

Self-Doubts

Another aspect of these women's personal characteristics is their self-doubts. Although they have achieved success and recognize their accomplishments, they suffer from the self-doubts that many women work to overcome.

Linda, a successful surgical resident, has fears of failure. She explains that she has never wanted to be the best, just be good at what she does. To be the best would mean that she would draw attention to herself.

I don't want to make myself look good! What if I fail? And that's the thing I think that was the most threatening was that everybody started talking about me and they started expecting *so much* and I thought I would look bad or stupid.

Despite her fears of failure, Linda received recognition as chief resident and has published several papers. However, her self-doubts still linger.

Wendy's self-doubts center on her comparison of herself to her siblings. Although she has earned a national award in her field, when she thinks of the accomplishments of her siblings, doubts about her own successes arise. Wendy speaks about comparing herself with her sisters.

I think I have done that a lot. Too much in my life. Sometimes I do it now, you know. [My sister] writes this book and I read it. And I think, "My God, she's done so much with her life. And look at me, I've done nothing." And I start feeling sorry for myself. And then I hit myself. . . . And I realize that I am fine. But sometimes I do have these lapses where I go and I think, you know, you're a failure.

Although both Wendy and Linda are very successful and have been recognized in their chosen fields, they still must work to overcome their self-doubts.

Career Choice Process

To gain greater understanding of the internal characteristics of these high-achieving women, one must understand their career-decision processes, the meaning of work in their lives, and their future plans. First, it is important to examine how each woman chose her career.

The career-decision process takes many forms for women. Some women may rely on their academic strengths to guide them. Others look at their interests and values; some are influenced by specific experiences that caused a gut-level reaction in them.

Wendy can remember when she first decided to be a producer/reporter. She worked on her school newspaper in high school, but hearing the news of the space shuttle *Challenger* accident sparked an interest she knew she would pursue:

I had been in my school newspaper. And the *Challenger* accident occurred. And I realized that day, when, you know, those astronauts died up in space, that I didn't wait until a newspaper article came out, where I could read it. I went straight to the first radio I could find and I turned it on. . . . I was getting the information I needed. And the way that they described it, I didn't need to see pictures. I could see exactly in my mind how the *Challenger* exploded. . . . And, it was then that I knew that I wanted to go into journalism.

A similar experience was described by Darlene. She remembers watching a Jacques Cousteau nature program about marine life that grabbed her attention and kept her interest for many years, and even today. These examples illustrate how one experience can spark an interest, grab one's attention, or reinforce one's direction. One experience was powerful enough for Wendy and Darlene that it had a lasting impact on their career dreams.

Other women were more systematic in their decisions. They matched their experiences, interests, and skills with a career. Linda, for example, knew she liked to work with her hands, and she had observed her father's career as a surgeon, so she chose surgery as a career.

The way I look at it, pretty much the reason I ended up in choosing surgery is, besides seeing it with my father, . . . I found out that I was good with my hands. And I liked science, so it all just kind of ended up that way.

Gena, the engineer, also relied on this very cognitive process to choose her career. She took physics in high school and enjoyed the material she learned. So she researched careers that involved math and science. Then she contacted colleges and evaluated their curricula. Gena and Linda used more rational, systematic means to choose their careers, as opposed to Wendy and Darlene, who experienced a reaction to a particular incident that sparked an interest. Yet all four women have achieved highly in their fields and are very satisfied with their careers.

To gain even more insight into their career-decision processes, our interviewers asked these women what advice they would give to students today about careers. The advice they offer provides much insight into their values concerning education and careers. Three themes emerge. First, they place high value on enjoying one's job, that is, on the individual finding a career that is of interest to her or him. Second, they emphasize the necessity of higher education. And, third, they provide information about how to choose a career, emphasizing researching career options.

Wendy believes that individuals should choose careers that make them happy. She offers her advice:

I would say that you got to do what makes you happy, you know. [It] may be one thing to have the respect of your family and everything. But it's another thing to have to live with that job every day. I've seen so many people make that mistake. . . . [T]o thine own self be true.

All of the women emphasized this theme—the importance of choosing a career one would enjoy. Darlene illustrates this by pointing out that no one wants to wake up in the morning and dread going to work.

The women also agree on the importance of education. Tonya believes higher education provides opportunities that people will miss if they don't get an education beyond high school. "Yeah, it's so hard . . . I just see too many people who didn't do that and they're, you know, you got to work three jobs." Education allows one to choose a satisfying career and to advance in that career. It provides more economic assurance and a lifestyle that leaves time for family and friends.

The last piece of advice emphasized by these successful women is about the process of choosing a career. Gena chose her career based on careful research into her interests and available careers, so she offers similar advice to others. She advocates a proactive position, encouraging others to start the process of choosing a career on their own.

Tell them to investigate career choices. See what they're good at in school, what they like, what they dislike. Talk to people in jobs that involve those skills. Actually go out and visit people at work, see what they do. Really just do research. . . . [D]on't wait for it to come to you. Because you'll be sitting there for a long time in most cases.

Value of Work

Their career-decision processes are only one piece of the puzzle. These women have achieved in the career and educational domains, so their careers hold important positions in their lives. They identify themselves by their careers and prioritize their activities around their careers.

When asked how work fits into her life plan, Tonya responded, "Oh, it's essential." She explains, "It gives meaning to everything." This attitude toward work is characteristic of all six of the women. They view work as a means of expressing themselves and as a way to enrich their lives. Darlene says it best: "It is an expression . . . of my goals." Their careers give them an arena in which to use their talents to contribute to society. Work is a priority because it provides a sense of self-fulfillment and accomplishment.

Gena describes her value of work:

It makes me feel like I have accomplished something. . . . I'm using the skills that I have to do something, hopefully something for a good reason or good purpose. And I wouldn't want to sit at home and waste my talents. I would feel like I was wasting my life away if I wasn't doing something.

Although work may be a priority in the women's lives, some express a desire for more variety in their lives, other avenues to express themselves. Linda is completing her residency training, which requires a rigorous schedule; she explains, "My life is work right now. There is very little time for anything else. . . . It's just like there is nothing else right now." Because she has focused her time and energy on her career for so long, she now wants to broaden her personal interests and learn new hobbies, like playing the piano and learning a new language.

Their careers are a priority in their lives, but with good reason. These women love what they do. They are in professional careers that require priority, but they choose the place work has in their lives because it fulfills them in so many ways.

When Linda talks about her career, she is passionate about surgery:

> You see a patient . . . who's been to several doctors and has been told she can't be operated on, and that she's going to die. You take out this tumor and within that same day you know the lady is now tumor free. And they go home and they're very grateful. . . . [T]here isn't any other job like it!

Darlene also finds fulfillment in her career because it provides her with an opportunity to research problems and find answers. She feels excitement when the drug she has been working on finally goes on the market. She describes her job as allowing her to work in "new frontiers."

> You know, the day-to-day stuff may be kind of boring . . . but that potential is always there to have a breakthrough. To work on something , you know . . . problems of today like AIDS, Alzheimer's . . . diseases that we don't even know about yet. [T]he potential is there to create a drug, so that's fun.

The potential of making a breakthrough provides motivation to Darlene to stay focused on her work, and it provides excitement and fulfillment that keeps her career a priority in her life.

These examples demonstrate the importance of a career in the lives of these high-achieving women, and they illustrate the fulfillment one may gain through work. Although the examples focus on different characteristics of the women's careers that continually motivate them, the fact that the women have located these characteristics in their careers is a unifying theme.

One's personality, attitudes, beliefs, motivations, and values may give one great opportunity for success. These women's stories, which demonstrate independence, curiosity, goal-oriented behavior, and self-motivation, illustrate the personal characteristics that assisted them in reaching their goals. Yet their personal characteristics are not the only factor in their success stories. Each woman's personal characteristics developed within a context of a family, a community, and a society. On all levels, this context exerted influences on the women that shaped their beliefs, developed their attitudes, and reinforced their motivations. This finding is in line with the sociocognitive framework offered by Lent et al. (1994). One powerful influence in this context is the women's families.

Family

Families of origin play an important role in the career development of women. Families send messages about the meaning of work and the value of education. Research by Parsons, Adler, and Kaczala (1982) and Entwisle and Baker (1983) suggests that parents apply gender stereotypes when forming achievement expectations and perceptions of ability for their children.

However, support from one's family can make the difference in overcoming negative societal influences that create barriers to achievement for many women. Research has demonstrated that parental encouragement is related to career success (Gaskill, 1991), and perceived parental support has a positive effect on school and university attainment (Poole, Langan-Fox, Ciavarella, & Omodei, 1991). Farmer (1980) also revealed that support from family members is one of the most important factors in girls' career motivation. Higham and Navarre (1984) agree that parents' treatment of their gifted daughters influences the girls' adolescent achievement patterns. Yet they reveal that parents of the gifted are disproportionately underrepresented at meetings for parents (Higham & Navarre, 1984).

The stories of these high-achieving women illustrate the effects of parental influence on the women's career and educational progress. All the women received messages from their parents that education is valuable. Although some parents did not have the opportunities to pursue higher education, they emphasized the importance of education as a precursor to success.

Gena's parents supported her emotionally and financially during her graduate training to allow her to continue her education:

My parents gave me every opportunity. I mean, they had the difficulties. I don't really think I did. I just learned from their experiences to see, you know, what they had and didn't have. And be happy that I have what I do, and take advantage of it.

Her father has a high school degree and her mother is a registered nurse. Not only did they offer her financial support, they supported her emotionally in her academic endeavors. While they encouraged her and emphasized their value of education, they never forced their own dreams on their daughter. Instead, her own goals and successes were reinforced by their praise and encouragement.

Darlene's experience was very similar to Gena's with respect to the encouragement and emotional support offered by her parents. Yet Darlene's parents were unable to financially support her educational pursuits. She explains,

If we wanted to go, "great" and they, you know, emotionally supported us. There was no way they could financially support all of us to go to college. So, they didn't force us, you know, say, "You live at home, you are going to college." They weren't anything like that. It was more like, you do what you want to do and we will support you . . . we will be behind you 100%.

Parental support for career and educational goals, and the valuing of education, are persistent themes that begin early in these women's lives. Not only do the parents provide encouragement, they often model the values and attitudes for their children.

Darlene remembers her parents' support for her early education. Her mother insisted that Darlene and her siblings complete their lessons before going out to play.

[In] grade school . . . my mom would sit us down in the summer and tell us we had to do our writing lessons and our reading things and math before we could go out and play during the summer.

Wendy recalls the importance her father, a doctor, placed on educational achievement. He monitored his children's grades and expected high grades for all his children. "Education was always very stressed, you know. . . . [Y]ou never came home with anything less than an A or B. If you came home with anything less than a B, you had a problem. A major problem."

Parental support for career decisions is also a continual theme in the women's lives. Most of the women remember their parents encouraging them to make their own career decisions, knowing they had the family's support behind them. Linda describes the influence of her father on her career decision. "The family has always given me a lot of support. I have to say that in this endeavor to become a surgeon, I haven't gotten a lot of support from other people. It's always been my father." While individuals in her world were discouraging her career-oriented behavior and dreams of becoming a surgeon, her father's encouragement was enough to sustain her dreams.

Wendy's father was also influential by providing her with a role model of someone who enjoyed his career. Because of her father's behavior and attitude toward work, Wendy learned to choose a career she would enjoy, one in which she could continue to grow.

My father loves what he does! And work was never, to me, just seen as a way to gain a living. It was always seen as, you know, something you do because you *wanted* to do it. And I think that's the approach that each one of us has taken, in the fields that we have chosen. . . . We've gone into things that interest us, and that will keep us active. We *enjoy* what we do!

While Wendy's father was a very positive model of the meaning of work in one's life, Wendy struggled against her father to choose a career she was interested in, rather than one her father wanted for her. Because of her decision to choose a career different than his wishes, Wendy's father refused her any financial or emotional support: "He said, 'If you go into journalism you will pay for your own career. And you will pay for your own schooling on your own. I won't help you. I won't support you.' "

Despite this obstacle, Wendy persisted and completed her education in journalism. It is only recently that Wendy's career success has earned her the respect and approval of her father. She now receives encouragement and support from her father and is pleased that her success has made him proud.

As is evident from the life stories of these high-achieving women, parental support for one's career decisions, and the valuing of education, are crucial to successful career development. Through their words and behavior, parents model attitudes, beliefs, and feelings that are transmitted to their children. In most of these women's cases, the messages they received created their attitudes toward education and reinforced their career decisions.

Another aspect of family influence involves siblings. Siblings provide a source of comparison, competition, and mutual assistance. These women use their families to provide a context or reference group to understand the importance of their own successes. For example, Gena's family history gives her college graduation meaning beyond simply receiving a degree:

I was the first one to graduate from college. You know, of the whole [family]. . . . There was this big event for the family. Their first . . . to ever graduate from college. So, the whole family was really proud of me.

Because she is the first in her family to receive a college degree, her accomplishment has added significance.

Darlene uses her career choice as a distinguishing characteristic in her large family:

My family, I am the only one that is actually in the sciences. Like I said, I have brothers and sisters . . . three of which are in the trades. . . . Then everyone else went into business!

Her career choice distinguishes her from her siblings and allows her to express her individuality.

A last example demonstrates how Wendy compares herself with siblings when judging her achievements. The comparison fosters competition, which can enhance her motivation or paralyze her in self-doubt.

> I did very well in math. And, you know, all the other kids always asked, "What did you get for this one?" But when I compared myself to my sisters I knew I wasn't good in math. It didn't come as easily to me as it did to them.

The competition in one's family may spur motivation to achieve and continue to move one toward success, or it may create obstacles of self-doubt. Families can be abundant resources of support, encouragement, and assistance or offer a dearth of emotional sustenance for an individual's dreams and pursuits. They provide a context in which to assert one's individuality or membership in the family, and to reflect on one's own accomplishments.

Teachers

Another theme that emerged in these women's stories involves the role of teachers in their lives. The women have vivid memories of positive and negative influences of significant teachers. These individuals are examples of the impact others can have on one's development.

Many of the women recall the influence of significant teachers on their educational and career development. Some of these significant individuals left negative impressions on the women. Some of the women remember discouraging words and prejudicial attitudes. Linda's experience with an adviser in college and another in medical school provide clear examples of the lasting impressions significant people may have on a woman's career development. Linda placed great importance on the advice she would receive from her college adviser. She went into a meeting with him thinking, "Whatever he said would really be important." Yet he advised her to give up her goal of going to medical school. Although his advice did not thwart her plans, his words created a lasting impression of the lack of support she received in her pursuits.

Linda's first experience with her medical school adviser also remains clear in her memory.

> My first day in the OR with him, I walked in. . . . So he was in this big surgery and I stood behind him and I didn't want to bother him, you know. . . . He has a big reputation for being an excellent surgeon. I just stood back there and so . . . I had been sitting back there for half an hour watching him and he suddenly turns his head but doesn't look at me and he says, "Who are you?"

So I introduced myself. . . . He says, "Dammit, another woman!" And then he says, "[A]nd a Chink too!" And then he said, "Killed a lot of them in the war."

Linda was very aware of his status and reputation, so rather than becoming enraged at his insensitivity, she blamed herself for making a negative first impression. Yet his statements demonstrate the damaging potential of words and "wisdom" that come from individuals one respects. His position awarded him her respect, which he misused to intimidate her.

Other women remembered teachers who positively affected their career development. They recall encounters with people they respected, who carefully gave advice, offered support, and assisted in their development. Wendy, who attended Farmerville High School, describes an early relationship with a teacher in grade school who took time to work with her on her reading and writing skills. The teacher read to her from classics such as *Canterbury Tales* and "The Rhyme of the Ancient Mariner," which Wendy loved to listen to. Wendy credits this experience as the creation of her interest in writing.

Many of the women remember both positive and negative significant individuals in their education and training who influenced them. The vividness of their memories speaks to the impact significant people have on one's choices, progress, and feelings about oneself.

High School Counselors

For many young people, it is during the high school years that they begin to develop career interests and educational goals. The support or lack of support these women received for their goals during their high school years is a microcosm of the larger societal expectations that affected them. One aspect of their high school experience that was consistent in the women's stories was their encounters with high school guidance counselors.

The high school counselor may be instrumental in guiding high school students to the right classes, helping them investigate career interests, and assisting them in developing educational and career goals. Yet it seems that all too often the counselor is unavailable to the student or offers hasty advice that has negative effects on the student. A study completed by Walker, Reis, and Leonard (1992) focused on the most frequent concerns of gifted women across the decades between 1910 and 1980. Some of the concerns included vague and traditional school and societal expectations, lack of challenging curricula, lack of role models, and unhelpful guidance. In fact, guidance counseling was rated the most inadequate of all the educational services (Walker et al., 1992). A similar experience is found in the life stories of our six high-achieving women.

Unfortunately, most of the women reported that guidance counselors were unavailable to them unless they made special efforts to obtain assistance. When asked if her high school had any career counselors, Kathy described the lack of guidance at Metro High School:

It wasn't anything that was really pushed or anything like that. I think you more or less had to seek them out, you know, it wasn't any kind of thing like you *had* a counselor that, you know, you would go talk to or anything. . . . I wouldn't say it was the best high school in the world.

Most of the other women describe similar experiences. For example, when Gena tried to get career planning assistance from a counselor at Metro, she found she had to do all of the research on her own. No one made information available to her about careers, colleges, or scholarships. It was only through searching through the counselor's files on her own that she became aware of engineering as a career. She explains, "If I hadn't gone out and sought it out on my own, no one would have ever recommended that to me. Even though my best subjects were math and science."

Linda recalls a negative experience with a counselor who advised her to change her career goals. The counselor at Country High School relied on one assessment instrument and hastily offered advice: "I told him what I wanted to do and he told me I'd be more suited to do something else."

Only one woman, Wendy, could remember a positive experience with a high school counselor. The counselor at Farmerville High School offered her support for her career decision when her father would not.

I went to her one day. And my heart was breaking. And I told her, "My father wants me to go into medicine but I don't want to do that. And he's so disappointed in me. . . . And she said, "Sometimes you know when you are right. Sometimes you just have to do what you know is right even though it means somebody may not agree with you. You have to make your decision for yourself. You are becoming an adult now." And she just *really* helped me make up my mind that, "OK, I'm going to go for it."

From the women's stories, one gains an appreciation of the role of the guidance counselor. The counselor has the potential to dramatically influence the direction of many students. Yet most of these women became disappointed and frustrated by the unavailability of the counselor or the inability of the counselor to assist them in an affirming manner. Because this resource was not a part of these women's career development, its absence does not mean it did not influence them. The lack of guidance provided a type of null environment in which no information was given to the women, no guidance or support was offered, and the need for all of these things was not even acknowledged. The lack of support sent a strong message to the women that reinforced societal messages that no one cares if they succeed.

Obstacles to Success

Although these women achieved their goals, success did not come easily to them. They faced barriers and obstacles that might have prevented their achievements had they not persisted. Experiences of racism and sexism abound in some of their stories, and others struggled against financial barriers. These obstacles and barriers provide insight into the context of their development, the environment in which they lived.

Some women describe early experiences with sexist attitudes in the messages they received about their career goals. Gena, a Native American who went to Metro High School, remembers a bias against women pursuing engineering careers. Although it was not overt discouragement, subtle sexism was evident in the lack of information and support given to her. She explains, "No one pushed me into engineering or even talked to me about it when I was in high school. It was like for the men."

Linda, an Asian woman who attended Country High School, also recalls sexism in the early messages she received about her career choice. However, Linda's experience involved overt messages of blatant sexist stereotypes:

The mothers of some of my close friends in high school would say . . . that I was being too ambitious to try and become a doctor. . . . They would tell me that really the woman's role in life is not to become the career person. That I would be throwing away my education once I got married.

Although these early experiences with sexism were discouraging to Linda and Gena, the women persisted in their determination to succeed. They rejected the attitudes that discouraged their goals.

Another type of obstacle experienced by some of the women is encounters with racism and prejudice. Wendy, who is Latina, remembers her father's warnings about racism:

My dad told me when I was young. . . . I remember he told me . . . "There's something called prejudice that you're going to encounter. . . . And, it means that people will not like you because you don't have blonde hair and blue eyes." . . . But, you know, the funny thing about it was that he also told me when I was a kid, "[P]robably by the time you have children there won't be this problem." He was wrong!

Linda, who attended Country High School, remembers specific experiences with racism. She has dealt with prejudice so often that she now blocks it out to defend herself against it.

When I was growing up, in high school, people used to tease me all the time about being Chinese. . . . I'm just kind of immune to it. . . . I guess it's because I grew up having people swear at me. Tell me I was no good because I was Chinese. The girls didn't want to play with me, that kind of thing. . . . But I learned a defense mechanism to block it out.

Another type of obstacle encountered by several of the women includes lack of financial assistance or support. Finances can help one realize goals or can be the insurmountable barrier to achieving success. Two of the women describe their experiences with this barrier and their persistence in achieving their goals.

As I have mentioned earlier, Wendy chose a career against her father's wishes, so he refused to help her financially. She worked 30 to 40 hours a week at odd jobs while a full-time student trying to support herself and her educational expenses. Yet, despite this obstacle, she finished her degree in four years and has achieved success in her chosen career.

Another woman's story of financial barriers creates a lasting memory of a dream deferred. Darlene's goal for many years was to become an oceanographer. Although she made plans to fulfill her dream by entering the Coast Guard Academy for training in oceanography, these plans were thwarted by a physician's inaccurate report of a physical injury. Alternative options of attending a university that offered a degree in oceanography were not possible due to her financial circumstances. Despite her financial obstacles, she has completed a master's degree and has plans to earn a Ph.D. in a science-related field. Although she was forced to change her specific career goals, she persisted in her education and a science-related career. When asked why someone might end up as an oceanographer, she explains that one's financial circumstances must have allowed it:

They had money to go to the West Coast! . . . They probably had opportunities open up to them. . . . [O]r the drive to overcome any obstacle that was
put in their way as opposed to being diverted into a different course. . . .
Guess I didn't have the money.

Financial barriers, sexist attitudes, and experiences with racism have created obstacles to the women's educational and career development. Yet several of the women have accepted the obstacles as part of their progress to their
goals and have developed ways of coping that allow them to persist.

Gena explains her encounters with sexism and ageism in the workplace.
"You are the only woman in the field, you're younger, you know. It's even
when you are a man and you're younger, you are going to get that. But it's
even worse when you are a woman." Gena expects to encounter sexist attitudes. One might expect Gena to react in outrage, to at least show signs of
frustration and aggravation, yet she comments, "Well, I expected it."

Linda is also in a male-dominated field and must daily deal with discrimination and harassment. Two incidents she recalls vividly illustrate the obstacles she must overcome in her career as a surgeon.

I was asked to review a paper. We have journal reviews. And in his rota-
tion we each received a journal article once. And then he would give a little
talk about some medical thing. And the journal article that I was asked to review was why women shouldn't be in surgery. . . . And I was just very ticked
off by this guy. I was just dumbfounded . . . but I reviewed it. I ignored him.
. . . What's more amazing . . . when I was interviewing, people were asking
me if I was on the pill and I couldn't believe it! It's none of their business!

Yet she does not allow her anger to surface. Instead, she has developed coping skills that allow her to ignore the discrimination for the time being. Linda
is repressing her anger until she is in a position to effect change.

My attitude has been that I am not going to be able to change *anything* as a
resident but I might be able to do something as a staff person. So my attitude
has been that I would just take it and let it go . . . for now. But when I become a
staff person I'm going to set up rules and regulations on the behavior. . . . I
feel powerless to do anything about it as a resident.

Not only do many of the women dismiss or ignore their encounters with
racism and sexism, they sometimes view obstacles as advantages. Wendy

views her ethnicity as affording her opportunities in her career. Although she has experienced racism and discrimination, she likes the idea that her ethnicity makes her visible. She explains her perspective, "I think being Latina and in this field has really helped me. Because in a funny way it makes me stand out more. And people take notice." Although the visibility due to her ethnicity could bring discrimination, she takes a positive perspective, acknowledging the benefits of being unique.

Wendy describes an early obstacle that she believes increased her determination to become a writer and reporter. She began school with English as her second language, creating a language barrier that impeded the development of her writing skills. Her first language was Spanish. One of her teachers worked with her on an individual basis to help her overcome this obstacle. She credits her difficulty with the language and efforts to improve her writing as the impetus that led to her above-average writing skills.

Gena also takes the perspective that what some may consider an obstacle for her is actually an advantage. While many women may be discouraged by the low number of women in engineering careers, Gena sees it as an advantage. In her college courses, her gender gave her visibility in male-dominated classrooms and increased her social opportunities. She explains, "The fact that there were a very few women in it was another inspiration to me. . . . Yeah, I like to be the center of attention in there. I don't like to be one of the crowd. I never did."

Although their career choices have presented them with many obstacles, these high-achieving women have persisted through these challenges, accepting barriers as part of the road to success, developing coping skills to help them deal with their own responses to the injustices they face, and viewing many of these obstacles as advantages and opportunities. Although their persistence and attitudes have brought them success despite racism, sexism, and financial barriers, many women who face similar obstacles find them insurmountable.

The examples of our six women present a theme of individual determination and eventual success, but these women are the exception rather than the rule. We must not dismiss the injustices that still prevent many women from achieving their goals. We must not focus on the individual's determination as the solution to these societal problems. Although these women's stories illustrate great motivation to achieve, the stories also describe daily encounters with racism and sexism.

Role Models

The women also describe a lack of exposure to nontraditional career role models. Role models may provide information that affects a child's stereotypes of appropriate occupations for men and women and defines acceptable educational options available to them (Eccles, 1985). Role models provide examples of career opportunities and successes. The lack of these types of role models in these six women's lives leads one to question the availability of role models for other young women. A role model provides an example of attitudes, beliefs, and behavior for one to emulate or reject. When women are exposed to individuals in professional careers, they become aware of the meaning work can have in one's life, the various professions one can have, the ways one can combine work and family, and the availability of success.

Walker et al. (1992) point out that gifted women are concerned about the lack of role models and inadequate organized mentoring for them. Higham and Navarre (1984) explain that although girls have no trouble finding teachers, nurses, and other stereotypical feminine occupational role models, they may not have encountered women in nontraditional careers. The literature emphasizes that for women to realistically aspire to a career, it is crucial to have role models who demonstrate lifestyles that incorporate work and family (Almquist & Angrist, 1971; Crosby, 1991; Keith, 1981). Yet Hayes (1986) points out that women are hampered due to the lack of these role models and mentors.

Some research has demonstrated that the influence of female teachers is an important predictor of career salience and level of educational aspiration for women (Hackett et al., 1989). Stake and Noonan (1985) have provided evidence that same-sex models have more positive influence than opposite-sex models. Gaskill (1991) also reports the importance of same-sex models in women's career success.

The existing literature is clear about the importance of role models in the career development of women. To gain a richer understanding of the influence of role models on women's development, one must listen to the stories of women who have experienced positive and negative influences from these individuals or have been influenced by the absence of role models in their worlds.

Several of the six women comment about the absence of people in their worlds who worked in professional careers. Gena, who grew up in the inner city, explains that she did not have assistance from her parents when seeking information about her career choice because her parents lacked that information too. She describes her lack of role models:

Where I grew up there weren't a lot of professional people that we were exposed to. People's parents worked in the mills, worked at the store, were policemen, nurses. There weren't any engineers, doctors, lawyers. We were never really exposed to that. . . . [W]e never had role models or people we could talk to that we knew.

A lack of role models can also result in a lack of preparation to effectively combat obstacles, such as sexism or racism. Linda, who grew up in a rural setting, did not know any women in professional, male-dominated careers. She wanted to work in a career in which she would have responsibility and independence, and her father supported these goals. Yet the lack of exposure to females in positions of authority left Linda unprepared to deal with the backlash of sexism. She says, "I never realized that . . . there would be *that* much resistance to doing it. I always just thought I would do it."

Kathy also experienced a lack of female role models in her career development. She was not exposed to career-oriented women because her mother did not have a career. Speaking about her husband and herself, she explains, "Neither of our mothers went to college and had any career or anything like that. . . . I think that if I didn't have a career I probably wouldn't have a problem with it." Her mother was a powerful role model of a woman who is not career oriented, and Kathy is unfamiliar with the experience of career-oriented women other than herself. Although she says she would be satisfied without a career, she expresses conflicting feelings about giving up her career once she has children, and she values the status she has in her current position.

Some of the women were fortunate to have a role model, whether it was a parent, teacher, or peer. Role models provided an example of what is possible, and instilled values in the women that they still rely on today.

Tonya remembers as a child handing out brochures and going to fundraisers to help her uncle in his political campaigns. Her mother worked for her uncle and a state representative, so she was politically active as well. These experiences made a lasting impression on Tonya, and she still actively participates in political and community activities. Not only did these early influences affect her choice of career as a regional planner, they also shaped her values that lead her to incorporate activism in her personal life.

Linda also found a role model who affected her career choice. Her father allowed her to help him in his medical practice, so Linda was exposed to medicine as a career.

When I was a young child, probably around the age of 7 to 9 . . . I used to go to my dad's office. He's a surgeon. And I would assist him, or help him with his work. If there [were] interesting cases he would bring me in and let me help him. . . . He didn't show me anything gory, he just showed me anything that was interesting. And, so I started out working in the atmosphere or the environment of a medical office or a surgical office.

Her father demonstrated the activities of a surgeon and allowed her to participate in activities that would nurture her interest.

For other women, teachers served as role models. Kathy encountered a teacher in college who worked in the human resource field, an area of interest for her. The teacher talked with Kathy about the field and provided information about courses she could take to become more familiar with this career:

So she knew that I was interested. And, yeah, I think that she did encourage me. . . . We didn't become like close and it wasn't like any kind of storybook thing or anything. . . . [S]he was probably the only person that I knew that was in human resources. . . . [I]t's not like, you know, a chain of people in my family or anybody else who I could have talked to about it.

Although Kathy did not have a close relationship to this teacher, the experience provided Kathy with her only occupational role model in the field she was interested in. As a role model, this instructor provided invaluable information to Kathy by sharing her experience.

Gena, a Native American, also describes a high school teacher who functioned as a role model and who had a lasting effect on her:

[He was] a real good physics teacher. I mean, that's really what probably turned me on to engineering, the physics. . . . He made it interesting and actually *taught*. If you had a problem understanding, you know, physics can be a little bit difficult, he could explain it to you so you could understand it. . . . [H]e was excited about the subject matter, you could tell. . . . He had actually taught in college, but he came back to teach in high school. . . . [H]e was going over to Nigeria to teach in his country. You know, he was just a real interesting person . . . [K]ind of a role model, I suppose. You know, if *he* can do this, you know. He came from Nigeria. . . . Wasn't easy for him to get where he was.

Not only did Gena's physics teacher provide a model of someone who loved science, he provided her with a model of persistence and determination to achieve.

Women must have career role models, but women also need role models who successfully negotiate multiple roles. A last example involves a peer as a role model of ways to combine work and family. While Kathy struggles with how she will balance her roles in the future, she has many different models of ways she can accomplish this.

Just about all of our friends are having kids or have already had them. . . . So you *do* start to think, What would I do? I don't know. And then I've got the girl at work who has a situation where she just works a couple of days a week, which is nice. That would really be perfect because the thing that scares me is to stay out of the workplace for a few years and then try to get back in.

Kathy's friends and coworker are in the midst of balancing multiple roles, so Kathy can see the positive and negative consequences of the ways they are managing their roles. By having exposure to role models who successfully combine these roles, Kathy can make an informed decision based on what is best for her, and can be confident that it is possible to find success in both spheres.

Future Plans

Although they are satisfied with their current careers, all of the women described future plans for their careers and personal lives. An interesting theme emerged in many of the women's stories that offered a perspective on their current positions as stepping stones to future success.

Several of the women have definite plans to move in their careers in the near future. Linda is finishing her residency and is making plans to progress in her career as a surgeon. Gena, an engineer, is considering returning to school to work toward an M.B.A. to broaden her employment options. Darlene wants to work on a doctoral degree. When asked what she would do if she could do or be anything, Darlene replied, "The only thing that I would change is the three letters after my name." A Ph.D. would allow Darlene to continue to advance and give her more autonomy in her career to search for answers to her own questions.

Other women express desires to move to larger companies with more opportunities or to narrow the focus of their careers and specialize. Plans for the future are a way to keep growing. Gena explains her perspective, "I'm accomplishing what I want to accomplish. And I'm learning new things. And I'm not stalemated. . . . I'd just like to keep going. I don't want to stay where I am." The lack of a future direction means the possibility of stagnation in one's career and in one's personal development. Kathy has no specific plans to advance in her career. However, she is not without plans for changing roles in her life. Her plans involve ways to balance her career and her family, a crucial issue for high-achieving women.

Although all these women have achieved success in their educational and work-related careers, they are not content with accepting their current positions as the end of their struggle to obtain their goals. Instead, they have definite plans to move toward greater challenges and self-actualization. Whether these plans involve education, advancement in their careers, or ways to succeed in both the home and the work spheres, they view their current positions as stepping stones to the next life experience. And, many times, the next step is children. Tonya and Gena were pregnant at the time of the interviews, yet all the women expressed concern and interest in how work and family will fit in their lives.

Planning for Future Roles

Because work is a priority in these women's lives, and women are still expected to be the primary caretakers of children, the conflict between home and work becomes all the more poignant in their life stories. In a society that offers little or no support for working mothers, and sends subtle but pervasively negative messages about mothers who work, planning for multiple roles becomes an essential task for career and relational success. High-achieving women receive dual messages telling them to work toward career success to use their skills and express their intelligences but to devote their time to their children when they have them. The messages they receive often tell them that career-oriented behavior and motherhood are incompatible. The quantitative literature reveals the increasing feeling of role conflict in women. In 1967, only one fifth of Tangri and Jenkins's (1986) longitudinal college sample felt conflict between marriage, career, and family, but in 1970, one third of the sample reported conflict, and in 1981, one half reported feeling conflict. The six women's stories illustrate this conflict and the various ways they are planning to balance their roles.

Kathy struggles with how she will balance her career and family life. Although she wants to spend time with her future children, she cannot see herself staying home full-time. And the option of working part-time has negative consequences for her because she would lose the status of her current position. She explains the different sides of the issue:

So there's one pull that says, "If I have a baby I want to be with it," and there's another one that says, "[I]f I didn't stay with it, what would people think?" And then there's this part that says, "[W]ell, I see these people staying at home and they're happy and they're smart women."

Even with the various competing messages, some women are clear about their multiple role plans. Gena fears losing her own identity in her future children. She doesn't want her life to be so consumed by her children that once they leave for school, she has to search for an identity of her own.

I don't want to be a person whose whole life is their kids. You know, "[M]y life revolves around my child," so I don't think it's good for the child or you. . . . I see people like that. Everything they do just revolves around their child. Take them here, take them there, going to see this . . . and what are they going to do when their child goes off to school? They have nothing in their lives.

Linda doesn't plan to have children, yet she still must negotiate her time to balance her career and her role as wife. Although she has focused most of her time on her career, she has come to value more of a balance in her life: "I always thought work was more important. In the last two years or so I would say I've come to decide that [my husband] is more important than work."

Although these high-achieving women may place high priority on their careers, their lives are not unidimensional. They do not escape the conflicts between home and work. Their personal lives are full of family and friends, who also give meaning to their lives. Therefore, planning for multiple roles and balancing the different areas of their lives are essential to career and relational success.

Conclusion

These women's stories illustrate internal and external influences on their achievements. Their stories provide us with a glimpse of the factors that may be related to women's career success and realization of their aspirations. Their stories have allowed us to view achievement through their eyes. The current findings support social learning theory as described by Farmer (1985; Farmer, Wardrop, Anderson, & Risinger, 1995) and Lent et al. (1994). The women's career choices and career behavior involved more than matching their interests to a career (Holland, 1985). It also involved how their unique learning experiences resulted in self-efficacy beliefs and outcome expectations, and how their structures of opportunity limited or broadened their choices. The women's gender, ethnicity, and socioeconomic status provided a structure of opportunity that included experiences with role models, family, and obstacles. The women's personal characteristics developed in and interacted with their environments and resulted in their high achievement strivings, interests, and career choices.

The women's stories illustrate their personal characteristics of independence and curiosity, their reliance on goal-setting, their liberating and transitional attitudes toward women, and the self-doubts that they must face. Their stories also let us in on their career decision process and how work fits in to their lives.

The women's stories give us a picture of their environments—the contexts of their development. We become aware of the influence of family, teachers, high school counselors, and role models. There is also a part of their stories that involves the obstacles they have overcome and that they face daily, such as sexism, racism, and financial barriers. However, these women have succeeded in their careers and are now planning future successes, for their careers and family lives. By examining these women's stories, we can begin to understand the interaction between personal characteristics and one's environment and the factors that may lead to women's success in career and family.

6

Gender Differences in Career Development

An understanding of the career development of women requires an understanding of how women both differ from and are similar to men in this area. That is why the study reported in this book obtained data from both men and women. In this chapter, I review the findings on gender differences from each of the three data collection phases. I focus on the information obtained from the interviewees. The stories told us by the men we interviewed are compared in this chapter with the stories I discussed in Chapters 2 and 3 provided by the women interviewees. Later in this chapter, I review the quantitative gender differences found in our longitudinal study.

Men in Science Careers

School Experiences

A question we were interested in was whether or not men and women had different experiences in high school that related to their choice of a science or math career. For the women, we found that some had liked science but didn't do well in or like math. Others had enjoyed and done well in both. The picture some of the women had of scientists, or of students who took electives in science, was one of unpopular students, the "brains," the "nerds." Were these themes evident in the stories of the men who had chosen science or math careers too? Table 6.1 provides the names, occupations, education, and marital status of the 25 men interviewed who persisted in a science career.

A surprise to us, many of the men in science- and math-related careers were turned off to academics in high school, then went to college and found themselves ill-prepared for the calculus courses required for engineering. However, they persevered and earned their degree in science or technology.

(text continues on p. 130)

Table 6.1 *Men Who Persisted in a Science Career: Grade in High School in 1980, Education, Current Occupation, Marital Status*

Name	Grade	Degree	Occupation	Children	Married
Garden City High School					
Ronald[a]	9	D.D.	Dentist		x
Clay	9	M.A.	Accountant		x
Nicholas	9	M.A.	Accountant		x
Isaac	12	B.S.	Computer science	2	x
Gary	12	A.A.	Chemist		
Suburban High School					
Chad	9	B.S.	Accountant	1	
Fred	9	A.A.	Electrical technician		
Metro High School					
Eduardo	12	B.A.	University physical education teacher		x
Bob	12	A.A.	Biomedical technician	2	x
Ken	12	B.A.	Computer science	3	x
Sam	9	B.S.	Pharmacist	1	x
Victor	9	M.B.A.	Computer science		
Ogden	9	B.A.	Biologist		
Keith	12	M.A.	Accountant	2	x
David	9	B.S.	Computer science	1	x

NOTE: *n* = 25.
a. Men of color: Ronald, Asian American; Joe, African American/Asian American; Norman, Hispanic/German; Paul, Native American.
b. Matthew attended college for one year and completed his training on the job. He designs parts for commercial trucks; his title is engineer.
c. Edwin's father was born in Germany and Edwin lived there for a time.

Table 6.1 *(continued)*

Name	Grade	Degree	Occupation	Children	Married
City High School					
Joe[a]	9	M.A.	Accountant	1	x
Paul[a]	9	A.A.	Electrical technician		x
Farmerville High School					
Charles	12	D.C.	Chiropractor	1	x
Norman[a]	9	B.A.	Computer science	1	x
Nathan	12	B.S.	Engineer	1	x
Jack	9	B.A.	Industrial engineer		
Country High School					
Matthew	12	A.A.[b]	Engineer technician	1	x
Ted	12	B.A.	Geologist	1	x
Edwin[c]	9	M.S.	Engineer		
Russell	12	M.S.	Engineer	1	x

NOTE: *n* = 25.
a. Men of color: Ronald, Asian American; Joe, African American/Asian American; Norman, Hispanic/German; Paul, Native American.
b. Matthew attended college for one year and completed his training on the job. He designs parts for commercial trucks; his title is engineer.
c. Edwin's father was born in Germany and Edwin lived there for a time.

129

An example is Matthew, an engineering technician who attended Country High School. He said,

In high school I didn't try all that hard to do things as I should have. I took classes that interested me, I was able to not take anything that didn't interest me. I guess that goes back to enjoying your work. I tended to take a lot more shop classes. I took architecture for a couple of years, and drafting and that was what really interested me. I didn't take the advanced math courses that a lot of people took, and I didn't take any of the science classes beyond what was required. At this point I know that I should have done that; I guess at that point no one was really prodding me or pushing me to do some of the more difficult things, I just didn't apply myself real well.

Bob, from Metro High School, is a biomedical technician. Similar to Matthew, Bob said,

I won art contests in grade school and everything. It ended up that when I got to high school I started taking a lot of architecture classes. When I started high school I was one of the top kids in my class, but I was very bored. Well, when it came to architecture I loved it. One thing about high school that really bothered me was that there was too much freedom there. Instead of taking more algebra or science they let me make my own schedule and I spent too much time in architecture so when I got to college it was a rude awakening as far as being prepared. Metro definitely did not prepare us for college.

There were several other examples of this kind of high school experience; either the men were turned off to academics or they didn't take advanced math, such as calculus, even though they wanted an engineering degree. Nathan, from Farmerville High School, is now an engineer. He failed the first time he took calculus in college. But he persisted and finally passed calculus after taking it twice. Clay, who attended Garden City High School and is now an accountant, was an average student in high school in his math courses. Clay had difficulty with calculus when he entered college in engineering and he switched to accounting, in which he was more successful.

Ogden, a graduate of Metro High School, was a chemist. He said,

In high school I played the drums. I lived for the band in high school. I did not study; as a matter of fact, my biology teacher refused to OK me for high school chemistry because I was a C student in his course. Well, my parents and my adviser overruled my biology teacher so I did get to take chemistry. If

I had it to do over again I would still go to Metro, but I would become more scholastically tuned in.

Edwin, an engineer introduced in Chapter 4, was a graduate of Country High School. He said,

In high school the spectator athletics, where people come to these meets and games, that's when I really started excelling in sports. I was in basketball. In PE class I tried hard. They give presidential awards in PE class if you can do something like six pull-ups, and so many situps, and all this and you get a presidential award. That was important to me. I got a presidential award. By the time I got in my senior year in high school I was captain of several sport teams. Most of my friends were not involved in academics in high school. From my freshman year in high school I was fixated on athletics. I was getting ready to graduate, it was the senior year and I had no idea of what I was going to do. In high school I never took math because I was in athletics. I just signed the test and they passed me. So senior year after I decided I wanted engineering, I took a night course in algebra at the local community college. My senior year it really hit me, the clock was running out you know.

Another aspect of the men's experience in high school involved a teacher or teachers judging them as not being college material and, as a result, encouraging them to take the vocational technical education courses and to participate in work-study programs that would prepare them for entrance into one or another of the skilled trades. Chad, a graduate of Suburban High School and now an accountant, described the work-study program called DAVEA conducted out of a regional community college. Chad said,

I went to DAVEA my senior year. It's kind of a vocational school. You take off half the day and kids from school all around the area would go there and come back later for classes. So I would go there specifically for the accounting classes. It got to be a game to where getting into my senior year I would be after every grade that came out in accounting. I thought I could get by in college without math, just doing accounting; addition, subtraction, multiplication, division, I could do all that. I was wrong!

Ken, another Metro High School graduate, now a computer scientist, said,

I was in the work-study program at Metro because I'd had a summer job at this car dealership where my brother-in-law worked, and wanting to continue to do that, I joined the work-study program at school. And it was good. I mean the working part was good and I really paid no attention to school. I had terrible grades in my junior year and my senior year. I didn't take any science or math either year. Prior to that I was in accelerated classes in math and science. So I turned [in] the other direction. I think if you are in a work program, the teachers say these accelerated classes aren't necessary. But at that point I didn't really feel like there was anybody watching what I was doing. So one of the things, when I look back, is the fact that I took no science or math classes my last two years and I feel that if I would have maybe that would have led me to a better college and maybe a higher level in my profession.

A couple of differences stand out between the men and women interviewed who were in science- and math-related careers. The men were frequently not turned on to academics in high school; instead, they were into sports, music (playing in the band), or just hanging out with their friends, and some were sidetracked into vocational training. None of these experiences prepared them for science and engineering majors in college. The women's experiences were similar with respect to not being prepared adequately for college. See, for example, Gena's story in Chapters 1 and 2. The women's experiences in high school were different, however, in some important respects. Sexual harassment, for example, was unique to the women's experiences.

Magic Wand Stories

In Chapter 2, I described the "magic wand" stories provided by women who were in science careers when we interviewed them. Their stories fell into three categories. When the men in science careers' magic wand stories were examined, their stories fell into similar categories with some additional ones. The first category of stories, which reflected essentially wanting to continue doing what they were doing with some upgrading, was told by 6 of the 25 men in science. Typical of these stories was that by Ronald, an Asian American who became a dentist. He said, "I would buy expensive dental equipment and a large building for my office and probably work part-time, leaving some time for tennis."

Norman, a Hispanic man who had attended Farmerville High School, was a computer scientist. He said,

Well, I'd be doing the same thing. But I would've been doing it a lot sooner, and I would have advanced a lot quicker. You know, if I had this magic wand I would have finished high school with good grades. I would've gone straight to a four-year college instead of a community college. I could go to any college in the world if I had a magic wand, right—but I still would've gone to the one I finished up in because my family's very important to me, and it's important to stay nearby. I would probably have my master's by now and be where I probably will be in about five years.

Other men in science- or technology-related careers—an accountant, a geologist, a pharmacist, and an engineer—also said they would continue doing what they were doing now because they were happy. One has to conclude that these men and the women who expressed similar themes are relatively satisfied with their choice of a career in a science or math field. Several of them would like to upgrade, or be more autonomous, but otherwise not change very much.

Other stories told by the men in science, similar to some of the stories told by the women, focused on having more time to spend with their families, to travel and take vacations with their families, and to have a nice place to live. Chad, who is first-generation Italian, said,

First of all I'd make sure that everybody in the family was taken care of for their future (i.e. life insurance policies). That they had something to fall back on if they needed it. And the house would definitely be right up there at the top, right up there. I'd have a nice home, a nice size house and go on a vacation every year. Then I'd probably start my own business I've always wanted to do that.

In addition, some of the men's stories were about helping others less fortunate, including finding a cure for cancer, bringing about world peace, and feeding starving children in Third World countries. Nicholas, also an accountant, said,

I've always said if I was ever to win the lottery and was able to retire, I'd like to volunteer somewhere and help somebody who is not as fortunate. I really feel good, even around Christmastime, when I am able to give, to work with church groups handing out food baskets. My father-in-law is president of a local community organization; I give them money to feed some needy families. I know there's a lot less fortunate people than me, there's people that are a lot worse off.

A gender difference appeared in these stories in that several of our men in science and math occupations wanted to be star athletes or star entertainers whereas the women who wanted to change things would travel the world, change the world for the better, or even change their own personalities. Five of the men wanted to be star athletes, including Charles, a chiropractor, who said,

I would go back and not stop gymnastics when I did. To this day I remember the day that I stopped. It was as simple as telling my mom I didn't want to go in that day. And it never happened again. At the time I was told that I was doing good. And I was doing back flips before the girls in high school were doing straight legged cartwheels. I was in grade school, so I was pretty amazing at the time in a small town. It was kind of a high. I would have continued that and probably gymnastics all through university. It would've been interesting to see how that path would have worked. If I could be given a voice, I definitely would be singing. Bette Midler and I would be doing a lot of duets and making big money in the movies.

Isaac, a computer scientist, said,

I'd love to play pro basketball, that'd never happen though, but it would be fun just to play basketball for who knows how long and get paid just to play basketball, that would be fun, I tell you.

Bob, a biomedical engineer, said,

If I had some of those things taken care of for me where I knew I was set in life, I would go do what the heart wanted. Play baseball, just because it has all those things. I'd have fun, money, be traveling, that would be right there and then I'd have to go ahead and be on TV and have those two coaches that told me I wasn't good enough watch me.

Some magic wand stories were "dream fulfillments" of careers aspired to but not achieved. A couple of these men had wanted to be doctors and ended up in lower-level health-related careers. Ogden, now an environmental biologist and chemist, had wanted to be a doctor, but on his first try he failed the MCAT (Medical College Achievement Test) and was unable to bring himself to take it over again. His magic wand story wish was "that career in medicine, maybe I will go back to it sometime."

Norman, one of the computer scientists mentioned earlier, dreamed of being a medical doctor. Victor, a computer scientist, dreamed of building a model city in the suburbs and being the mayor. Gary, a chemist, dreamed of owning his own restaurant with live entertainment. Chad, born in Italy and an accountant, would be a coach and teach. Paul, an electrical technician and a Native American, would be one of the richest men in the world, would "run the world," and would improve the U.S. economy.

These "magic wand" stories are similar in broad outline to those the women told us. The stories in which the men told us they wanted to be in an entirely different career frequently involved being a star athlete, which was not a theme among our women in science. But other themes, such as helping the poor, healing the sick, bringing about world peace, were common for both genders.

Guidance Stories

Five major themes emerged from the women who had chosen science careers when they were asked what they would be sure to say to high school students today if they were invited to give a talk at their former high school. A dominant theme was to tell current high school students to pick careers they knew they would enjoy over those that were popular or that seemed to guarantee a good salary. Other themes were to encourage exploration and planfulness. The women also would encourage "hanging in there" when the going gets tough and choosing a career that would ensure economic independence.

Several of the men in science careers also said they would emphasize the first theme to today's high school students. They said, for example, "Go with your heart," not "the big bucks."Joe is an African American whose mother is an immigrant from Asia. He has an M.B.A. in accounting and he said,

I would want to be sure to get across to students to find out what's important to them and why. I mean the most important thing is self-discovery. The way you discover the world is to look inward and find out what's important to you and why, then think about whether those things really are important in the grand scheme of things. And that will allow you to prioritize in the right way. Once you find out that, it's not so important to get a car at 17. It's important to understand what's really valuable to you, and I think once you have that then it gives you the ability to prioritize and to delay gratification.

Another theme evident in the women scientists' guidance stories was to encourage young women today to explore a lot of different careers before choosing one for themselves. This was a prominent theme among our men in science as well. Several of the men, reflecting back on their high school experience, also said they wished they had been more serious students back then. These men would encourage students today to get serious about their careers when they are still in high school so they can plan ahead.

Isaac, who was interested in architecture when he was in high school and is now a computer scientist with a master's degree in information systems, said,

Be more serious about high school, your grades, and start thinking about your future; try to think in terms of things that you like to do. I guess trying to leverage your likes and wants into a profession. If you like a science of a certain type or what not, try to investigate what other sciences are out there, what schools are out there that offer the things you want to do. I'd stress the seriousness of high school. I could see how I did OK in high school. I did a little better in college though, so I'd say work with your counselors and try to develop a plan that you are interested in pursuing.

A third theme among the women in science was to "hang in there no matter what the obstacles." This theme was less evident among the men in science, but some of our men in science emphasized this as well.

Nathan, the engineer also had attended Farmerville High School, said he would encourage students today to work hard in high school—not to pick the easy classes but instead to pick challenging courses and stick with them for the long term. As we noted earlier in this chapter, he had a bad experience with calculus when he went to college, but he persevered and graduated.

Ken, a computer scientist, said,

I would tell students to set a goal for themselves and don't make it too high; try to achieve that goal and then when you do, set another one somewhere above that one. And I would say if they wanted to be a doctor, I would tell them to pursue medical school first and don't look down the road to the M.D. yet, because maybe they'll give up in their first year saying I'll never make it through the next eleven years, but if they just try to make it through the first four, maybe they don't become a doctor but they can still be in the health field. If there were heroes presented to the students, I think it would help a lot of people to be inspired and set goals.

These men encouraged students to read up on the economic projections for careers and to choose carefully. Some said to learn about career financial prospects before choosing a career—this is more important than whether or not you like the career. But this theme, a focus on salary, was atypical.

Summary of Gender Differences and Similarities in Science Careers: Interview Data

The major differences for women and men in science careers were related to sex discrimination and sexual harassment experienced by women in science and math classes, which the men did not experience. Some of the women in science we interviewed were not discouraged by these experiences; however, as I noted in Chapter 3, many women were turned off to science because of sexual harassment. Another difference was that for the men, vocational technical high school "tracks" were recommended when teachers thought the students were not college material. Many of these men went on to college and found it difficult to compete because they were poorly prepared in terms of college course requirements.

Several men and women had the common experience of not being turned on to academics in high school and not planning ahead for their careers. Both men and women spoke of the students who took advanced math and science as being "nerds." The image of the scientist was not so much male as it was "nerdy."

The magic wand stories and the school guidance stories of the women and the men exhibited similar themes. There was one difference that stood out, however, which was the high number of men who dreamed about being star athletes. The magic wand question elicited various types of responses from both the women and the men. For most, it was an opportunity to get in touch with what would make them most satisfied with their lives. However, some, whose current situations were overly stressed"for example, a single mother working two jobs or a father working two shifts—might dream of lying on a beach doing nothing or some such self-indulgent activity. Such wishes, if satisfied, might provide only temporary pleasures because they meet a need for reduced stress. In light of this possibility, it is important to use caution when interpreting the magic wand stories that described radical change. These stories may or may not reflect regrets and unhappiness with long-term career prospects.

Gender Differences in Science and Technology Career Choice: Quantitative Findings

Occupational Prestige Differences

The prestige levels of the science-related careers chosen by women were, on average, significantly lower than those chosen by men. Crabtree et al. (1995) compared men and women who had remained in a science or technology career in 1990 on occupational prestige. They found that the prestige level of the men's occupations compared with the women's in these fields was significantly higher (84 versus 62). Further examination revealed that women compared with men were clustered in the helping sciences, especially nursing and health technician fields (46% versus 4%). Men, compared with women, were clustered in engineering (35% versus 3%). At the physician level within the health fields, 12% were men and 5% women. These data suggest that we need to continue to focus resources and interventions for girls on developing interests in engineering and on higher levels within the health field such as physician. Project Talent (Card, Steel, & Abeles, 1980) and the High School and Beyond study (Hilton, Miller, & Brown, 1991; J. Miller, 1986), which were both longitudinal, found—similar to Farmer (1985)—that high school-age boys and girls aspired to relatively similar career prestige levels, but that they majored in less prestigious career fields and ended up in lower-level careers. In our study, for men, persisting in science was strongly related to having high career aspirations both in 1980 when they were in high school and in 1990 when they were young adults—but not for women (Farmer, Wardrop, Anderson, & Risinger, 1995). It seems that aspiring to a high-level career is related to choosing one and persisting in it. It would seem important to stimulate such aspirations in women during the formative early school years.

But women may be resistant to such attempts because they continue to view their future role related to child rearing as less compatible with occupations that demand a high level of commitment in terms of willingness to travel and relocate and willingness to work evenings and weekends. When we interviewed the women who had entered nursing, they gave as one of the most important reasons for choosing nursing its high rate of employability anywhere they might choose to live and the flexibility of the hours they could choose to work. These women viewed nursing as a career that would fit well with having and raising children and also with a single or divorced head of household lifestyle. They were hedging their bets against the challenges they anticipated in their future related to multiple roles as well as divorce. These reasons for choosing nursing were more important to the women nurses we interviewed than their perception that their personal attributes fit this career. These women could benefit from the knowledge that some employers of engineers, such as Gena's, are willing to arrange to have some work done at home when their female engineers have babies. Such flexible work arrangements make engineering a career that women with multiple roles might consider.

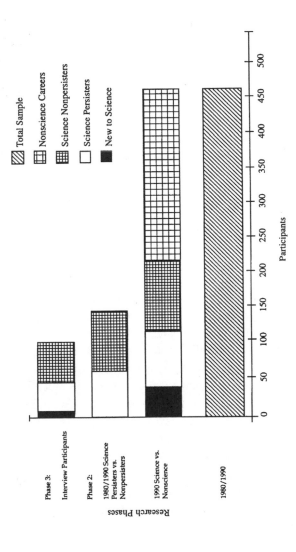

Figure 6.1. Subsamples for Data Analyses in the Longitudinal Study
NOTE: For the longitudinal study, see Farmer, Wardrop, Anderson, and Risinger (1995) and Farmer, Wardrop, and Crabtree (1995).

Taking Advanced Science Courses in High School

Farmer, Wardrop, Anderson, and Risinger (1995) reported that taking elective science courses in high school contributed more to the choice of and persistence in a science career for women than it did for men. Figure 6.1 provides information on the subsamples we used for both interview and quantitative analyses. It was not that the women took more elective science courses than men, but that for women choosing to do so was a strong indicator of their interest in these fields. Farmer, Wardrop, and Crabtree (1995) found that valuing math for its relationship to their future career was more characteristic of women who chose science careers than of women in other career fields. Mean differences for these measures were similar for men, but math utility did not contribute unique variance to the structural equation that predicted group status for men, whereas it did for women.

For both men and women in science, taking elective science because they wanted to, rather than because they were expected to, discriminated them from persons in other career fields. This might be described as "intrinsic interest."

Attributions and self-efficacy. We also found that attributing their successes in math to their ability, and rejecting the attribution of their failures in math to lack of ability, was more characteristic of both men and women in science compared with those in other career fields (Farmer, Wardrop, & Crabtree, 1995). This pattern of attributions has been found by Weiner (1979) and Frieze et al. (1982) to be positively related to continuing interest in an activity. Betz (1990) found that higher math self-efficacy is related to women choosing higher-level careers in science. Our data did not indicate that math self-efficacy was a significant predictor of persistence in science for women or for men. However, the combined direct and indirect effects for math self-efficacy predicting persistence in a science career was .20 for women, indicating a meaningful relationship when all variables in the model were considered (Farmer, Wardrop, Anderson, & Risinger, 1995). Of interest, when the focus shifts from comparing women who persisted in science with those who did not, to comparing women in science with those in other career fields, math self-efficacy was significantly higher ($p < .01$) for the women in science. This result was also true when comparing men in science with men in other career fields.

Valuing Science Because It Affects Future Success and Satisfaction

Valuing math and science course work because it is important for achieving future career aspirations and plans was not an important predictor of persistence in a science career for women or for men. However, when the comparison was between men and women in science careers and those in other career fields, mean differences were significant between groups for both genders. Men receive clearer messages from their families, teachers, counselors, and society at large for the importance of a career in their lives. Women still receive mixed messages in this regard and therefore are more reactive to the support or lack of support provided by significant others with respect to their career planning. The "null environment," one that is indifferent to women's career aspirations and achievements, still exerts its influence (Betz, 1990). This idea is based on the experience of many girls and women of the indifference of parents, teachers, friends, and the community at large to their accomplishments in school. Girls report significant others including parents, teachers, and counselors saying to them, "Do what you want to, be happy, have a good life," whereas boys are told: "Get good grades so you can get into the best schools and succeed in a career" (Eccles, 1994). Even more undermining of a career interest in science is a statement one girl reported from her high school counselor, "For a pretty girl like you, what you do is not very important. You're going to get married in a few years anyway." Underlying these messages is the acceptance of the idea that women are not only the child bearers but also the child rearers, and therefore they cannot be as involved in career pursuits as men. Until this societal view changes, we cannot expect full parity for women in the workplace. Norma, described in Chapter 3, is a good example of a woman who experienced a null environment with respect to her career. Women need encouragement and support from significant others to enter nontraditional careers in greater numbers. According to Etzkowitz, Kemelgor, Neuschatz, Uzzi, and Alonzo (1994), a critical mass of about 15% is needed to provide support within an occupation.

Men's Career Choice Development Better Understood Than Women's

One of the clear findings from the quantitative phases of our study is that we were better able to account for antecedent influences on men's career choices than we were for women's. For example, Farmer, Wardrop, and Crabtree (1995) reported they could account for 74% of the variance for differences in antecedent influences on men's choice of science, compared with men in the humanities, whereas they could only account for 36% of this variance for women. This was the case even though we added variables to the models we tested that were thought to be relevant to women such as sex role socialization, sex discrimination, home role commitment, androgyny, and cooperative achievement style, among others.

Gender Differences in Planning for a Career

I have argued, with others (Farmer, 1971; Harmon, 1978), that women have a more complex task confronting them when they make a career choice because this choice is not independent of their other life plans. Dual-earner couples have become the norm in the 1990s and men frequently make their career choices within a life planning framework too (Gilbert, 1994b). A later chapter in this book by Lenore Tipping explores the career and life planning of the twenty-something generation, based on our interviews. Findings from the high school phase of our study indicated that the women and the men valued both their home or family role as well as their career role. However, for women, the more they valued their home role, the less they valued their career role. This interaction effect was not present for the men (see Figure 6.2).

Summary of Gender Differences and Similarities in Science Careers: Quantitative Findings

A persistent finding in our study as well as several others, including the most recent findings from the National Science Foundation (1994), was the prestige difference in the science occupations chosen by women and men, with women's being significantly lower in prestige. Women chose nurse and health technician most frequently, whereas men chose engineer and physician. Career aspiration level—a combination of occupational prestige and educational level—was an important predictor of persistence in a science career for both genders; however, the strength of this relationship was stronger for men than for women.

Another difference, evident when these men and women were in high school, was the effect of their homemaking commitment on their career commitment. For men, no effect was evident, whereas for women the effect was significant: When homemaking commitment was high, career commitment was low. Combining multiple roles is complex and places more need to compromise on women than on men. Chapter 14 discusses some ways to help women with planning for their multiple roles.

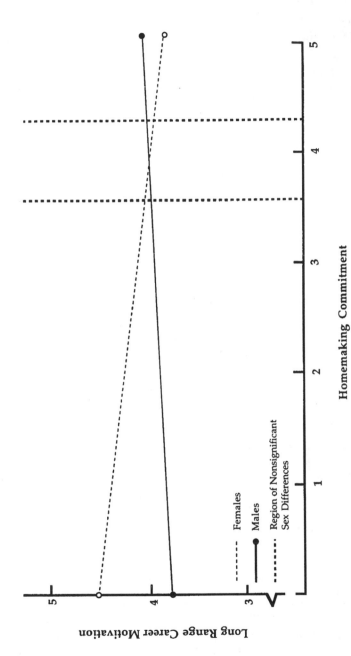

Figure 6.2. Graph of significance ($p < .01$) interaction effect for gender on long-range career commitment and homemaking commitment.

Some differences for gender were more subtle. For example, both men and women in science took more elective (i.e., advanced) science courses in high school; however, this behavior was predictive of persistence in science for the women, but not for the men. Both genders said they took elective math and science for intrinsic reasons, rather than to please someone else. Similarly, both genders valued math for its relationship to their future careers, but the predictive power of this valuing for persistence in a science career was much stronger for women than for men. Both women and men attributed their successes in math to their ability rather than to effort or luck; they rejected the idea that their failures in math resulted from lack of ability. These attribution patterns are found to predict persistence in an activity.

It appears that the best predictors of persistence in a science career were fairly similar for women and men, but the relative strength of these relationships differed. For women, taking elective science and valuing math for its contribution to their future careers was most important for persistence perhaps because they had to compensate for the null environment at home and in school. For men, having high career aspirations in high school and beyond and having high science grades in high school was the most predictive. It is tempting to think that these gender differences reflect the differing messages men and women receive from important others—parents, teachers, counselors, and friends. For women, the messages are mixed and not clear in their support; for men, the messages are clearer, "if you have the ability, go for it."

Men Who Changed Their Careers From Science to Other Career Fields

We interviewed 21 men who had wanted a science career in 1980 and by 1990 had changed their career to another field. In comparing these men with the women who changed, who were described in Chapter 3, I reviewed their stories for the similar themes: choosing a popular career in high school, choosing a better fit 10 years later, choosing a better fit in spite of obstacles, and choosing a less satisfactory career because of circumstances beyond their ability to cope. Table 6.2 presents the current occupation, educational level, and marital status of all 21 men who changed from science to another career field. Table 6.3 presents their 1980 science aspiration as well as their current career and includes occupational prestige level (Stevens & Cho, 1985) as well as Holland occupational interest codes (Gottfredson & Holland, 1989). The Holland codes are explained in Chapter 1.

Table 6.2 *Men Career Changers: High School Grade in 1980, College Education, Marital Status*

Name	Grade	Degree	Occupation	Children	Married
Garden City High School					
Steve	9	B.A.	Personnel worker		x
Ledyard	9	H.S.	Minister	1	x
Tad	12	B.A.	Business manager	1	x
Suburban High School					
Nate	9	A.A.	Business owner	2	x
Lennie	12	B.A.	Sales		
Titus	12	B.A.	Business manager		x
Donald[a]	12	A.A.	Business owner		
Jim	9	A.A.	Sales		
Metro High School					
Ned	9	H.S.	Plumber	2	
Tom	12	B.A.	Sales		x
Patrick	12	H.S.	Machinist	1	x
Miguel[b]	9	B.S.	Sales manager		
Dorian	12	A.A.	Air Force recruiter		
Harry[b]	12	B.A.	Trainer, industrial	2	x
Kevin[b]	9	M.A.	Business administrator	1	
Vinnie[b]	12	H.S.	Corrections counselor		
Ethan[b]	9	M.A.	Marketing		x
City High School					
Jesus[b]	9	H.S.	Business owner		
Farmerville High School					
John	9	A.A.	Machinist	3	x
Country High School					
Gene	9	H.S.	Plumber		
Eliott	9	H.S.	Construction foreman	1	x

NOTE: *n* = 21.
a. Donald, born in Italy
b. Men of color: Harry, Ethan, and Kevin, African American; Miguel, Vinnie, and Jesus, Hispanic.

145

Table 6.3 *Men Career Changers: Occupations Aspired to in 1980 and in 1990s: Prestige and Holland Code*

Name	1980			1990		
	Code	Occupation	Prestige	Code	Occupation	Prestige
Tad	CRS	Accountant	78	ESR	Manager	84
Jim	CRS	Accountant	78	ESA	Sales	70
Vinnie	CRS	Accountant	78	SAE	Corrections counselor	72
Eliott	CRS	Accountant	78	REC	Construction foreman	66
Gene		Agricultural technician		REI	Plumber	34
Steve	AIR	Architect	90	ESR	Personnel worker	62
Donald	AIR	Architect	90	ESR	Business owner	84
Patrick	AIR	Architect	90	RIE	Machinist	
Ledyard				SAI	Minister	56
Miguel	ISR	Chiropractor	75	ESA	Sales manager	70
Lennie	IRE	Computer programmer	62	ESA	Sales	70
Nate	IRE	Computer programmer	62	ESR	Business owner	84
Jesus	IRE	Computer programmer	62	ESR	Business owner	84
Tom	ISR	Dentist	96	ESA	Sales	70
Dorian	RES	Engineer	87	SRE	Air Force recruiter	66
Kevin	RES	Engineer	87	ESC	Business administrator	72
Ethan	RES	Engineer	87	ESC	Marketing	72
Titus	RIS	Forest ranger	48	ESR	Business manager	84
John	ISA	Physician	92	RIE	Machinist	41
Ned	SIR	Podiatrist	92	REI	Plumber	34
Harry	IES	Sociologist	81	SAE	Industrial trainer	72

NOTE: *n* = 21.

146

Career changers who went into business. Nine of these men had earned four-year or higher college degrees and had changed to a business field; four of these nine were minority group members. First, we focus on the five men who were from white, lower-middle-class families and whose parents typically had not gone to college. In 1980, these men had chosen architect, forest ranger, accountant, computer programmer, and dentist; by 1990, they all had changed to some form of business career. Their 1980 choices were not particularly popular choices but were made based on some important experience with a family member or a class in high school. They were also choices that the men knew very little about. The five men are Tom, Tad, Lennie, Steve, and Titus.

Tom, who was a senior at Metro High School in 1980, said he wanted to be a dentist at that time. However, 10 years later, he had ended up in sales. Why did he change? Well, for one thing, he found the predentistry curriculum difficult in college and so he switched to a business major. He had chosen dentist as his career goal in high school because of the lifestyle it seemed to promise, not because of an intrinsic interest in dentistry. Neither of his parents had attended college and he felt that he had lacked adequate guidance in choosing a major and succeeding at college. His grades in his business major were not good either, although passing, and this hurt him in finding a good job when he graduated. He values money and status as goals for himself in his work. He is happy with his life and wouldn't change anything if given a magic wand. So he did find a better fit for his abilities and values, and one that offers the potential for a good life.

Tad was a senior at Garden City High School in 1980 and wanted to be an accountant at that time. He began college with an accounting major but found the math too difficult. He earned his B.A. instead in education. In his student teaching courses while he was still in college, he found that he didn't like teaching, so he went directly from college to a sales position. He is a manager at a real estate agency and oversees 20 agents. He loves his work. He has found a better fit for both his abilities and his skills in working with people.

Lennie had chosen computer programming in 1980 when he was a senior at Suburban High School. He had applied to study computer science in the business school at a major university but was not accepted. He then switched to the major his brother had pursued and earned his B.A. in public environmental affairs. When he graduated, he didn't get a job related to his major; instead, he immediately went to work in an investment business. He stayed there five years, then shifted to a sales job, which he has now. All his siblings went to college. Unlike most of the men in this group, his mother was a kindergarten teacher and thus familiar with college and able to help Lennie more with his career planning. If Lennie had a magic wand, he would quit work today and play golf. He works for the money, not for the intrinsic satisfaction of the work itself. He seems happy with his life. He doesn't work too hard, and he has time for golf and, what he terms, the good life.

Steve was in ninth grade at Garden City High School in 1980 and at that time he wanted to be an architect. His parents were "blue collar" and had not gone to college. Architecture appealed to him because he liked to draw and he enjoyed his drafting classes. Although he wanted to be an architect when he was in high school, his high school counselors steered him toward the construction trade. He went to community college right out of high school for one and a half years, with business as his major. He had a lot of fun but his grades weren't very good. Only in the last few years has he pursued his college degree in earnest, because he now realizes that his head is against the ceiling at work without this degree. He was employed as a personnel worker processing employee benefits for large companies, and was about to complete his B.A. degree. He had four more courses to take to graduate at the time of our interview, and he was earning mostly As in his courses. Steve would tell high school students today: "You gotta have some kind of guidance or else you're spending a lot of energy going in circles." If he had a magic wand, Steve wanted "to be smarter." He says he is happy with his work, but he has some regrets related to college.

Titus, from Suburban High School, had wanted to be a forest ranger in 1980 and he is now self-employed. He had always been good at math and science in elementary and high school. Neither of his parents had attended college, and when he went to college he had no particular major in mind so he spent a couple of years just taking courses he liked. Titus said,

> I had some accounting and some economics and at that point I was going to be a business major, that's what I ended up doing. However, I was one of those guys that could have been an economics major, a philosophy major.

Titus still loves the idea of being a forest ranger, studying earth sciences, even being a petroleum engineer. As a child, he would go with his uncle on excavation trips and collect fossilized bones, and that experience has stayed with him. But he didn't choose a college major until he was nearly finished. He has accumulated experience in various industries since leaving college, all in marketing and sales. At the time of the interview, he was self-employed, offering consulting services to various businesses and using his prior experience in marketing and the telecommunication business. Titus, even though he has a college degree, is not very happy in his work and he would encourage high school students today to find out about different jobs and to explore and visit with persons employed in those jobs. When Titus was asked what he would do with a magic wand, he said, "I would have to change everything. It would have to be a big swoop of the wand. . . . I would have a ranch in Montana or Wyoming, and own my own business." For Titus, more information and career guidance in high school might have made a difference in where he is today.

This group of five men included two who had been somewhat derailed by circumstances from their original career goals, Titus and Steve. Four were handicapped in their career development by lack of adequate guidance from family and school and from lack of experience and information about their 1980 science choices. Tom and Tad, however, seemed fairly well satisfied with their present careers in sales and real estate. Lennie, whose family was more middle class, was not very career oriented. He was content to be in sales, similar to his dad, and he had no regrets about not getting into the computer science program.

Minority career changers with four-year or higher college degrees. The experiences of the minority men in our study are of interest. Several of them switched from their science aspiration to a more people-oriented career such as education, marketing, or management. They typically earned master's degrees and were from the two inner-city schools, Metro and City. Metro was about 32% minority, and City was 85% minority. The minority students at Metro complained about discrimination from teachers and white students, with the possible exception of students in athletics. Chapters 7 and 8 by JoAnn Cohn and Kirsten Peterson provide insights into the experiences of some of these men at school and in the community.

Ethan and Kevin, African Americans, were in ninth grade in 1980 and both had wanted to be engineers. They had been selected because of their high school grades to participate in INROADS, an inner-city-based program to introduce promising minority youth to engineering while they were still in high school. In their sophomore year in high school, INROADS broadened its focus to include exposure to business as well as engineering. At this point, Ethan also became involved in the business part. At that time too, the guidance counselor at Metro told Ethan his grades were not good enough to get into engineering at one of the big 10 universities.

Ethan's parents, although not college graduates, had taken some college courses and gave him strong support for going to college. As predicted by his counselor, he was accepted at a big 10 university but not in engineering. He began with an undeclared major, hoping to transfer into engineering. Ethan said,

At any rate, when I got into college, I had gotten accepted at a couple of schools for engineering but I did not get accepted at the major university for engineering so I went down there as an undeclared major and they said after 60 hours of course work, if you want to transfer into engineering you have that option. Well, I went down there and I met enough people and I saw enough people going through the engineering curriculum, that it really didn't interest me. I had no interest in being an engineer. I saw a close enough view of what they were doing and what they were going through that I didn't want to do it. I wanted something different. So, I started to look around, you know—what skills do I think I have and what skills do I think I can use and what do I like to do? Trying to develop what you really want to do is tough. So, I don't really know how I came up with business In all fairness, my roommate was probably an influence because he was in a business curriculum and he was selling me on some of the features, and some of my friends were in business school. So I looked at that and I said, Yeah, I think I could do that. The marketing side had an appeal because it was more of a wide range of opportunities because there was sales, advertising, and a lot of different areas, like hotel management so you could branch off without deciding exactly what you wanted to do and that was one of the big things when I graduated in selecting companies to work for.

It was important to Ethan to have variety in his work and to have options open to him to shift his focus if he wanted to. He was hired immediately out of college at a big manufacturing company and is still there. He seems to be happy in this job; however, in response to the magic wand question, he said he would be a commercial airplane pilot. It seems that he joined the Air Force ROTC in college but a heart murmur disqualified him for pilot training. He still has a dream about being a pilot. On the other hand, he is not unhappy in his work. There is more of Ethan's story in Chapter 8, which indicates that his experience at work was not free from racial discrimination.

Kevin, as a result of his experience in the INROADS program, began his college studies in engineering and then transferred to business at the end of his sophomore year. He was given a personality test during college and scored high on people orientation. He believes this estimate is correct and that he belongs in business, working with people. He returned to graduate school in 1991 and majored in business management. He worked as a recruiter for the university during his graduate school years. His dream job is to consult with companies and help them develop day-care centers for employees' preschool children. He definitely has found a better fit. Kevin experienced many obstacles in his career development. He was adopted as a baby but didn't discover this until he was 12. We tell more of Kevin's story in Chapters 4 and 7.

Miguel is Hispanic and was in ninth grade at Metro High School in 1980. Neither of his parents had attended college, but they were very supportive of their children's academic endeavors and encouraged them to attend college. In 1980, Miguel wanted to be a chiropractor. In 1990, he had earned a B.S. degree in premed and was employed as a sales manager at a pharmaceutical corporation. Miguel had entered college majoring in radiological technology but was soon disillusioned by the bleak economic prospects for graduates in this major. He switched to premed and took five years to complete his degree. He applied to several medical schools and was accepted in at least one, but decided at that point to take a job rather than continue in school. The feedback from medical school wasn't encouraging. Miguel said,

Gosh, probably about midway into getting feedback from the application process when I started seeing that I wasn't getting into the places that I wanted to get into. Whereas, I didn't really see my want to be that [a doctor] to be that bad, to where I was going to do that. It wasn't that big a deal for me. OK, well I'll try—this just didn't work out, let's see what else I can do. What do we have here?

When Miguel was reminded during the interview of his choice of chiropractor in 1980, he said, "Really? That's funny. Guess I did kind of start out in the medical route." Now he is taking graduate courses in business management and plans to complete an M.B.A. Miguel might be said to have chosen a popular career in 1980, and now he has a career that combines his early medical interest with his interest in sales. His answer to the magic wand question was that he would own his own business and take more time for golf. So he seems to have a better fit as a sales manager in a pharmaceutical firm than he would have had as a doctor.

Harry, an African American, was a senior at Metro High School in 1980. He said at that time that he wanted to be a sociologist. When he was reminded of what he had written in 1980, he said, "Oh God, we had career days and things but looking back it was mailman one week, fireman the next week, just kind of varied, professional basketball player, doctor, lawyer." It seems that sociologist was not a serious choice for Harry but a momentary one. Harry was a basketball player throughout his schooling, both in high school and in college. He entered college in an education major thinking he might teach physical education. When he found that his athletic skills were not good enough for professional leagues, he changed his major to human relations. He currently works as a trainer for a bank in the credit card department. He is unhappy with his current career, both the salary and the prestige it offers. He aspires instead to be a recruiter or a manager in this industry. Harry's magic wand story indicated that he regrets not being more serious about a science degree when he was in high school. He said,

I guess if I had to do it all over again, I'd probably choose subjects in high school and in college that would lead me on a professional course, probably medicine or engineering. I'd try to do better in the sciences. I have no doubt that it was just the fear of not knowing and the people around me really not understanding the importance of science, chemistry, physics, those type things. When the people around you aren't doing those things, then you tend not to do these as well. So, knowing what I do know today, I would go into the sciences a little more.

Harry attended the same high school that Kevin and Ethan attended and both of the latter had been involved in the INROADS program to introduce them to engineering while they were still in high school. Harry was a senior in 1980; Kevin and Ethan were ninth graders. It seems that Harry missed out on exposure to engineering and now regrets it.

These four minority men, Ethan, Kevin, Miguel, and Harry, are all in business-related careers. Three of the four are relatively happy with their current work. Harry is not.

Career changers with A.A. degrees. Five of the "changers" had earned A.A. degrees and were either thinking about or planning to complete a four-year degree. The mean occupational prestige for the career choices these men made in 1980 was 82, and in 1990 it was 69, much lower. Table 6.2 indicates that three of these five men are now in business, another is an Air Force recruiter, and another is a machinist. Their magic wand stories indicate that they are aspiring to achieve a high salary or more education.

For example, John, who is working now as a machinist, aspires to earn a B.A. in business and become a business manager. Earlier, he had enrolled in a four-year college but found he didn't like the accounting courses. Then he switched to business management but couldn't keep up tuition payments. Several years later, he went back to college part-time. He is a keen observer of his fellow workers and he has a well-articulated philosophy about how management could be improved at his shop. John said,

I'll tell you what. When you are a worker out on the floor, I don't care if you are union or nonunion, whatever the case may be, if once in a while, someone that you work for tells you, Hey that's a good idea, or that's a wonderful job you did or something like that, and gives you some kind of recognition for what you have done—it makes you feel good, it really does. That's another thing I believe in.

His magic wand story indicated he "would be the president of the U.S." He went on to elaborate on what is wrong with the present government and with politicians. He would fix it, put it right. He is an optimist with a cause; he wants to make things better. He believes that once he is in management, he will make things a lot better in his factory.

Dorian, who wanted to be an engineer in 1980, is now an Air Force recruiter. When he joined the Air Force, he was still planning on obtaining training in aeronautical engineering but he tested color blind and this disqualified him. He finds that his recruiter career uses his leadership and people skills well, but his magic wand story indicated that he would want to earn his B.A. and fly in some capacity for the Air Force.

Nate, who had wanted to be a computer programmer in high school, now owns his own construction business and is optimistic about his future and quite content with his career. He said he was not college minded.

Jim, who had wanted to be an accountant in 1980, is now a sales account executive for a marketing firm. His college training is in marketing. His magic wand story indicated a desire for more autonomy at work as well as the flexibility to spend about half of his time playing guitar. He has kept up his music and plays on weekends with a small band.

Donald was born in Italy and in high school wanted to be an architect. He is currently running his own printing business. His interest in printing began in high school, as an assistant to the graphic arts teacher. He began college with a major in architecture but found it difficult and switched to graphic arts. He seems to have found a better fit. His magic wand story indicated that he would win an Oscar for acting, and then he would expand his print business and make it the best around.

These five men didn't go as far in college; they stopped with two-year degrees. Many of them have dreams about how different their lives would be if they had them to do over. Some, like John, are working toward a four-year college degree.

Career changers who did not earn a college degree. Of the 21 men originally aspiring to a science career, 7 either did not go to college or did not complete a college degree. Were they derailed by circumstances or was college just not for them?

There were some themes that emerged among these men that were not evident among the women changers. One of these themes was a concern with economic security—the long-range prospects for employment that a career offered. Ned, who had wanted to be a podiatrist in high school, chose to be a plumber as an adult. He said,

I would tell students to make sure they are going to be happy in what they are doing, that . . . good money has a big part to do with careers and it's going to be something that's going to be long term, that they can rely on, that their job is going to be secure, that it is going to be there and not something that's going to be folding. You got to be happy, the money has got to be there, that is what I think.

Two of these men were Hispanic, Vinnie and Jesus. Vinnie had indicated accountant as his career choice in 1980 when he was a high school senior. He recalls his high school years as a blur of drug use. He is currently engaged in counseling convicted men and seems committed to helping others, especially Hispanic convicts. His response to the magic wand question was that he would move to Mexico, own horses, and enjoy his newfound luxury.

Jesus, on the other hand, had indicated computer programmer in 1980. He told us that he had entered college and taken a few courses in this major and found them very unappealing. He had chosen computer programming because his high school counselor had encouraged him to do so. He dropped out of college after one semester and took a job at a local steel mill. He said,

And back in 1983 that was a big thing. The big movement was to get into electronics, computers, computer programming, whatever, something that had to do with a technical field. Now I know that that was not what I was supposed, that was not my true calling. Because what happened was that you don't take a hyperactive kid who gets into a lot of trouble, not bad trouble, just mischief because I was a goof-off, class clown, and you don't take them and sit them down and have them playing with little knobs and a resistor and compositors and electronics.

At the steel mill, Jesus found recognition and success, and he moved through the ranks to become one of the first Hispanic men in the sales department. He was exceptional. All other employees in sales were Anglos with college degrees. He credits the steel company with giving him his "college degree." He then branched out to establish his own business in international steel sales, with several clients in Mexico. He is very excited about his business prospects. However, his magic wand story indicated that he has a dream. He said,

> I would have to come back to my favorite one, which I couldn't believe I
> . . . didn't . . . put it on here when I was about fifteen or sixteen, but I always
> wanted to be an airline pilot. Yeah, my uncle flies and there's something
> about that that just fascinates me, you know, the feeling of being free, just get-
> tin' up in the sky and doing a cartwheel without having the cops stop you. Just
> that type of—I would have loved to have been an airline pilot and I think that,
> depending on how this situation goes, I would probably be interested in, down
> the road, taking aviation lessons as a hobby.

He had flown as a child in Mexico with his uncle and that experience remained with him. Jesus' response to the magic wand question, however, continued:

> Well, actually I still would want to do this, because what I am doing here
> is trying to create something for myself and if I had a million dollars I'd have
> the capitol and I could go put up a warehouse in Mexico and sell until I am
> blue in the face. Because this is more than just a job. Because whatever I cre-
> ate it's going to be mine. If I create nothing, nothing will be there for me. But
> if I create something, then it will be mine, and I can pass it on to someone
> else—what I've created—and have them run with it. This is what I would want
> to do.

Jesus' story has many facets. Many of the experiences he had moving to the United States from Mexico at the age of 9 were painful. JoAnn Cohn tells more of his story in Chapter 7.

Ledyard, who had wanted to be an astronomer in high school, was derailed from this aspiration by his chronic depression, beginning about age 17. His depression seemed to have its roots in his father's philandering, which led to his parents' divorce. At about the same time, Ledyard's girlfriend rejected him. His depression lasted five years until he had a "conversion" experience and turned to the Christian ministry as a career that would satisfy him.

Eliott indicated accountant for his career choice in 1980, and in 1990 he was a foreman in the construction business. He went directly to work out of high school and has come to value a college education for his own children. His magic wand story was that he would have that education.

Patrick had wanted to be an architect in high school and now he is a machinist. He attended college to obtain training as a machinist and he plans to obtain his machinist certificate. This would qualify him to design parts of a machine as well as repair them. In high school, he had enjoyed drawing and designing houses. He took courses in architecture in high school and found he was good at reading blueprints. His magic wand story indicated that he would like more autonomy in his job but that otherwise he is quite happy.

Gene, who had originally aspired to be an agricultural technician, is now apprenticing for his electrician certificate. He feels he has found his niche. From an early age he enjoyed fixing things and working with his hands. He also enjoys outdoor activities such as hunting and fishing, and in his magic wand story he told us he would move to Colorado, where he could combine work with his hobbies of hunting and fishing.

These seven men, none with a college degree, displayed a range of reactions, from satisfaction with their present lives and work—"excited and happy"—to regrets about their work prospects and about not having gone to college.

Prestige Level of the Career Changers: 1980 and 1990s Compared

For the 21 men who had changed from a science field to another field, their average occupational prestige had changed from 72 to 65. Looking just at those men who had earned college degrees, their occupational prestige had changed from 78 to 72. Earning a college degree appears to provide a slight advantage in terms of prestige. The differences for gender are too small to make much of. For the women who had changed from science (Chapter 3), their occupational prestige had changed from 69 to 66. For the women changers who had earned college degrees, their occupational prestige changed from 72 to 71. When these prestige comparisons are made for gender and science careers, however, as we reported earlier in this chapter, the gender gap is much larger (84 versus 62).

Summary of Gender Differences Among Career Changers

We examined the stories of the men who changed from an interest in science to some other field to see if their reasons for switching were similar to those the women changers gave us (Chapter 3). The main reasons the women had given us were having chosen the popular career in high school, finding a better fit, finding a better fit in spite of obstacles, and being derailed from their career choice by circumstances beyond their ability to cope.

Of the 21 men who were career changers, several had chosen a career in high school without knowing too much about it, and often without too much thought, similar to the women who chose popular careers. Men making this type of career choice were Miguel, Ethan, Kevin, Lennie, Harry, John, Titus, and Steve. Career guidance from family and school was relatively limited or misguided in the experiences of these men, as it had been for the women. For some, such as Ethan and Kevin, who chose engineering, their choice was influenced by a special high school program aimed at increasing minority participation in engineering careers. Later they found a better career fit.

Several of the career changers ended up in business careers. Most of them were happy with this choice, and when they reflected on their earlier aspirations, they often said, Well I didn't like math, or I didn't like the isolation involved in some of the technical careers like computer science. Examples of men who had earned a college degree, and who found a better fit in business, were Tom, Tad, Lennie, Steve, Ethan, Kevin, Miguel, Donald, John, and Jim. Among the career changers who had not earned a college degree, several had found a good career fit in business or the skilled trades. These included Jesus, Patrick, Gene, Ned, Eliott, and Vinnie. Some of these men had found a better fit only after persevering when discrimination or lack of money to meet their responsibilities made it difficult. Such men include Jesus and John. The careers these men changed to had somewhat lower occupational prestige than the careers in science they had originally aspired to, similar to the women who had changed. However, the differences in prestige were not large, and there was no gender difference of any size. This finding contrasted with that found for men and women in science careers, with men in those careers having much higher occupational prestige than women.

A few of the career changers among the men were seemingly derailed from achieving a good career fit by circumstances beyond their ability to cope. Ledyard was derailed by family circumstances, and had fallen into a deep depression until he found meaning in the Christian ministry. He originally had planned to become an astronomer. Dorian had wanted to be an aeronautical engineer but was disqualified because the pilot training aspect of this career excluded persons who were color blind. He still dreamed of being a pilot, although he found some degree of satisfaction in his role as an Air Force recruiter. Titus had chosen forest ranger for his career when he was in high school and he still dreamed of this occupation. He had been prevented from achieving it, it seems, because of lack of guidance from both his family and his college advisers, and so he had drifted through college without a major. He is now working in business but is not very happy. Harry, an African American, had wanted to be a sociologist when he was in high school. He is unhappy in his current work as a trainer for personnel in the banking industry. He wishes his family and his teachers had emphasized the importance of science to him. He regrets not having majored in science. He seems to have been derailed by a kind of null environment not unlike that many women experience.

It seems clear from the stories told by the men, as well as the women, in our study that the classical career development and choice theories (Holland, 1985; Super, 1990) are adequate for some but inadequate for many of the women and also for the men. Circumstances beyond their ability to cope often exerted a strong influence on their preliminary choices, and their lack of information and planning frequently led to wasted years spent floundering or to discouragement, frustration, and compromises in career choices. Personality seemed to play a role in determining whether a person persisted in spite of obstacles or made a compromise in her or his career choice. We will take up this theme again in Chapter 14 on career counseling and Chapter 15 on future directions.

Part III

Issues Related to Careers

Ethnicity, Culture, and Socioeconomic Status

The Effects of Racial and Ethnic Discrimination on the Career Development of Minority Persons

JOANN COHN

Career development has been viewed as a lifelong, stepwise process by Donald Super (1990), who developed what he called the "life span, life space approach to career development." According to Super's well-accepted theory and model of career development over the life span, each individual moves through five stages of career development. The stages are growth, exploration, establishment, maintenance, and decline.

During the growth stage, ages 4 to 14, curiosity and fantasy play are ways in which awareness of interests and abilities develop. During the exploratory stage, ages 14 to 25, tentative choices are made (i.e., electives in school, part-time work), which later evolve into trial work and study choices and lead to crystallization of a career choice. The establishment stage, ages 25 to 45, involves stabilization, consolidation, and advancement or frustration within the chosen career. The maintenance stage, from age 45 to 65, involves either stagnation or updating and innovation. The decline stage from age 65 on involves either disengagement and retirement from the career or specializing in some new career field or hobby.

The cultural and social lenses through which I viewed the experiences of the minority individuals in this study were shaped in part by my own experiences of being outside the norm as a bicultural woman. My lenses also have been influenced by growing up in New York City, where I was surrounded continuously by the edgy, awkward motions of people different than one another struggling to coexist comfortably such as commuters crowded on a rush hour train. My worldview as influenced by these factors led me to focus in these interviews on the experiences and effects of being crowded out, pushed aside, overlooked. I may have, as a consequence of my subjectivity, missed seeing themes that run counter to exclusion—namely, inclusion, support, and positive acknowledgment. With this caveat in mind, and with the knowledge that a sample size of nine is not large enough to support generalizations, I believe it is valuable to examine the following stories for what they call to our attention about the effects of racial and ethnic discrimination on the career development of people of color.

In the interviews of the 22 persons of color who participated in Phase 1 of this longitudinal study, a common thread emerged that ran through nine of the interviews. This thread illustrated some ways in which racial and ethnic discrimination experienced early in the career development process of a person of color had a negative effect on later stages of the process.

Experiences of Racial and Ethnic Discrimination in the Growth Stage (Ages 5–15)

The early years of the growth stage are the childhood years. The later years of this stage include junior high. Little of what can actually be called career development occurs during this stage, but it encompasses crucial formative years in which ideas and attitudes about careers begin to be formed as well as the foundations for self-efficacy and self-esteem. These are the years of elementary school and playing with other children in the neighborhood. During these years, children learn to interact socially with their peers and to relate to others outside of their home and family. They begin to learn that they have a role in a larger context than that of their family, and they begin to be affected by feedback and reactions from others.

Some people of color who were interviewed for this study grew up in neighborhoods that were predominantly white. Theirs were among the first families to "integrate" the neighborhood, and they remember vividly that they were not welcomed with open arms by their white neighbors. Sometimes they and their families were simply ignored by their new neighbors. Other times, however, they encountered violent hostility. Linda, now a surgeon, recalls,

It was very hard to live in the country. Because, we were, you know, an Asian family. Asian . . . We went through all the name-calling and the rock-throwing and the beating-up, and all this other business.

Of the people of color we interviewed, most had an awareness when they were growing up that certain neighborhoods, certain streets, and certain areas were "off limits" to people who were different than those who lived there. Although many communities are segregated ethnically and racially, not by law but by long-standing tradition, individuals who test the boundaries or innocently cross them can pay a severe price. Susan, an African American with a B.A. in psychology, remembers:

The neighborhood wasn't that conducive to minorities . . . Some of the guys would get jumped . . . it's really prejudiced over there . . . the young men weren't safe at all. A couple of them got jumped every now and then, because they went too far south trying to get a seat on the bus . . . they couldn't do that because if somebody saw too many of them walking together they would get jumped. And these people had weapons.

The people of color in this study who experienced ethnic and racial hatred in their neighborhoods learned early that others would not hesitate to mistreat them simply because of their cultural background or the color of their skin. Such unjust treatment at an early age caused them to expect discriminatory treatment and to take the attitude that there was nothing they could do to stop it. Some came to hate themselves for being different and to believe on some level that they deserved to be treated poorly. When an individual becomes used to being discriminated against, he or she may have trouble later in life mustering the courage to fight back.

Experiences of Racial and Ethnic Discrimination in the Exploration Stage (Ages 15–25)

During the Exploration Stage, young people enter high school and begin to develop and identify their interests and learn about their capacities. The world outside their homes begins to open up to them, but it does not send children of color the same welcoming message that it sends to white students. This is particularly evident when young people are in high school.

The high school years are years of transition into young adulthood. Students select some of their own classes, thereby gaining experience in choosing what they wish to learn, and they involve themselves in extracurricular activities that enable them to begin developing an understanding of the kinds of things they like to do. These opportunities move an individual further along the growth stage of career development. Interests and abilities are discovered and developed, while interpersonal relationships advance to further levels of complexity.

In this context, ideally, an individual's confidence in him- or herself develops and the special talents he or she possesses provide initial clues as to the kind of work that might ultimately be satisfying and enjoyable. Interpersonally, this is an awkward time, as hormones rage and the need for limits and boundaries collides with the desire to be independent and treated like an adult. Nevertheless, this usually does not have a long-term negative impact on an individual's progress toward choosing and pursuing a career.

Some of our interviewees had more trouble in high school than could be explained by hormones and the natural rebelliousness of youth. In the midst of trying to identify their interests and abilities and participate in extracurricular activities during high school, some of our interviewees were constantly affected by racial and ethnic discrimination from their peers.

In his book *Savage Inequalities: Children in America's Schools* (1991), Jonathan Kozol describes the vast differences that exist between the high school experiences of white and minority students in this country. On average, most white students attend high schools that are clean and safe, have staff who are well paid, and boast state-of-the-art learning resources. Most minority students, on the other hand, attend high schools with a crumbling infrastructure, outdated learning materials, and poorly paid teachers. Part of the reason for these inequalities is financial—"the immense resources which the nation does in fact possess go not to the child in greatest need," writes Kozol (1991, pp. 79-80), "but to the child of the highest bidder—the child of parents who, more frequently than not, have also enjoyed the same abundance when they were schoolchildren." Kozol goes on to point out that those who control the purse strings for our schools feel that good educational resources are wasted on poor children, who are perceived as not as bright or motivated and as having less potential for success than children from wealthier families who live in better neighborhoods.

Most of the minority individuals in our study attended high schools that were racially and ethnically mixed. A majority of them (18 of the 22) were in our inner-city schools. However, they did not feel that they received the same treatment as their white counterparts. Wendy, who is Hispanic, recalls, "I always felt as if the teachers treated me different, as if the other kids treated me different."

Vinnie, who is Hispanic, remembers:

We didn't get treated very well by our fellow students and we didn't get treated very well by the administration. . . . Even our teachers . . . we didn't get treated very well by them either. . . . It was racial. I mean, it wasn't any lower expectations, it wasn't *anything*. . . . You weren't given the opportunity to do what they did. We were degraded the whole time we were there.

Calabrese and Underwood's (1994) article "The Effects of School-Generated Racism on Students of Color" supports these students' statements of their experiences. The authors' research uncovers the sobering truth that "schooling is different for white middle and upper class adolescents than it is for people of color . . . systemic racism . . . is expressed overtly and covertly [in our schools]" (p. 267). The authors go on to say that "although school-generated racism is ignored, denied, or suppressed, it is available in the stories carried in the hearts of people of color. Their stories describe acts of emotional and physical violence, and are nearly universal to minorities" (p. 269).

The minority students in our study often encountered uncaring teachers and school administrators, none of whom seemed to consider these students an integral, important part of the student body. It was almost as if they were invisible. Susan said:

[The teachers] never did anything for or against me. . . . I went to class, they taught it, and then I left. . . . When I went back, nobody remembered me.

What emerges from the stories of these individuals is a picture of an environment that made the people of color living and going to school within it feel despised, ignored, and as though no one cared in the least whether or not they succeeded. As a result, these individuals felt isolated, alone, and not very hopeful about the future beyond high school.

When ethnic and racial prejudice surround an individual at an early age, the feedback that person receives during this time of crucial identity development is that to others, he or she is not as worthy of attention as white peers, does not fit in among white students, and is inherently inferior. Such feedback can have lasting effects. Wendy said,

[My high school] was 99.9 percent white people. And I think it made a difference. Because it always made me feel as if I wasn't . . . one of them. I was an outsider . . . And I think that had a lot to do with why I grew up the way I did.

Instead of immersing themselves in their schools and communities and experiencing the joys of learning, growing, and looking toward the future, several of the people of color with whom we spoke reported that they felt stagnant and sought only to make it to the end, when they could leave school. They were unhappy with their schools and how they were treated every day, and this took its toll on them emotionally. It caused them to see school as a place to be endured, not an environment in which they could develop their abilities and find positive reinforcement for a job well done. Sometimes it affected their ability to succeed academically. Juanita, who is Hispanic, said,

> I couldn't quite understand why we couldn't have some of the stuff other people could have. . . . I don't understand why we had to go to Bayside Grammar School when our neighbors would go to the better school or another public school. There were other schools in the area but I could never understand why I had to go to that really bad school . . . there were fights every day . . . My whole purpose in school was to survive . . . I mean the fighting and . . . the drugs and stuff like that . . . I just had to survive. I'm sure I could've done a lot better. . . . I had so much potential in grammar school, and it was just that other people slowed me down.

Discriminatory treatment was highly stressful and hard to cope with at such young ages. It was damaging to the self-esteem of these young people, who were already in a stage of development that is painful and anxiety producing under the best of circumstances. Vinnie, who is Hispanic and a corrections counselor, recalls that the discrimination affected his motivation to try to think about the future in a hopeful, positive way and to see school as part of the process of developing himself: "I didn't look ahead. I didn't look ahead at all. I looked to getting out of school."

Some of our interviewees sought ways to escape the feeling of being unwanted and disliked simply because of their facial features or the color of their skin. Linda said:

> When I was growing up, in high school, people used to tease me all the time about being Chinese. I was "The Chink." So that kind of response gets a reflex in me, where I'm just kind of immune to it. . . . I guess it's because I grew up having people swear at me. Tell me I was no good because I was Chinese. The girls didn't want to play with me, that kind of thing. . . . I learned a defense mechanism to block it out.

Vinnie tells a similar story of coping:

> I won't let people ever get me angry. And I think that kind of stems from back when I was in school when I would let people get to me. You know, when they would call me names, and they would get to me. And they saw my emotions and they won. But if you don't let them see your emotions, you win, you know.

In the absence of an ability to turn off his emotions or not show them, Vinnie looked to other sources for a way to escape the pain in high school.

I was in [a high school] I didn't want to be in. We didn't get treated really well there. . . . Blacks and Hispanics didn't get treated very well there. It was a big racial thing. So I didn't . . . I didn't get along well with a lot of people. I did a lot of fighting. A lot of fighting, a lot of arguing. So, a way to escape was through drugs. You know, it's a sad thing. But it happened. I mean, it just happened.

Some students became involved in athletics in high school and were able to obtain attention and equal treatment in this arena. Miguel recalls,

My brother and I transcended racial barriers. I think a lot of that was due to our involvement in athletics. . . . There were little cliques, you know. The Hispanics all hung together, and the blacks all hung together. Being in athletics, I obviously transcended the white barrier, the white-Hispanic barrier. And we also transcended the black-Hispanic barrier. I think we were looked at kind of oddly by our Hispanic peers, because they kind of saw us as traitors.

Sports teams were not always the avenue to acceptance and better treatment, however, as Susan explains:

When I did make the volleyball team, I think I was the only black on the team. I think that coach was a little prejudiced. She wouldn't let me play, and when she did let me play, there was so much pressure that I didn't do well. Because I never got to play, and then, you know it's like a catch-22. You don't play because you don't do well, but you don't do well because you don't play.

The exploration stage spans the ages from 15 to 25, and thus includes the college years and the first couple of years of postcollege career development.

Racism and ethnic discrimination on college campuses is rampant in the United States and has become more pronounced during the past several years. Incidents of race-related violence on campus have been on the rise, as well as publicly stated insults against minorities, written or pictorial insults in graffiti or on posters, and organized protests over race-related issues (Jones, 1991). Jones points to economic, social, and political factors that contribute to this trend, and emphasizes the connection between the increasingly intolerant political climate in this country and the steady increase in strained race relations on college campuses.

For some of our interviewees, the discrimination they experienced in college affected their feelings about pursuing their career interests. Vicky said,

For a while I was pretty passionate about journalism. I went to [a certain university] for a little while, and they have an excellent daily student newspaper there. It's a great training ground and it was a lot of fun, but [this school] was just not the place for me. I just didn't like it. . . . It was a place where I met 17-year-olds who had never met a black person in their life. . . . It was really tense. I mean, swastikas on the door, hate mail. It was not fun. I found myself seeing fewer and fewer black people in the classes. . . . I got tired. You kind of get sick of being a role model. You just want to be left alone. So I came home.

Later in the Exploration Stage: Encountering Discrimination in the Early Stages of the World of Work

Many career development theories depict a career pattern with a continuous forward-moving and uninterrupted flow (Super, 1963) in which, it is implied, every individual possesses all the psychological and economic resources to meet the challenges of planning for a career. E. Smith (1983) stresses that this is simply not the case for most minorities in the United States. For them, external constraints that include limited finances may make steps forward along the career path very difficult, if not impossible. The reality in terms of work for most minorities in the United States is that planning for a fulfilling career is a luxury within the context of trying to survive by earning enough to pay the bills, pay rent, and buy food. The notion of implementation of self-concept and personal fulfillment through work (Super, 1963) does not apply to the way most minorities in this country think about work. Super recognized this in his later work (Super, 1990), stating that "the nature of [an individual's] career pattern . . . is determined [in part] by the individual's parental socioeconomic level . . . and by the opportunities to which [s]he is exposed" (p. 207). He goes on to say that

> the fact that self-concepts are learned by experiences with people, objects, and ideas makes it seem very likely that socioeconomic status functions as a career determinant in at least two ways: it tends to open up or close opportunities, and it helps to shape occupational concepts and self-concepts. (p. 229)

Smith (1983) states that racial discrimination may also be an obstacle to forward movement along the career path. The successful member of minority groups, she says, are generally the ones within their racial or ethnic group who are the most socially desirable. Lighter skin and limited use of Black English both contribute to social desirability. Smith also points to a minority individual's level of personal persistence as a factor affecting his or her career success.

People of color have a hard time finding work when they are in high school, so work experiences that might have helped them make the transition from youth to adulthood are not available to them (Smith, 1983). This has been hypothesized to affect the way they think about their own potential for future career success. Gottfredson (1981) writes,

> Perceptions of job accessibility would be expected to influence vocational as-pirations through their impact on one's expectations for obtaining those jobs. People are likely to weight their preferences according to these perceptions in order not to waste time pursuing "poor bets." People will balance their prefer-ences with their sense of what is possible. (p. 570)

When they entered the workforce, a number of the participants in our study had trouble with discrimination there, often because they were the only person of color on staff. Juanita said:

> I went to work in a hospital. And, how can I say it? I broke the color bar-rier. . . . They made it real hard on me.

Jesus said:

> You hear about the glass ceiling? It exists. It exists. And I became very disenchanted with the corporate structure. . . . I peaked, and I couldn't go any further. . . . I could not fit in. I couldn't fit into that world because, and I hate to even say it. Because I'm Hispanic. . . . That's a big cultural problem, there. . . . I was the only Hispanic salesman in that department. . . . The clique was that if [a person] came from the same university as the bosses or managers, they could relate to each other. Both academically and socially. Socially maybe by going and playing golf. Academically by coming from the same college. I could not do that. And it was like hitting the wall. Hitting the wall.

Business organizations place a high value on conformity and give their employees positive reinforcement for marching to the same drummer and be-ing just like everyone else. This can be difficult for people of color who may not look like everyone else, dress like everyone else, or speak like everyone else. Wendy said,

> I have an accent . . . and I didn't know if I'd ever be able to overcome that. . . . The first job I went to, they wouldn't let me anchor any newscasts. For al-most a year they wouldn't let me voice anything. It was probably the worst year of my career. At one point, I went out and did all the legwork and wrote a

three-part series on AIDS. It was a very moving piece. And my boss said, "You can't anchor it. Sound is everything. You can't anchor it." So he did. And it won an award. And what made me so mad was that he had entered this thing in his name. I never got *any* of the credit. And I thought, "I'm gonna overcome this accent problem . . . and no one is ever going to cheat me like this again."

More often than not, pressure to conform to the corporate standard was covert rather than overt. Managers and supervisors often expected conformity but did not discuss their expectations with their employees who were people of color. Some managers or coworkers simply did not like having a minority person on staff and found it difficult to treat the minority staff member as they treated other employees and colleagues. Kevin had to deal with a prejudiced boss:

My manager, he had a problem communicating. I think he had a prejudiced bone or it was just difficult for him to work with . . . a minority . . . I think he had a problem with that. He didn't know how to communicate or share with me whatever he wanted me to know and learn. And it was hard for me to tell him that I was resigning. Because I knew he was a good guy at heart. He just had fears about . . . racial relations and that kind of thing.

Some bosses were more up front about their biases. Linda tells us:

My first day in the [operating room] . . . I stood behind my mentor and I didn't want to bother him, you know. Here I am this little medical student, and he has a big reputation for being an excellent surgeon. . . . I had been back there for half an hour watching him and he suddenly turns his head but doesn't look at me and says, "Who are you?" So I introduced myself. "I'm your medical student for the next six weeks." He says, "Dammit, another woman! . . . And a Chink too! . . . Killed a lot of them in the war."

The short-term effects of discrimination on the lives of those discussed here were decreased self-esteem, decreased enthusiasm for school and for seeing school as a bridge to a successful future, impeded success in educational and work settings, increased stress, and generalized feelings of discouragement.

Experiences of discrimination early in the career development process had long-term effects as well. Several of the individuals discussed here reported that it took them a long time to find a good fit for themselves in the world of work. Most reported that they continue to feel like outsiders, even when established in their careers. They describe persistent feelings of doubt that their talents will ever be fully acknowledged in their work settings, and seem resigned to receiving little or no encouragement to develop these talents. They have had to learn, it seems, to be their own champions.

Where From Here? Some Thoughts

Research has shown that special programs aimed at helping youth of color overcome obstacles to success, such as discriminatory treatment, have had success. These programs provided minority youth with individualized attention from caring adults in their schools that focused on helping the young people think about jobs and careers and understand how to plan for them. This communicated a "you can do it, and we expect you to" attitude that positively affected the students' self-esteem. Programs such as these (Bloch, 1989) succeeded in reducing student failure in classes, increasing their knowledge of the relevance of school and extracurricular activities to possible future jobs and careers, increased ability and enthusiasm for setting goals, and increased motivation to pursue further education. Also increased were self-esteem and self-awareness.

In addition, Hawks and Muha (1991) has suggested that career interventions involve talking openly with minority young people about the realities of racism and discrimination, and the effects these can have on minority career development. She proposes helping these young people think about cognitive and behavioral strategies they can use to effectively cope with discrimination in the future so that it does not deter them from pursuing their career goals.

Social learning theory builds on Super's life span approach to career development by showing us that experiencing negative consequences for engaging in activities related to particular educational or occupational goals can have a detrimental effect on a person's career development process. Such consequences discourage further pursuit of natural interests and chosen goals. The nine stories presented here bring this concept to life in a very powerful way. They illustrate that, indeed, "the specific nature of the learning experiences to which one is exposed and the environmental conditions and events that influence career choice are heavily influenced by . . . race . . . and cultural background" (Mitchell & Krumboltz, 1990, pp. 163-164).

8

Success in the Face of Adversity

Six Stories of Minority Career Achievement

KIRSTEN PETERSON

During the course of the interviewing portion of this project, it happened that I worked most closely with a portion of the interview sample who had attended the two urban high schools selected to participate in this project. Many of these former students continued to live in areas close to the neighborhoods they grew up in, and most were ethnic minorities. What struck me about these interview experiences was that, for the most part, not only were these interviewees doing well for themselves in the material sense, but they also had well-thought-out personal philosophies and self-concepts. In many cases, I was also impressed by the resilience of these interviewees, their ability to overcome obstacles, and their knack for uncovering opportunities for advancement and self-enhancement. Although much has been written about the obstacles that individuals from ethnic minorities and lower socioeconomic levels face with regard to career development and fulfillment (Burlew & Johnson, 1992; Lucas, 1993; Miller, Springer, & Wells, 1988), little has been noted regarding those individuals who transcend those obstacles and how they accomplish this.

As I began developing this topic, it became clear to me that I had to be careful in how I fleshed out the stories that follow. Having sensed the phenomena of individuals who impressed me with their abilities, perseverance, or sheer force of personality, I warned myself to be careful to look for the complete picture represented by these and other individuals I interviewed. Once having noticed the phenomenon of success in the face of adversity, for example, I found myself "wanting" it to be part of all that my interviewees experienced, and therefore had to tread carefully during interviews to allow people's stories to emerge—positive, negative, successes, and failures—as truthfully as possible. I grew up in a relatively privileged middle-class family and school environment where giving high effort generally led to success experiences, and at times had to challenge my assumption that a lack of success could only be a product of a lack of effort. In addition to contrasting socioeconomic backgrounds, I had also to confront my subjectivity as it pertained to how I differed ethnically as a Caucasian, from my interviewees, all of whom were individuals of color. This often meant consciously challenging my own stereotypes regarding different ethnic groups and reminding myself to think of each interviewee as a unique individual who could be affected in any number of ways by his or her economic and ethnic background.

In addition, it was helpful to think specifically about what I could also learn from those interviewees who perhaps were not able to succeed in the ways described below. Indeed, those stories helped provide a necessary perspective for me in my understanding of what is described in this chapter. Chapter 7 tells the stories of some of these less successful participants. Finally, I also had to be wary in my analysis to make sure that I did not confuse my personal feelings for a particular interviewee who might have been more forthcoming or personable with the ideas that he or she shared with me.

This chapter begins with a short description of some of the past and present obstacles to career as well as personal fulfillment these respondents faced. Next, I'll turn to a description of some of the events, environments, people, and personal philosophies that these interviewees felt assisted their development. In formulating the themes for this chapter, I drew from the stories of many of the 19 interviewees I personally spoke with, but will focus here on the responses given by 6 of these ethnic minority interviewees: Vinnie, Gena, Ethan, Margaret, Joe, and Vicky. These interviewees were nonrandomly chosen, each for his or her unique "take" on life as well as with an eye for variety in terms of gender and ethnic minority status. One respondent was Hispanic, one was Native American, and the remainder of the sample were African American. Two respondents were biracial. All names are purely fictional, and some other details have been changed to ensure the privacy of these people.

Obstacles

As the focus of this chapter is on how the interviewees found opportunities in their lives, less emphasis will be placed on the discussion of obstacles per se. As has been mentioned, all of the interviewees focused on here grew up in urban areas and attended two inner-city high schools. Several interviewees struggled to overcome the burden of a low-income upbringing. One high school was located in a steel mill area that had experienced the economic misfortunes associated with the demise of the steel industry. Others, although not victims of the steel industry depression, noted how their lower-income households added to the emotional pain of being a high school student in a more affluent high school, because it was harder to fit in. Other researchers have validated these findings in a number of realms, noting that one's socioeconomic status can be a powerful determinant of what careers appear available as well as attainable.

Another source of difficulty for several of my interviewees was having to deal with discrimination. This could take any number of forms, including that which biased against ethnicity and gender. Some respondents were exposed to this from early on and in a near constant form, such as Vinnie, who was consistently hassled by police in his neighborhood for simply looking Hispanic. Other interviewees noted a more periodic pattern of discrimination; Gena for example, admitted to working hard to overcome the limitations placed on women in her high school, but found later, in college, that her gender was at times even a valued commodity.

Joe, a biracial man of both Japanese and African American descent, viewed the obstacles to his development as primarily coming from society's treatment of minorities, which negatively influenced his own self-image. He and others talked about the media playing a part in propagating discrimination through dissemination of the "Big Lie," that African Americans in particular cannot be successful. Several interviewees talked about the difficulties of being a minority in a predominately white professional culture, and the extra effort they have to make to "fit in," an adjustment the majority culture members rarely have to confront. This phenomenon also has been noted by other researchers (Leung, 1995). The effects of this type of societal obstacle also ring true with the tenets of social learning theory (Bandura, 1986), which suggests that having similar role models from whom to learn appropriate behaviors is vital for both skill and self-efficacy development. Farmer (1985), while speaking specifically about women's career development, provides further support, noting the powerful effects on women's career development of the media's positive portrayals of working women.

Ethan, an African American engineer with a well-regarded and successful firm, also noted his concerns about the differential performance expectations placed on minorities even after they get a job in a corporation. Although white men are automatically "on the team," according to Ethan, minorities have to prove themselves first. This observation underscores the work of Ibarra (1995), who found that although minority managers were as able as their Caucasian counterparts to make appropriate social connections, these networks were seen as less beneficial in terms of career advancement.

Other obstacles mentioned included not having career information or role models; a lack of support from school, family, or work; a lack of identity; low self-esteem; the need to juggle too many roles; and a lack of perceived skills/interests. The existence of these issues here validates the findings of previous research in this area (Bandura, 1986; Green-Powell, 1993; Luzzo, 1993; Rakow & Bermudez, 1993).

Opportunities

In this section, I will focus on three areas within which my respondents were able to fashion opportunities and support for their career or personal development. I will first talk about environmental influences, the important people who provided social support, and finally several significant or unique personal philosophies that allowed my respondents to make their way more clearly and successfully through their lives.

Environmental Influences

School environment and/or programs. Although, for some individuals, the high school experience was marred by racial discrimination or a lack of basic career information or role models, other respondents saw good things coming to them as result of their high school years. Both Vicky and Joe attended the same high school, and both validated its multicultural basis as that which gave them a better, more balanced view of their world. Joe described the social scene and the effects it had on him:

It's funny because there were definitely cliques in high school. There was the black clique. And there was a Hispanic clique. And then there was this hodgepodge of people that I belonged to. Consisted of a Puerto Rican, a Mexican, a Colombian, a white guy who thought he was black, me, and Filipinos. And they were male and female. I mean, we were a weird group of kids. And a lot of successes out of that group, though. And I was amazed at how honest we were with each other. And a white guy from Boston. . . . It was a pretty mixed up school, which was really nice, I thought. I mean, there were Hispanics, and whites and blacks and Filipinos and Asians.

Other respondents mentioned benefiting from school programs that were structured to help them overcome the lack of career information or minority role models. Ethan described a program for minority students with potential that he was enrolled in that exposed him to accelerated classes, occupational role models, career information, and job search skills, which he found helpful.

Eighth grade, I got into a program called INROADS. That was a minority, at the time, it was a minority engineering program for high school and college-aged people. They were very selective. And I got in, and then in the summers, it was preengineering, I guess, in high school. And then in the summers we went to a pretty much like summer school. So you took algebra, you took drafting and took physics and biology and they gave you an exposure to it so that when you got in that class, you'd excel even more. I saw the whole focus was, "Hey, we can get more of a population and provide these services to individuals for their own needs."

Gena, on the other hand, did not feel at all supported for her career choice of engineering during high school, which she attributed in part to being discriminated against as a woman desiring that field. She did, however, find support as a woman engineer once in college, through participation in a Women in Science and Engineering program.

In the absence of, or sometimes in addition to, these more structured alternative activities, several of my interviewees talked about the influence of other interests, with a love of reading often taking center stage. For Ethan and Vinnie, this came about as a result of their high school English classes, which exposed them to a broad range of literature. This also gave each of them the sense that there was more to the world than what was in front of them, and opened their eyes to alternative options. Joe became exposed to the philosophical literature as a result of his mother taking classes to finish her undergraduate degree. This had a profound effect on him.

My mother, she was going to college to get her degree while I was 12. And she took a class of philosophy, a couple of them. And I read her philosophy books, they got into deep questions about morality, ethics, and the meaning of life, and I thought, "This is what's important." I spent a lot of time in my room just thinking, "Oh we get older, we get a job, we vacation two weeks out of the year. Then we retire and then we die." And it was like, "There has got to be more to life than that. There has got to be a reason for it." And I just wanted to know why I should go through it. And Plato was the first person that kind of gave me an idea of what I think is a reasonable meaning for this whole existence.

Other activities include an interest in religion, particularly on the part of two female interviewees, Vicky and Margaret. In both cases, these women used their religious beliefs to counterbalance family experiences that were unsupportive or dysfunctional.

Significant Others

Families of origin. All respondents talked about people in their lives who influenced them in various ways. Most had families who modeled the values the respondents ultimately adopted, including Vinnie, Joe, Margaret, and Ethan. Vinnie talked about the many ways his family impressed the importance of serving society upon him, which he saw as instrumental in his career choice of counselor for a prison population.

It has a lot to do with our upbringing. I mean, my parents were always there for everybody, I mean everybody they knew, their friends and stuff. My dad owned this building before my sister did. The one that I live in right here. And it was always full of renters who would come in, and, the American Dream, you know. And he would rent to them until they were able to buy their own home. And, you know, they [my parents] instilled those kind of values in us.

Vinnie's comments appear representative of the Hispanic culture in general, which has been recognized by others for its emphasis on the importance of a larger family network in the development of the individual's values and career goals (Leung, 1995).

It is noteworthy that few interviewees spoke of their families in terms of providing a great deal of emotional support, particularly as they were growing up. These was a sense among interviewees that life was tough enough for parents trying to keep their families above water, and that it was of little surprise that less attention was paid to open expressions of love or emotional support. Gena framed her experience of this phenomenon this way:

Well they never, I suppose I just did my own thing. I mean, I did so well in school that they never really had to. They never really said much about my work. I never, they never said, "Go do your homework." They just assumed I would do it because I would. . . . And they were, well, my mother was always on my brothers' backs, because if she didn't, they wouldn't do anything. Plus, since both my parents worked, we had baby-sitters and we had to become independent. I never liked being told what to do, either. And as long as we were doing OK, they never really did say, "Well do this and do that." If you're proving yourself on your own, then they would let us go ahead. I know my brothers, they were always getting yelled at because they were always getting into trouble. So, but if you weren't, OK, fine.

Whereas Gena saw her parents' laissez-faire style as a boost to her independence and self-esteem, Joe wondered what it would have been like to have more concern and supervision:

I mean they [my parents] were two very busy people, handling the businesses and my mother was going to school at this time, finishing her degree. And it just seemed, since we were all basically good kids, we weren't doing any ridiculous things, it *seemed* like we didn't need a whole lot of supervision, but in hindsight, I guess we did. So I can't help but thinking that with a little more guidance or a little more urging, maybe I would have done better in high school or something like that.

Interviewees noted that parents did express their concern in terms of how much they pushed onto their children the idea of college and becoming successful. Joe saw this happening for him through both his stepfather and his mother's statements that he was going to college. Similar to Joe's experience, Margaret remembered being told by her mother to start thinking about college, even though she had already ruled it out for herself. Margaret described her experience this way:

And I wasn't thinking about college when I was in high school. I didn't think that I was going to go to college. It was just something that, although my sisters are going to college, it was just something that I didn't think about. And my mother said one day, "What colleges have you picked out?" And I said, "College?" I said, "I'm going to work after high school. I am not going to school. I'm tired of school." She said, "No, you are going to college." I said, "Oh, okay." So that was my senior year. Usually it was like near to graduation before you take those tests and all that. The ACT test or whatever those tests are called. And after I took the tests, it still didn't dawn on me that I was going to go to college, my mother is preparing me for college. But she said, "Yeah, you are going to college." And so I started looking for colleges, right in my last quarter of school.

Both Joe and Margaret viewed being pushed into college as a positive act, as they each discovered the motivation to do well once in college, and found rewarding careers.

Vicky, on the other hand, had come from a dysfunctional family and often lived in fear of her mother's strong control over her:

My mother can be a very domineering [person] and she's a very control-ling person. I think that's why I grew up Catholic because the discipline is just so intense. She just loved that. And she tended to smother me, control[ling] me and it made me crazy so I just ran away from it because you can give her an inch and she'll change your hairstyle, buy you brand new clothes that look like hers and you're just like, "Aah!" I can't deal. I'm [an] only child, born late, and she thought she was infertile. So it's like, "Oh God!" And she's al-ways really concerned, "You'll get surprised, you'll get hit by a truck, you'll die, you'll leave, no!" And it was a really smothering, lonely childhood.

Vicky too received the consistent message that she would go to college:

Whether or not I was going to college wasn't something that was up for discussion. I was going to college. My mother made this *very* clear to me. "You are going to college. Pick a major, pack your stuff."

Rather than college initially becoming an opportunity, Vicky's reaction to be-ing so directed led her to prematurely foreclose on a major in journalism. Two colleges and several jobs later, Vicky was finally able to identify and come to terms with her own values and is now a community activist. For Vicky, the preordained expectation of college was initially an obstacle that she had to work hard to overcome before she could realize her true potential.

Family support helped these individuals move toward at least a goal of higher education and in general a sense that there was more opportunity in the world than may have met the eye. Social learning theorists point to family support as being very beneficial in the career development of children so in-fluenced (Bandura, 1986). The parental influence highlighted here, however, appeared in general to be geared less toward support for a specific career than merely to attending college as a way to "be successful." Interviewees inter-preted their parents' words in a variety of ways, not all of them helpful. Vicky's experience, for example, suggested that her mother's strong insis-tence on college forced her into a maladaptive career choice and actually de-layed her career fulfillment. For most of the other interviewees, however, families' influence was often the most important determinant behind their pursuit of a college education.

Friends. Friends were an important source of inspiration, providing nec-essary support that some interviewees were not getting at home. For Ethan, his group of friends helped motivate him to read more than was required for school and foster his later lifelong love of reading:

It was like a competition and it spurred us on and I remember in seventh and eighth grade we kept *on* going. There was a group of books that we were reading and we used to just transfer them back and forth between each other and we all read them. There was like five or six of us and we'd just hand them back and forth every week. We'd rather sit there and read books in class than listen to what was going on. These books were good and we enjoyed reading. I don't know, that was a big deal, of course, and I really enjoyed reading in high school.

Joe's friends helped bolster his self-esteem at a time when teachers couldn't reach him. He knew he was smart but talked about being afraid to try for fear of finding out that he wasn't as smart as he thought he was. Hanging out with other kids who weren't afraid to try and excel impressed Joe enough to put out some effort on his own behalf:

He [a friend of Joe's] was our resident example of how to be studious. Excellent student. He was in all the honors courses, just by virtue of the fact that he was brilliant and he always said, "Aw you should do this, that, and the other. Oh you can do this," and I was like, "Yeah, I probably could." . . . He encouraged me because I guess he wanted me to be around. He liked me and he thought I was bright too. He had no idea how I passed and actually, I guess one quarter, as a bet, I got on the honor role, just to say "Okay, I can do it." I just kind of paid more attention in class and so I got on the honor role. And he always said that if I tried, I'd just blow him away. And I thought, "Ooh, that's a pretty big statement because he's intelligent, he's a pretty smart guy."

Few of these respondents talked positively about individual teachers they were exposed to. Several individuals, including Vinnie, Ethan, Gena, and Vicky, suggested that their teachers seemed unmotivated and "just went through the motions." Okacha (1994), in response to other observations of this phenomenon, called for teachers not only to become more involved with their students of color but to appreciate cultural differences and act as advocates. Despite these problems with their teachers, the respondents did manage to glean much from their school years in other ways.

Spouses/partners. Nearly all of the individuals in my sample were married and spoke eloquently about the positive role their spouses played in their lives. In some cases, this important other person seemed to buffer the respondent from a neglectful or dysfunctional upbringing. This seemed especially true for Vicky, who feared she was unlovable prior to meeting her husband:

[I wasn't] in a great hurry to love people because past experiences taught me that if you love people, eventually they are going to hurt you. And I found out through my husband that wasn't really the case. It was early in our relationship that got kind of hard because I found myself waiting for him to hurt me and it never happened. And that frightened me and then we talked it out and worked through it.

Meeting his future wife had a similar self-changing effect on Joe, who attributed his desire to value himself and succeed academically to his decision to create a worthwhile life for *both* himself and his wife:

The reason I didn't do very well in school is I just didn't see the value in it and I wasn't very motivated. And she [my wife] motivated me to do well because I thought we'd have a future together. While I was prepared to face the consequences of not doing as well as I should, I wasn't prepared to face the consequences for both of us, you know, take the responsibility for making both our lives difficult. When I couldn't study for me, I could study for her. So that gave me the motivation to really put that extra effort in.

Ethan and Gena both married people who were engineers, as they were. They both expressed the importance of having the support of a significant other who could understand their particular work situations. Gena valued the work-related support she obtained from her husband and saw their common work interests as a foundation of their marriage:

That's one nice thing, we [my husband and I] can talk about each other's work and we both understand exactly what we're talking about. I can feel what he's going through at work if he's having problems and he can do the same for me. I'm working in electrical engineering, so some things that I'm not too sure about, I'll call him up. That's what brought us together. We started dating our first year of college. So we have common interests and goals, which just help build our relationship.

Clearly, these interviewees underscored the importance of at least some supportive others in their lives, although the composition of such support differed among these individuals. This finding is supported by social learning theorists who emphasize the effects of social support in helping individuals overcome other barriers to success (Bandura, 1986; Betz & Hackett, 1983).

Internal Influences/Philosophies

Initiative/independence. Most of these respondents learned to assert themselves in different ways to get what they wanted out of life. For the women in particular, this happened relatively earlier in their lives as they negotiated their way through environments that were at times less open to listening to a female's needs in terms of career. This was particularly true for Gena, when she decided she wanted to be an engineer, and is worth quoting again.

Because when I was in high school, engineering, if I hadn't gone out and sought it on my own, no one would have ever recommended that to me. Even though my best subjects were math and science. No one said, "Go out and be an engineer." I sought that out on my own. And so I was looking in fields that involved math and science, that would also be lucrative, and I started looking in engineering and it really sounded like it would fit my particular skills. And it sounded interesting to me, solving problems. And the fact that there were a very few women in it was another inspiration to me.

Joe too had to seek out extra information on his own about his chosen career, investment banking. It became a sort of game to him, turning the lack of information about his chosen field into the sense that he was doing something not only new but even unique among his peers. Once attaining that career became a goal, he was then able to maintain this initiative by applying it to, as he put it, "putting himself in the best position for success."

I thought I was going to do investment banking. And I said, "Well, how did these guys do it?" And I read about investment banking and read about their backgrounds. A lot of them were born into it. But a few of them weren't. And 90% of them went to business school. And so, in between my sophomore and junior years, I said, "Well I got to go to business school." So I went to this conference on graduate education for minorities and I met a guy there and said, "I'm interested in the your business school and here's where I stand now. What do I have to do between now and the time I apply to put myself in the best position for success?" And he told me. And then he put me in touch with a lot of other people. So I had an ongoing relationship with the university I ended up at.

Although more serendipitously, Vicky found that by going after what she wanted in a job, even if it was a volunteer position, her strongly held values were satisfied, which was what ultimately mattered to her. She was rewarded for this effort when the volunteer job she obtained ended up being a paying one.

On the whole, these respondents were go-getters, ready to reach out for opportunities rather than waiting for something to come to them. Lack of finances and a college degree slowed the process down for some, like Vinnie, who made ends meet with a series of unrewarding but important positions in which the experiences provided him with a valuable background. This job progression bore fruit when he was able to land a job in his chosen field of counseling, despite a lack of academic credentials.

The ability to persevere in the face of a lack of information and support appeared to be vital for these respondents and has been noted in the literature (Bandura, 1986) as being an important mechanism for successful career development. Without the mitigating influence of these personal variables, environmental obstacles like these have been documented elsewhere (e.g., Lucas, 1993) as powerful deterrents to career fulfillment.

Focusing on core values. There seemed to be a sense, at least for some of the respondents, that they had to spend time living and working to find out what was most important to them, and only then could they focus their efforts and satisfaction on the few things that actually mattered. Of interest, those interviewees who talked most movingly about their own self-actualization processes were those who placed more emphasis on the enhancement of their family relationships, with their careers actually taking second priority. Joe saw it this way:

For me [gaining status and prestige], it's not that important. Like I said, I have no plan. My only plan is to continue to move forward in my own mind and as long as I'm feeling happy about where I am, then I'm doing all right. The way I self-actualize is trying to be the best person in whatever role I'm in, and I'm doing *very* good, I think, at being a good husband. I think that's my main priority right now. I hope to do very well at being a good father. *Then* comes the career, definitely want to be a very good professional and what it takes to do that.

Vicky described how she came to decide what was important to her:

It's finding myself, finding where I fit into the world and I know I'll never be the type of person I saw in *Seventeen* magazine and I wanted so very much to be. And after a long series of introspection and looking around, I latched onto stuff that suited me, made me happy. I think if you know who you are, there is nothing you can't do. I think the most successful people in the world have a very strong and clear sense of self, "I know who I am and this is what I have to do." And they don't really see any obstacles as something, a character judgment or a reflection on their quality as a person. It's like, "Well, I'm doing this thing. I mean, how can you stand in my way doing this thing. This is my life. This is who I am. Get out of my way!" And I think if I have a strong and clear sense of self, I'll be a more whole person and a lot better to the people I care about.

The sentiments expressed so eloquently here reflect findings from previous work in this area, suggesting that successful identity development is a clear precursor for successful career development (e.g., Burke & Hoelter, 1988). This is considered particularly important for individuals from minority and lower socioeconomic backgrounds who, as has been mentioned, must overcome significantly more obstacles on their way to personally fulfilling careers and lives.

Creative reframes. I was impressed by the ability of some interviewees to take and make use of something in themselves or their environment, turning into a positive attribute in their lives what others may have seen as a detriment. Gena, for example, took pride in her differences from others and saw her Native American heritage as a way to get ahead:

Well I always thought it was neat. For one, me, I was always different because there weren't any [American] Indians anywhere so, then again, I stood out. "Hey, I'm American Indian! Ah ha!" It never really had any effect on my life because I've never, I hadn't had to live on reservations, or my mother never did, or. . . . It was always good to put down you're minority. When I was applying for colleges and stuff, it was good to be a minority. . . . That's who I am. I never looked at it as being a negative. That's who I am and I'm proud of who I am, who my mother is.

Similarly, Vinnie, in spite of the discrimination he experienced at Metro High School, came to value his own heritage and in particular see an advantage to being bilingual:

Now, it's [being Hispanic] a real big influence. Because, I mean, I'd say by the year 2000, you know, the Hispanic population will be a third of the population. I think it's a real plus that I am bilingual and everything too. Yeah, that helps a lot. It helps a lot now, [and] I think that will be a big plus in the future.

And, finally, I was impressed by the broadened worldview of some of the interviewees who, through their own experiences of dealing with oppression and discrimination, were able to see the world around them in a fundamentally different way. Joe described it this way:

I hate to say it, and you feel bad about it, but you can't help but feel superior to these [underprivileged] people. But if you buy into that, you have to be careful about that and you have to remember the circumstances that *they're* in. The way you should think about that, you should understand why they are the way they are. If anyone would understand that, we should, being black people. And it's important to realize that, given different circumstances, if I were in their circumstances, and they were in mine, they might have turned out to be far more intelligent and far more successful. And that's the thing you have to remember, because if you buy into that, then you give credence to white people feeling superior to these people. You have to realize, it's the circumstances that shape that person. A lot of it is environment and, yeah, a lot of it is hereditary as well, but we don't know what that person could have been if they had been born in different circumstances.

Summary and Suggestions

In conclusion, I believe that these stories can provide some insight into the environmental issues, social influences, and personal dilemmas that young people of color face. Several themes emerged, including the value of school programs and culture as well as involvement in activities outside the academic realm. Although family emerges as an important influence, their emotional support was less instrumental than their firm direction guiding interviewees toward the goal of college. Families also instilled important values. Friends and spouses often took the place of parents or teachers who were too overburdened to take individual time out for their children or students. Finally, several interviewees displayed finely tuned personal qualities that helped them negotiate their way to personal and career fulfillment. These included the desire to keep pushing toward goals despite setbacks, the recognition of and initiative to go after what they wanted most, the ability to reframe their own situations into an advantage, and, finally, a broadened perspective and appreciation for their own situations in the context of the world at large.

As has been illustrated throughout this chapter, many of the influences, both positive and negative, mirror suggestions put forth by social learning theorists, in particular Bandura (1986). This conceptual framework may be a starting point from which to continue exploration in this area, particularly in the way social support and learning can mitigate other more negative influences.

The perceived barriers and strategies for solutions suggested by these interviewees also provide some direction for potential interventions with today's urban, ethnic minority students. As has been suggested by others, career information continues to be needed. Several interviewees somehow managed to circumvent the lack of any type of specific information on their careers of interest, but only through their own sustained efforts and at times against the advice of others. Education quality could be improved merely by getting teachers more involved and enthusiastic about their duties and about the lives and interests of their students. Interviewee comments on the value of special programs and attainment of valued skills (e.g., reading, math, science) provide some specific directions for educators. By helping students attain these milestones and skills, teachers can help them feel special and competent—both sought-after attributes noted by the respondents who spoke in this chapter.

These suggestions appear particularly salient in light of the delays in career choice and fulfillment experienced by some of the interviewees in this chapter. Support for some more structured career programming may help prevent premature career foreclosure and encourage more helpful career exploration, as has been advocated for fulfilled career development (Holland, 1985; Super 1990).

Parents can be encouraged to provide more consistent support rather than allowing children so much time on their own. Although some interviewees thrived on their own, others expressed doubts about being too independent and wished for more structure in their lives growing up. At the same time, extended families and friends should be honored for the important roles they played, sometimes in the absence of more direct parenting.

I would like to close by extending a heartfelt thanks to these interviewees for their time and willingness to open their lives to a virtual stranger. Their stories stimulated my interest and taught me much about what is most important in life.

9

The Career Development of Children of Immigrants

VERONICA LUGRIS

Fifteen children of immigrants were interviewed. The eight children of immigrants who share their stories in this chapter are of different ethnic and racial origins representative of the larger immigrant group. Most of the four women and four men studied are first-generation Americans who share the impact that their parents' migration had on them. Two of the men immigrated along with their parents when they were still children. Six of these children of immigrants grew up in traditional two-parent, blue-collar families, thus they also share experiences with the socioeconomic group discussed in the previous chapter. The two Asian children of immigrants grew up in families where one or both parents were college educated. All but one of the fifteen children of immigrants graduated from college.

As a first-generation child of working-class Spanish immigrants, I hold a perception about children of immigrants that, no doubt, has influenced my work and my life. This perception stems from the assumption that immigrants generally come to the United States because of difficult situations in their homelands, whether economic, political, religious, or the like. Once in the United States, immigrant families strive to survive the difficulties inherent in living in a different culture, often with a different language, and away from familiar support systems. Survival becomes possible through the predominant immigrant view that the United States is a land of opportunities and such opportunities are especially available to their children through hard work and sacrifice. Not a surprise, I expected the children of immigrants interviewed here to have incorporated this view of the United States as a land of opportunity, along with a strong work ethic.

The eight children of immigrants represented in this chapter share several common themes in their career development. These themes include an early interest in their current careers as well as parental support for their career plans. These children of immigrants also share environmental obstacles in the form of traditional gender role obstacles and language obstacles. In addition, they share the view of hard work as an avenue to success. Finally, the women and men that we interviewed share a commitment to family and career roles.

Early Interest in Current Careers

All of the women and men except one had a very early interest in their current careers. Like Eduardo, who is now a high school math teacher, most of the participants had known their career choices since high school. Eduardo, a first-generation Polish American, recalls his early career aspirations:

I remember being a sophomore in high school and actually envision[ing] myself, whether through daydreaming or whatever, teaching math. Even though that wasn't my major. . . . And I always thought that that was really kind of funny how I ended up teaching math.

A few of the respondents discovered their career interests at even earlier ages. Beatrice, of Italian descent, shares her own early interest in a helping profession like teaching:

I just remember from like fourth or fifth grade wanting to be a teacher. Playing school, you know . . . we had a little back porch and I had the chalk board and my teachers would give me all the old books that they were going to throw away. And so I just always remember being a teacher.

Linda, a first-generation American of Asian descent, is now a surgeon. Linda not only developed an early interest in her profession, she also had the opportunity to become involved in her chosen career at an early age. As noted in Chapter 5, Linda told us:

When I was a young child, probably around the age of 7 to 9 years of age I used to go to my dad's office; he's a doctor. And I would assist him. . . . Like if he was going to be removing a hangnail or an ingrown toenail, I would just kind of hold the toe . . . I used to help him box his medicines up. Not anything that would require any great amount of responsibility. But I was in the office and I was seeing things. And so I had a pretty good idea of what medicine was. And I've always wanted to do that.

Seven of the eight children of immigrants interviewed share an early interest in their current careers. Most common was an identification of their current career interests in high school, although a few children of immigrants claim to have even earlier interests in their careers. The remaining child of immigrants developed an interest in his career while in college. Such an early interest in the current careers of most of the women and men that we interviewed might be explained by their immigrant parents' perception of the United States as a land of opportunities. Such a perception might have influenced immigrant parents to encourage their children to pursue their interests early on.

Parental Support for Career Plans

Like Linda's father, most of the respondents' parents supported them in whatever career decision they made, which offers support for some researcher's claims that immigrants view the American educational system as an opportunity for mobility (Caplan, Choy, & Whitmore, 1991; Delgado-Gaitan & Trueba, 1991; Gibson, 1991).

Eduardo echoes the feelings of many of the respondents' parents:

Their dream was for all of us to get a college education. Of course, we all have, I think they were just happy with that. Because they knew that once we worked and achieved that, we would work toward whatever else we wanted. I think that their thinking was as long as we were happy, they were happy with whatever we had chosen to do.

Although they eventually came to respect their children's career decisions, some immigrant families were not initially supportive of their children's career choices. Wendy, a reporter, struggled to put herself through school because her immigrant father initially disapproved of her career choice. When Beatrice pursued a master's in counseling, her immigrant Italian father was proud of her efforts to further her education. However, he had difficulty seeing the merit in an occupation that conflicted with the traditional worldview of resolving problems within the family:

I know he was very proud that I went for a master's degree. It could have probably been in anything, you know. He just was so excited about that. But from the old school . . . Italy, you know. There's not much counseling. And out of the family. . . . So he kind of thinks a lot of this is like hocus-pocus, kind of weird stuff.

Some researchers have found that immigrant families support the education of their sons as a means of improving the family's financial status, while the education of daughters receives more limited family support (Becker, 1985; Gibson, 1988; Goldstein, 1985). They report that immigrant families' limited support for their daughters' careers results from an effort to prevent

daughters from abandoning their traditional responsibilities as primary caretakers of home and children (Becker, 1985; Gibson, 1988; Goldstein, 1985).
There was no such evidence of limited support for the career development of
the female children of immigrants interviewed.

Linda credits her father with complete support for her career choice:

> The mothers of some of my close friends in high school would say, you
> know, that I was being too ambitious to try and become a doctor. And that,
> really a woman's role . . . in life is not to become the career person. That I
> would be throwing away my education once I got married, etc . . . There have
> been people that have told me that I shouldn't do it along the way and my fa-
> ther has always encouraged me to do this anyway. So I ended up with his sup-
> port making it.

All of the women and men interviewed share parental support for their career choices. Those immigrant parents that were initially opposed eventually
came to respect their children's decisions. Contrary to previous research
findings, parental support crossed gender lines.

Environmental Obstacles

Traditional Gender Role Obstacles

Although immigrant families encouraged the women that we interviewed
to pursue their career goals, they continued to maintain expectations for traditional gender roles within the home sphere. Thus the daughters and sons of
immigrants interviewed live by these expectations.

Linda, a doctor who is married and has no children, maintains a belief in
her traditional household role:

> Currently my husband and I try to take equal part in cleaning the house be-
> cause I'm never home. And the house gets messy if he doesn't help. And I in-
> tend to have a housekeeper in the future to help me with it. I should say "to
> help us" but I always think of it as being primarily the woman's job to keep the
> house clean.

Although Eduardo is not married, he has already internalized his parents'
traditional gender role expectations within the home. Thus, although Eduardo claims that he would leave it up to his future wife to decide how to combine her career and home responsibilities, his opinion that the woman has primary child rearing responsibilities is evident:

Whatever she would like to do. If she wants to stay home with them, or if she wants to go to work. They have a regular day care program at work. So she can even take the kids with her when they get a little bit older or whatever.

Despite immigrant families' support for their daughter's careers, traditional gender role expectations in the home appear to have a considerable impact on their daughters' career development. These daughters of immigrants agree that women should assume the traditional role of primary child caretaker with preschool children and that they should adjust their career plans to fit their roles as mothers. However, they also express conflict over having to put the careers they value on hold.

Juanita, a first-generation Mexican American, is a nurse who is married and has a school-aged child. Juanita saw her traditional responsibilities in the home as foremost over her career during her child rearing years:

When my child was going to come along, I knew motherhood was going to be first and that was going to be my priority before anything. . . . I always said when he [her son] comes along I'm going to have to really dedicate my life to my son and marriage and I have to put my own life on hold.

Juanita admits that she feels that being married and having a child have interfered with her career plans. Although she has recently started a business, she feels pressured by her family to have another child. Avoiding these pressures makes her feel guilty, even though her preference is to wait for her business to stabilize.

Although Beatrice views her child rearing responsibilities as a mutual agreement between herself and her partner, her role as primary caretaker of her daughter and its impact on her career is evident:

He [her husband] was saying, "Well you know I wouldn't want you to go back to work now with her being this little," but it's not like he's telling me, 'cause I don't want to either and we both think that's best.

Beatrice firmly believes in the importance of staying at home with her child, but she does not intend to completely abandon her career goals:

I think it's important now to stay home for most of the time. But then again, I would like to work at least sometime. I have my master's and I feel like it was a complete waste of time if I am not doing anything with it.

All of the women and the men sampled have incorporated the traditional gender role expectations in the home that their immigrant families instilled in them. Although such expectations often present home-career conflicts for the

women interviewed, they attempt to accommodate both family and career interests.

Language Obstacles

English was not a first language for several of these children of immigrants. This posed a barrier in these children's educational process.

Donald, who immigrated from Italy at age 9, shares his experience with
English as a second language: "When we came over I felt like a dummy because I always had some girl translating to me." As a result of this experience,
Donald avoided his Italian friends and pursued relationships solely among native English speakers. Donald earned an A.A. degree and currently owns his
own business. Donald's experience provides evidence for Goldstein's (1985)
assertion that immigrant youth often seek friendships with native students.

Ronald, who immigrated from Vietnam at age 11, could not understand
English at age 13. It was not until Ronald was placed in an advanced English
class in junior high that his teachers realized that Ronald was memorizing all
his subjects without understanding English. Ronald's need to learn English
was then addressed. Years later, while in dental school, Ronald found an important use for the memorization skills he had honed earlier.

Wendy, whose first language was Spanish, was told by a teacher: "You're
never going to be any good at reading. You're the slowest reader in the class
and it's shameful." Wendy's teacher's words were not prophetic, as Wendy
went on to become a successful journalist.

Thus these children of immigrants whose first language was not English
had negative experiences with acquisition of English as a second language.
According to many researchers, such negative academic experiences deter
immigrant students from learning (Becker, 1985; Goldstein, 1985; Trueba,
Jacobs, & Kirton, 1990). This claim was not substantiated in our study. On
the contrary, these children of immigrants appear to use these negative experiences as incentives to work harder to succeed.

Hard Work as an Avenue to Success

Negative academic experiences did not deter the children of immigrants
interviewed from achieving in their careers. Their immigrant families had instilled in these children a sense that education would allow them to overcome

obstacles to success (Gibson, 1988). Thus all of the respondents are driven to work hard at what they do with the expectation that hard work would bring success.

Eduardo summarizes this perspective best: "The majority of the time you can control your own destiny. And I mean a lot of it you can control through hard work."

Juanita states that she has always persisted in her endeavors because she knew that she would accomplish her goals through hard work. She explains that it was important for her to complete something and be successful through such hard work.

Donald states:

People who were born in the United States . . . don't appreciate the opportunity they got here. . . . It's just too many people are followers than leaders. . . . They always want to see what the other person is doing instead of going out there and just do[ing] it. . . . I never thought of it that way. . . . I say, Well, if I'm going to do it, I'm going to work hard on it.

Ronald, the dentist who could not understand English two years after arriving in the United States at age 11 from Vietnam, believes:

I think that anybody can make it through dental school, medical school. It's just, whoever graduates is whoever can tough it out. . . . You just got to be real consistent and you got to try real hard.

Wendy, who is Hispanic and is now a journalist, was told that she would never read well. She says,

I firmly believe this. If you want something bad enough, you'll find the way. No matter what the circumstances. . . . I had that accent problem. . . . That was murder. I was practicing rolling my tongue and all this other stuff. . . . I did stories and other people got the credit. But if you believe in yourself and you don't give up, you can do it.

The children of immigrants studied here work hard in many different facets of their lives, often juggling multiple work roles. As we have witnessed, the women interviewed pursue careers outside the home while taking primary responsibility for work in the home and child rearing. Linda, a doctor who is married, admits:

I find that I'm not one that sits around much. I mean when I'm home on the weekend the house is cleaned. And when I go to work I have something to do.

Juanita works as a nurse, has her own billing business, and volunteers at her son's school, in addition to her traditional role as her son's primary caretaker:

My life is like . . . everyday is something. I'm working or it's the business day or it's my family day or it's my son's day at school.

The men interviewed also juggle several jobs at once. Eduardo works as assistant dean, math teacher, and volunteer basketball coach at a parochial boys' school. In addition, Eduardo has a painter's union license, which he uses in the summer. Chad, of Italian-Irish descent, works full-time as an accountant, coaches soccer after work, and still finds time to study for his CPA exam and play with his daughter.

These children of immigrants unanimously attribute their work ethic to the messages they received from their immigrant families. Immigrant parents labor long hours to provide their families with necessities.

Linda, whose father immigrated from Southeast Asia, states:

Something my father always taught me was to be goal oriented. And that, you know, the really hard things, the really good things that you want in life are worth fighting for and persevering for.

Speaking of her Mexican father, Juanita says,

He's the hardest working man that I've ever met in my entire life. . . . All I could remember was him working. . . . He worked all day long and sometimes [would] come home at 9, 10 o'clock at night, eat dinner real late, and go to bed and just start another day like that.

Eduardo speaks of both of his parents, their hard work, and how this influenced him. Speaking of his Polish father, Eduardo acknowledges:

He was an extremely hardworking man. He is still to this day, even though he is retired, he's still a very hard working man. Now he just spends a lot of his time fixing things at other people's houses. He's a very handy person. So he spends his time jumping from his six children's houses fixing things and he is very, very dedicated, very committed to his family. You know, a very, very loving man. Always working, a workaholic. I think that has kind of rubbed off on all his children. I think we are all very hard workers. You know a lot of that is due to him. He would work endless hours . . . . There'd be many times in the winter where he would work construction during the day and then he would plow at night.

Of his mother, Eduardo states,

She worked just as hard as he did, if not harder sometimes . . . She would get up with him every morning and make his breakfast and lunch. And she would make the lunches for the kids. And her job was full-time as well. Being a house wife is no easy job at all. Seeing her commitment to him and her love and devotion to him and her family . . . I think that has definitely rubbed off on me as well.

The children of immigrants sampled share a belief that hard work will allow them to overcome obstacles and achieve success. Such a belief inspires the different facets of their lives. Thus they tend to be involved in multiple work roles. The respondents learned the value of hard work in their families of origin, through the messages and examples of their immigrant parents.

Family and Career Roles

Just as Eduardo was influenced by his parents' dedication to family, the other children of immigrants interviewed were also influenced by their parents and they too share a commitment to family. The importance of family for children of immigrants may, at times, conflict with the individualistic values inherent in American education (Caplan et al., 1991; Gibson, 1988; Goldstein, 1985; Trueba et al., 1990). Thus family plans influence career plans for most of the women and men in this first-generation children of immigrants group.

Ronald, who immigrated with his family from Vietnam at age 11, attributes his emphasis on family over career to his upbringing:

My parents [would] always tell us: "Education . . . is a means of making a living, and it's a way to support your family, and you shouldn't look at it [as] anything more than that. If education interests you, then you can pursue it to its limit if you want, but you always have to consider that we're here to live and enjoy life and have a family. And that's pretty much where your basic values and support come from. And without that, you really can't go very far."

Chad, first-generation Italian, is divorced and has a young daughter. He talks about the influence that his daughter has on his accounting career:

I'd rather be able to spend more time with my daughter. I don't want to have a job where I have to work 14-15 hours a day. . . . I'm a firm believer that work is work, and if work cuts into the time you spend with your family, then you're in the wrong line of work. . . . I work to make a living and I make a living for my family, so if I can't enjoy it with my family, what's the point?

Despite these children of immigrants' emphasis on the rewards of hard work, family commitments remain foremost for them. Like their work ethic, this family ethic was passed on by their immigrant parents.

Summary

These first-generation children of immigrants display career and family commitments that reflect the work and family values learned in their families of origin. Supported by their families of origin, they remained committed to their early career choices.

As first-generation Americans, many of the women and men that we interviewed faced environmental obstacles to their career interests. Traditional gender roles in the home posed significant conflicts for women's career pursuits, while English language acquisition posed barriers for those children of immigrants whose first language was not English. Despite these barriers, all of these children of immigrants share a belief that hard work will bring success. Such hard work is often displayed in this group in their juggling of several jobs at once. These children of immigrants agree that this work ethic was learned and reinforced in their families of origin. Immigrant families also instilled in their children a commitment to family that significantly affects career commitments, in particular for the women interviewed. They attempt to cope by adjusting their schedules to incorporate both family and career commitments.

Implications

The experiences of the children of immigrants represented in this chapter offer support for a theoretical framework based on social learning theory, which provides for the impact of environmental conditions on career planning (Mitchell & Krumboltz, 1996). Similar to what this chapter reveals, social learning theory underscores the contributions of families as communicators of values and expectations for achievement (Mitchell & Krumboltz, 1996).

As a result of the learning experiences within their respective families, these children of immigrants developed what social learning theorists term "world-view generalizations" about the opportunities available in this country and the required efforts to successfully make the most of those opportunities. Social learning theory also allows for the influence of environmental obstacles on career planning (Mitchell & Krumboltz, 1996). Thus obstacles in the form of English language acquisition and traditional gender role expectations appear to have affected the lives of those interviewed here. Finally, social learning theory also provides for the interaction of gender and culture and its influence on careers (Mitchell & Krumboltz, 1996). In particular, the experiences of these children of immigrants offer support for earlier findings of home-career conflict for women (Harmon, 1970) and the negative impact of this conflict on women's careers (Farmer, 1984; Farmer & Bohn, 1970; Tipping & Farmer, 1991).

Although it is well established that immigrants view the United States as a land of opportunities, opponents of immigration often fail to acknowledge the hard work and contributions of immigrants. In addition, immigrant families appear to harbor important clues as to how to instill family and work values in their children. Immigrant families are valuable resources that can inform the American educational system about the importance of fostering an actively supportive role in children's educational progress, pride about ethnic identity and cultural heritage, and a sense of collectivist responsibility.

Immigrant families are sometimes viewed as having strict traditional gender role expectations for their children. Although traditional gender role expectations prevail in the homes of the children of immigrants studied here, such expectations do not apply to their career goals. Given that this study contradicts previous research that finds that daughters of immigrant families are often discouraged from pursuing career interests in favor of home responsibilities, more research is needed to examine differences in career expectations for immigrant daughters and sons. Furthermore, although traditional gender role expectations cause some home-career conflicts for first-generation American women, it is not clear how these conflicts differ for later-generation American women.

Finally, barriers such as English language acquisition continue to inspire divergent views in the controversy over bilingual education versus immersion. Although this study appears to offer support for the idea that such language barriers do not prevent children of immigrants from succeeding, there is no evidence here to suggest that other forms of education such as bilingual teaching would not have been helpful to such students.

10

Socioeconomic Leaps

Achievement in the Next Generation

AMY CARTER

class /klas/ n, 1 a: a body of students meeting regularly to study the same subject; 2 a: a group sharing the same economic or social status (the working —);
b: social rank; esp: high social rank; c: high quality: elegance; 3: a group, set,
or kind sharing common attributes; 4: a division or rating based on grade or
quality. (*Webster's,* 1991)

Social class is a complex concept. In reading *Webster's* definition of
class, we can see its many facets. Class says something about our economic
power and our social status. It provides information about where we have
come from and alludes to where we are going. It involves a value judgment by
implying quality, or a lack of it. It groups us together, and it divides us. No
doubt, social class exerts a powerful influence on all of our lives.

It is likely that we know what social class is and have a rough idea of
where we fall on the socioeconomic continuum (Sewell & Hauser, 1975).
What is less clear, however, is how it affects us. How has our social class affected our experiences, our values, our perceptions of ourselves, and, particularly for the current purpose, our career choices and development?

My interest in social class, and belief in its importance, stems from the
different social atmospheres I have encountered. My father comes from a
working-class background and has worked in a factory for more than 30
years. My mother, who comes from a rural background, entered college several years after she finished high school. She balanced being a mother and her
education while she was completing her degree in teaching. I am currently in
a doctoral program in psychology and worked as a waitress for several years
while attending college. The variation of my own experiences, as well as
those of my parents, fellow students, and coworkers, has led me to believe
that social class is an important personal variable that shapes individuals' beliefs and expectations related to their career achievement and life in general.
Certainly this belief influenced my interpretations of the participants' stories.
Writing this chapter on social class provided me an opportunity to continue to

explore this interest and, in particular, consider the experiences of working-class individuals who have moved into a professional field. I hope that the heightened awareness of issues related to social class, which these individuals experienced as their social economic status changed, can provide career counselors and psychologists with important information about this underexplored variable.

Gottfredson, in an explication of her developmental theory of occupational aspirations "Circumscription and Compromise" (1981), suggests that our knowledge and images of social class are learned much in the same way our knowledge of jobs and sex roles are—largely through observation and social modeling rather than through any direct "teaching," and over a period spanning several years. Gottfredson (1981) uses Stendler's (1949) work with the development of social class awareness in grade school children as an example. Children first tend to view class in a dichotomous black-and-white fashion—rich is seen as good, and poor as bad. As children reach the late elementary school years, their conceptualization of class becomes more refined; they begin tying jobs to economic rewards; and their awareness begins to resemble that of adults. Gottfredson (1981) points out that as children became more aware of social class, they approach it less directly: "As youngsters became more sophisticated in their understanding of social class, they were more sensitive about displaying that knowledge, which is a sign of understanding in itself" (p. 562). It seems that although we obtain an intimate knowledge of social class and its relationship to job status, we also learn at some point that this subject is taboo.

Social Class Neglected and Misunderstood in the Literature

Gottfredson (1981) points out that although the importance of social class is often acknowledged in theories of career development, this variable is often largely ignored or minimized by vocational psychologists. Much more attention is paid to weaker predictors, such as parental values and individual interests. Richardson (1993) also highlights the lack of attention that has been paid to class in this field: "The theoretical and research literature in vocational psychology-career development is notably oriented toward the White middle class." She goes on to comment about the failure to attend to this problematic gap: "Moreover, there is almost no acknowledgment that poor and lower class populations, regardless of race or ethnicity, are almost totally absent from this literature" (p. 426). It seems that experts in the field of career development, much like the children in Stendler's (1949) study, have learned to step politely around the issue of social class.

Typically, sons and daughters tend to aspire to and obtain careers with levels of socioeconomic status similar to that of their parents' occupations (Sewell & Hauser, 1975). Perhaps it is this lack of change in socioeconomic status across generations that has allowed it to be largely overlooked in the field of career development. The underachievement of working-class students in comparison with their higher socioeconomic peers has been documented and attributed to various factors—limited financial resources, lack of motivation and home values, and little support from parents and schools (Burwood, 1992). This gap in achievement, however, has been treated more as a fact than a potential problem to be solved. The lower achievement of working-class students is particularly troubling because a gap in ability does not accompany it. Gottfredson (1981) points out that, regardless of ability, higher class students have the highest aspirations. Similarly, Burwood (1992) reports that children of higher social status are more likely to be tracked for college and receive the curriculum relevant to higher education, again, regardless of ability. Burwood describes this as a waste of talent and stresses the need to "attack traditionally entrenched conceptions of a limited pool of educable ability" (quoted in Karable & Halsey, 1977, p. 312).

Although levels of socioeconomic status and career achievement tend to remain consistent across generations, there are exceptions to this pattern. Overall, eight (six men and two women) of the 105 participants were exceptions, defined in the present study as individuals from lower-middle-class families (as defined by the Duncan Socio-Economic Index; Sewell & Hauser, 1975) who aspired to and ultimately obtained careers of higher socioeconomic status. The stories of six of these individuals, four men and two women, will be the focus of this chapter.

Common threads run through the experiences of these men and women. In examining their life stories, the same themes emerged again and again. The move up in socioeconomic status for these individuals began with strong aspirations. Hard work was the vehicle for realizing these aspirations and overcoming financial obstacles. The concept of the "work ethic" came up again and again in the interviews; participants clearly saw hard work as the vehicle they would use to change their lives. Once they became established in their careers, many participants found themselves struggling to maintain a balance between work and other areas of their lives. Individuals dealt with this struggle in different ways, but the theme of prioritizing work and family and the possible consequences of these decisions were a primary concern in these participants' lives.

Beyond the more logistical problems of providing their own financial support, working very hard to realize their aspirations, and learning to balance this work with other areas of their life, these men and women also struggled with adjusting to a way of life and a social world they had not grown up in. Individuals coped in different ways, but throughout these struggles, respect for their parents and the sacrifices they had made were evident. More generally, they spoke with a sense of pride in their working-class backgrounds and respect for the blue-collar world.

I hope that by examining the stories of these six participants who made significant leaps in socioeconomic status, and each of the themes in turn, we can understand more about the possibilities for change across generations and the impact class has on individual's lives.

Strong Aspirations

The origin of the move up the socioeconomic ladder was a dream. Some participants reported that a parent's dream of success was handed down to them. In these instances, the framework for success was outlined for them and they grew up knowing they were expected to fill it in with their achievements. Tad, a manager for a realty company, reports that there was never any question that he would go to college; it was an expectation his father had had for him as long as he could remember. In his own words,

My father's dream was to put his three kids through college, and that's what he did. We were raised to say that we would do that. We were going to go to college and that was it.

Tad had not even decided on a career path and reports that his ending up in real estate was a "fluke" as well as his father's suggestion. He received his B.A. in history and had planned to teach, but found after a semester of student teaching that he would not be happy doing this job. Tad says that he never had a strong sense of what he would like to do:

I didn't ever know what I wanted to do, not even in college! In high school, I never thought about it because I was on the college track—I didn't really think about a specific job. Teaching was something I was interested in, but I just felt like it was time to pick a major and so I decided to go that route.

His father suggested real estate to him at this time, reasoning that with three months off in the summer, he could teach and practice realty on the side. The realty worked out well for Tad and became his full-time job. He is now a manager in charge of training in a small company.

Chad, whose father immigrated from Italy, also reports that his career aspirations were heavily influenced by his parents. One of four children, he felt that he was specially selected by his parents as the child that would achieve:

They had these expectations of me that I felt I had to live up to. I always did well in school and it got to the point where if I did poorly in a class, whatever the reason, I'd get in trouble. If my brother did poorly in a class, they would just say, "OK, try harder next time." But by the same token, they recognized that fact. I got a car before my brother did; I got a lot of things before my brother did. He's my older brother and that has caused a lot of friction between us.

Chad is now an accountant for a life insurance company and a head coach for a high school soccer team on the side. He reports that the decision to go into accounting was largely made by his parents.

It was my father's decision mostly. He said, "You have to do something where you will make money." Accounting isn't the greatest thing in the world but I can do it. Whether I liked it or not, they saw to it that I was going for that. I don't know if they were worrying more about what I wanted or what they thought I should be doing. In their defense, I guess they just figured, "You've got this potential to do something that none of us could do, so don't blow it. Do it."

Other participants report that their parents instilled in them the importance of career choice and financial security but felt the career choice was their own. Miguel, who is Hispanic as well as working class, got his degree in biochemistry and now works in the upper marketing division of a pharmaceuticals company. He reports that his parents always had high expectations for him but did not force any particular career on him.

They always let us know that we should do better than they did. It was never forced upon us. They never said you *have* to go to school, but it was always kind of an implicit thought in my mind. College was definite for me.

Clay, an accountant who is pursuing his master's degree, reports a very different experience. His aspirations were completely internal; they came only from himself. Clay points out that he is the first person to receive a degree on his father's side of the family and that he never received any pressure or encouragement from his parents to go to college. His parents' lifestyle did, however, strongly affect his own aspirations.

I knew I wanted something better than what I had seen growing up. At least a chance for that. It seemed like going to college was one way to do that. My parents didn't have the opportunity to go to college. They worked hard, very hard, their whole lives, but I knew I didn't want to do what they've done.

Sandra, who is now the supervisor of the inpatient billing department at a hospital, felt neither an internal nor an external push for her achievement. Rather, she views it as somewhat of a fluke. In speaking of her current position, she says,

It's just something I fell into and fortunately for me, it has worked out great. It's nothing that I planned. I just needed a job and they offered it to me and it just went from there.

The Work Ethic

Regardless of the origins of their aspirations, hard work was the means by which individuals achieved them. Many of the participants paid for their education themselves. As a result, their lives were devoted almost exclusively to work during college and early on in their careers. Miguel comments on his situation:

We fared pretty well in terms of grants and scholarships and once we were able to get into college we supported ourselves. Once I left high school I don't think I had one day when I didn't work. My freshmen year I was working about 25 hours a week, and towards the end of my college career I was working about 30 hours between my research co-ops and everything else. So I was putting in quite a few hours by the end, in addition going to school full-time. But it taught me responsibility, you know, I had to do a little of both to make things go.

Chad also describes the struggle to support himself and still do well in his studies.

I was working full-time and going to school at night, which was no picnic. I was getting home late and it was hard to find the time to do homework. No rest and that didn't make a difference. My parents still expected my grades to be where they were.

Clay reports that he was also financially independent. He says that his parents helped him out to a small extent, but he feels he would have done it without their help. In his own words:

By going to a junior college and working, I took care of two years and I saved enough for a good part of the next two years. I did end up borrowing about $3,000 from my Dad to finish my undergrad. But I paid him back my first year out. That was something that was important for me to do.

Many of the participants see their parents as being responsible for their strong work ethic. Cindy, who is an English teacher at a Catholic junior high school, describes how her parents affected her feelings about work:

Work is very important to me. I think a lot of it has to do with the way I was brought up. I was raised on a farm and there was always something to do. Today people think that kids should have all these luxuries. Parents today would probably look back at my Mom and Dad and think that they were abusing us because of the way they made us work, but I know the value of a dollar bill.

Sandra describes a similar sentiment:

Nothing was handed to me. . . . I worked for it. If you want anything from the workforce you have to prove that you can do it and do it right. I have gotten where I am by proving that I can do it, and do it well.

A Place for Work: Fitting in Other Life Roles

Even after becoming established in their careers, participants found themselves struggling to maintain a balance between work and other areas of life. For many, this struggle was a familiar one because they had often felt their own parents' absence due to work while they were growing up.

Tad has a particular concern with maintaining a balance between work and his family lives. He intends to always give his family priority over his work. This decision is partly based on his father and mother's divorce after all the children had grown up and left home. He feels certain that his father's working 80 hours a week and the lack of time spent with the family were contributing factors in their split. He sees his grandmother, who successfully combined career and work, as a good role model. He comments,

She worked full-time when my mom was growing up, but she didn't lose the family. She still set time aside to spend with them and they have a lot of fond memories of growing up. I guess that's what I want to have. Having a career is very important, but it's also equally important to have a happy family life and a happy marriage . . . because after you're done and retired, that's who you're with.

Miguel also talked about his father's absence due to work:

Dad worked way more than 40 hours per week. I'd never see him. He worked rotating shifts so he was always either sleeping or at work and he wasn't around a lot for us kids. But we knew that he supported us in everything we did. The support was known and obviously the love was known.

Miguel, who reports that he is currently "living his job" and gives it 110% of his time, feels that he would like to cut down on work when he starts a family, but work will still be his first priority.

When I get married, I'm not going to be able to dive into things 110%. If I start raising a family I might have to cut down to 90%. I'll take 20% away from my job and give it to my family. Some people will neglect a family. But family is important to me. It was important when I was growing up and I would like to have it be the same in my family.

Chad, in contrast, strives to give his family priority over work. One of his primary motivations for working is to earn enough money to buy a house for his daughter. He says,

The main reason I want a house is for her. She hardly ever gets to go outside because I won't let her go out and play by herself. A lot of times it is dark by the time I get home from work so we can't go out. If she has a backyard that she can just run out to, I'd be a little more comfortable. She'll ask me, "How come I don't have a house like the other kids?" and that just gets you right in the heart.

Sandra, who is active socially and very involved in her church, also works 50 to 60 hours a week. She comments on her struggle to make time for everything:

I think it's a matter of continually trying to balance personal things with business. I'm always juggling. If I take a little bit of time from personal, I always try to give it back. Or if I take some time from business, I try to make up for it.

Cindy reports that her father was a workaholic when she was growing up. She stresses the fact that work is very important to her, but she tries not to let it consume more than half of her time.

I don't think you should give everything to your work. I don't want to focus only on work and ignore my family. I also think that being a teacher is a good occupation, as far as having a family is concerned. My own immediate family was very scattered and one thing I enjoy about teaching is that I get time off at Christmas and time available in the summer. That's very important to me. I feel that I can have a career and still have the flexibility and freedom to raise a family.

From Working Class to Professional

Even after the achievement of their career aspirations was well under way, social class still remained a key issue for many of the participants. Some participants described feeling estranged from their families and their backgrounds. The change in socioeconomic status was not merely a matter of a higher tax bracket, it also involved a change in identity.

In one of the few studies considering the adjustment of working-class individuals in the professional world, Granfield (1991) explored the struggles of lower-class individuals in a prestigious law school. Granfield suggested that the struggles encountered by individuals in their new environments are due to "identity ambivalence." He comments, "Working class students who sought to exit their class background could neither embrace their group nor let it go. This ambivalence is often felt by working class individuals who obtain upward mobility into the professional-managerial class" (p. 343).

Granfield reports that this identity ambivalence manifests itself in different ways. Some students felt different and had a sense of not fitting in with the professional world. As a result, they often learned to mimic the behaviors of their higher-class peers. As they began to adopt behaviors that differed from their backgrounds, they were perceived by family members and individuals of the own class as having "sold out." Others are plagued by a sense of guilt and are unable to completely enjoy their success.

Conflict with family was particularly relevant for Chad, who had been singled out as the child who would achieve. He says,

My father is a barber and my mother is a waitress. One brother distributes car parts, the other works for Frito Lay, and my sister is a receptionist. Their jobs are all different from mine. I wear a shirt and tie and sit behind a desk all day.

The fact that he has a degree has caused conflict with his older brother in particular, who coaches the high school soccer team with him.

On paper I'm the head coach. Technically, I have to admit that the only reason he is not the head coach is because he doesn't have a degree. He can't do it and that's just the rule. I go out of my way to never let it be a head coach/assistant coach relationship. We had a big blowout about a decision I had made. What it boiled down to was the fact that he was uncomfortable being second fiddle, not because of anything I'd done but just because he felt his opinion didn't count, but it did.

The different social skills Chad has learned as a result of being in the professional world also have been a source of conflict.

With my family it's kind of free for all—do what you want and just be yourself. Whereas with me there is a proper way to do this and a proper way to do that. We once went to a buffet and I told them they should get a new plate whenever they went through the line, instead of using the same one. I worry about things like that. I have a hard time letting them be and letting them enjoy themselves, and that's how I'm different. Since I started my job I've picked up all these habits. Suddenly, I'm paranoid at restaurants. I have to realize that I can't force that on everybody else. I feel like I'm in the middle because I'll be with one group of people, and at other times I'll deal with my family and all of a sudden it's completely opposite. So I always sit back and wonder, is it me or is it them?

Chad also sees that his concern with doing things the proper way is affecting his relationship with his daughter:

I don't want her to be an adult when she is just a kid, but I just want her to know the proper way to do things. Sometimes she'll say, "Dad, I think you're making too many rules for me." But she is very well mannered so that's the positive side of it.

While adopting a set of rules more similar to his professional peers has become an issue for Chad, Miguel says he was perceived as a "sell-out" in high school. Miguel is worth quoting again on this theme:

In my school the Hispanics all hung together, the whites all hung together, and the blacks hung together. Being in athletics, I transcended the white-Hispanic barrier and the black-Hispanic barrier. We were looked at oddly by our Hispanic peers because they saw us as traitors. My middle sister was just the opposite—she would not transcend racial barriers, no matter what! She feels a strong need to maintain her ethnicity. It's her choice, but it may make things difficult for her. I feel that you need to get along with everybody.

Unlike his sister, Miguel describes himself as a free spirit and seems reluctant to align himself with any particular group. Such a perspective seems to help him avoid conflict as he transcends barriers—both racial and socioeconomic. He reports that his experience interacting with many different people has also helped him by exposing him to different perspectives. He comments,

I still to this day try to apply diversity to everything that I do. You can't keep a narrow perspective on things. You need to have as broad of a scope as you can possibly obtain.

Sandra seemed to have conflicting feelings about her success. At times, she describes her work as the supervisor of the hospital's billing department very positively:

I like my job. I'm very satisfied with it and I think that has a lot to do with it. You have to like what you're doing if it's going to be beneficial to you. Sure it's been hard at times, but I like my job. It is a great sense of accomplishment to me.

When asked how she perceives work in the context of her life, however, she says that work is for survival. She reports that she lives with her parents, and things are taken care of as far as a house payment and food, yet she still views work as survival. Her insistence that work is just for survival seems to conflict with the status of her job and the obvious pride she has in her achievements.

Participants also seemed to qualify their high aspirations; they seemed to feel a need to justify them. For example, Clay, when asked about his desire to go to college, said,

I wasn't disappointed with what I had when I was growing up but I just came to a point where I was hoping to have more, to be able to provide more when I'm a parent. I saw my parents working lots of hours and I wanted more structure for myself. And when I was training as a night manager at a grocery chain, I was starting out work at 10 o'clock at night and working until 7 o'clock in the morning. It seemed more blue-collar work, and I have nothing against blue collar by any means because my parents came from that. I have a lot of respect for them and what they do and for what blue collar does, but that isn't what I wanted to be doing. I wanted to be more white collar.

Clay's obvious pride and respect for his background is apparent in his explanation. Other participants expressed this strong sense of pride for their backgrounds. They also expressed gratitude for their parents—for the sacrifices they had made and what it taught them. Cindy, for example, talks about her parents' hard work and how it affected her values:

That is one thing I will say for my parents, they raised us to realize where money comes from, and how much there is and what you do when you don't have it. I really do appreciate my parents for that. I know that the only way I'm going to get what I want is by working for it. When I get it, it makes me feel proud to know that I worked for it, because I don't want anything given to me.

Tad also expressed a deep sense of gratitude and a sense that his parents had sacrificed a lot for him.

The stuff they did for us—they gave up so much! And my father gave us a work ethic, because he worked 80 hours a week. So I just figured, hey, this is how you can be successful and do what you want. You can control your destiny by working hard. And he is *very, very* very proud of me now. It's a good feeling to know that the person who raised you is actually so proud of you. I see the smile on his face when he introduces me. He says, "This is my son," and it is like *wow!*

Chad is particularly grateful to his father:

I admire my father because he literally came off the boat from Italy. He went to barber school here and now he owns his own business. My father still doesn't write extremely well and he doesn't spell that great. In grade school when he would sign my notes or a permission slip, the teacher would think that I had forged his name. So he's had to struggle. He's done very well for himself but I think that he still believes that he hasn't done as well as he could have, and therefore I should do better. One reason I want to do better is to pay him back. I always picture myself pulling up in the driveway in a nice car and asking him, "What do you think about the car?" He would say, "I like it," and I would just hand him the keys. I always picture giving it to him because if I needed a car to get to school when I was in college, he'd give me the car and he would walk to work. That's just the kind of person he is. He didn't work far away, but he shouldn't have been walking. Even if it was a block he shouldn't have walked . . . it was his car.

Summary and Implications

As we have seen, some women and men can make considerable upward movement in their economic status. Their achievements show that the class-achievement gap can be bridged. For the six individuals interviewed, this move involved high aspirations, dedication, and a lot of hard work. Their success suggests that workers in the career counseling field should become aware of their biases, and avoid tracking individuals according to their parents' socioeconomic status, which has often occurred (Burwood, 1992).

We have also seen that their change in social class was not simply an economic move, it was also a change in identity. Their stories illuminate the salience of class in people's lives. The change in socioeconomic status they experienced provided many of these individuals with a keen awareness of the largely unspoken rules that accompany different social groups. Renegotiating their working-class heritage in the professional world was a struggle for some participants. The experiences of these men and women suggest that career counselors should not make assumptions about people's class status—whether lower, middle, or upper. Class is an important life variable and should be treated accordingly, in the literature and elsewhere.

The lack of emphasis paid to social class in the vocational psychology literature is also likely to change as more working-class individuals enter the field. As Tinsley (1993) points out, "people focus on that which they find interesting" (p. 108) and

> vocational psychology will begin to make significant progress in investigating issues that are of relevance to minorities and working-class individuals when a significant number of persons who have intrinsic interests in, and insights into, these issues have been educated as psychologists. (p. 110)

As diversity increases in our society and the professional world, these problems may begin to resolve themselves.

Although much more emphasis on social class is needed in the vocational literature, Bandura's social cognitive theory (Lent et al., 1996), with its emphasis on the interaction between the environment and the individual, is a useful framework for understanding the complex influence of social class on career development. This "reciprocal interaction between behavioral, cognitive, and environmental influences" was apparent in these six individual's stories. While the desire for something better and changes in behavior often led to their improved status, many experienced strong reactions, from themselves as well as their families, and experienced what Granfield (1991) has termed "identity ambivalence." The action/reaction element was an important feature for these individuals. The theories of Super (1990) and Holland (1985), which do not emphasize the dynamic, interactive quality of career development or as explicitly address issues of access to resources and social barriers, were not complex enough.

Finally, the stories of these individuals challenge some of the negative stereotypes of lower-class individuals. These biases are apparent in some of the factors to which experts have attributed working-class children's lack of achievement—lack of motivation, poor home values, and little parental support (Burwood, 1992)—and also in Stendler's (1949) finding that children view rich as good and poor as bad. Class discrimination can be particularly damaging because it so often goes hand in hand with minority status, particularly gender and race.

In our achievement-oriented society, discrimination against the lower classes cannot be as cleanly argued against as discrimination against other minority groups. Granfield (1991) points out that "because social class position is frequently seen as the outcome of individual talent and effort, the assignment of stigma to lower socioeconomic groups is not seen as being based on arbitrary evaluation" (pp. 347-348). Although this argument may have some merit, it does not seem relevant to the six individuals considered here or to their families. The lack of effort and talent, which is supposed to accompany the lower-class lifestyle, was not apparent here. I hope that the obvious struggles and hard-won achievements apparent in these six individuals' stories will encourage people, particularly those who work in the vocational psychology field, to reconsider their stereotypes.

11

Career Development of Rural Women and Men

Different Priorities

REBECCA L. CONRAD

There has been little research devoted to understanding the career development of students and young adults from rural environments. The empirical findings available reveal significant differences between rural and nonrural students with respect to education and employment (Cobb, McIntire, & Pratt, 1989; Murray, Keller, McMorran, & Edwards, 1983; Pollard & O'Hare, 1990; U.S. Department of Education, 1994). These differences are important, as are the actual experiences and values of individuals from rural environments, in shaping a clearer understanding of their career development. Therefore, this chapter will briefly review what is known about the career development of rural students. To advance this knowledge, it will portray the life stories of the seven young rural persons (four women and three men) from the two rural schools that participated in the longitudinal study who were most representative of the themes evident in the stories of the 31 rural persons interviewed. Themes that emerge across the individual stories will often illustrate what sets the rural experience apart. I hope the journey through their stories will increase our understanding of career development in rural students and young adults above and beyond the research overview and stimulate ideas for improving career education.

First, let us define what is meant by *rural*. The U.S. Bureau of the Census defines *rural* as areas that are not metropolitan. *Metropolitan* refers to counties with a city of at least 50,000 population and may include other counties having strong social and economic ties to the central county (Sherman, 1992). Therefore, an area is categorized as rural if it is not in a county containing a city of a least 50,000 population or a county having strong social and economic ties to the central county. According to Murray and Keller (1991), rural people constitute approximately one fourth of the U.S. population.

According to these definitions, research has pointed to several differences between rural and nonrural populations. Parents of rural students tend to have less formal education than their metropolitan counterparts; a greater proportion of rural students enroll in a general, noncollege curriculum; a smaller proportion enroll in a college prep curriculum; rural students take fewer math and science courses, obtain less formal education, and earn less income than their nonrural counterparts, on average (Pollard & O'Hare, 1990; U.S. Department of Education, 1994). Despite these clear differences in education and attainment, it is important to note that since the 1980s, rural students have matched the average scores in virtually all national tests (U.S. Department of Education, 1994). Therefore, differences in educational and career attainments cannot be explained by lower abilities and school performance.

Certain attitudes and values are also more common among rural than nonrural students. In 1980, seniors in rural high schools reportedly valued their part-time jobs more than academic course work (Cobb et al., 1989). Also in 1980, significantly fewer rural students than urban and suburban students planned on attaining bachelor's and other advanced degrees, and more planned on acquiring vocational education or had no postsecondary educational plans (U.S. Department of Education, 1994). The literature suggests that educational attainment is influenced by the lower prevalence in rural communities of technical and professional jobs that could otherwise serve as role models and potentially be viewed as occupational goals by young people.

The socioeconomic status of their families also may influence rural students' educational aspirations. An important element of this status is parents' education levels. As mentioned earlier, rural students' parents are more likely to have ended their formal education with high school graduation and less likely to have obtained college degrees than nonrural parents (Pollard & O'Hare, 1990). Furthermore, the value parents place on education conveys a strong message to their children. Rural high school seniors were more likely to report that their fathers were inclined to encourage them to obtain full-time jobs or to attend trade school. Similarly, proportionately fewer rural students thought their mothers were supportive of their full-time college attendance (U.S. Department of Education, 1994). Rural students are more likely to get this message not only from their families but also from their guidance counselors and teachers. The proportion of rural students who received encouragement for college attendance was smaller than that of nonrural students (Cobb et al., 1989).

We can discern several general themes in the quantitative data alone. With respect to formal education, rural students attain less and value it less on average than their nonrural counterparts. They also seem to receive less encouragement for educational pursuits. Further, the data show that rural individuals earn less and experience more unemployment than those from urban and suburban schools (Pollard & O'Hare, 1990).

How do these themes "fit" with the actual experiences of rural students and their families? What other factors are important in these individuals' lives that affect their work lives? What can these other factors tell us about the rural experience that we cannot learn from the lists of statistics? To begin our exploration of these questions, we will look at seven individuals (four women and three men) and see what we can learn from their stories.

I am interested in this group of women and men because, like them, I grew up and attended school in a rural area. The lack of research and the differences between rural and nonrural students that have been shown concern me. Therefore, I am personally invested in expanding my own understanding of these differences as well as contributing that insight to the career development literature. Furthermore, as I explore the stories of the rural men and women, it is important to note that I am expecting to find some of the same educational and career findings that have been shown in the research previously mentioned. However, I am not assuming that a lack of advanced educational or career pursuits comes from a lack of ability or overall motivation. Instead, I am searching for other factors influencing their career lives.

Looking past these statistical differences and at the lives of seven rural people, several themes emerge and will be discussed. First, the low value that is placed on formal education by the men and women in this study is an important factor in the development of their careers and lives. The second theme that emerges pertains to the incredibly meaningful role of work in their lives, despite the fact that most of these individuals do not highly value formal education. Another major factor in their career lives, especially for the women, is the incorporation of family into all decisions that are made. Finally, the life stories of these men and women reveal the need for greater support and encouragement when they make early educational and career decisions in high school.

The Value of Education

As previously mentioned, the men and women in the study do not highly value formal education for its own sake. In fact, of the seven, one man and one woman earned bachelor's degrees. Four others attended community college for various lengths of time, but did not obtain degrees. One man did not attend college, but is currently involved in an educational apprenticeship for his trade. All but the two who earned bachelor's degrees expressed a lack of desire or need for more education; the view that, without a specific plan, education is a waste of time; and the valuing of experience over education.

Elaine, a tracking clerk for a large package delivery company who has succeeded in many aspects of her job, values her community college experience only for the job-related skills it gave her. She explained her view of education:

As far as college, I just took the classes that I knew I needed to get a job. . . . [My older brother] always asks me when I'm going to go back to school and finish up and I just tell him I have no desire to do that and no need to do it. I don't think I ever will.

Norma, whose story was told in Chapter 3, is currently working as a forms design analyst at a large manufacturing company, a position that entails extensive word processing skills. Like Elaine, she attended community college and, also like Elaine, she does not seem to have focused herself on this education: "I felt since I didn't really have a definite plan of what I wanted to do, if I was just going to go to college to take stuff, it wouldn't be worth my time or their [her parents'] money."

Similarly, Matthew, who works as an engineer but has less than two years of college education, could not see how college was worth the expense: "I always tend to be fairly practical and seeing all those years of spending six or eight thousand dollars, whatever it was back then on college, seemed to be just ridiculous."

Matthew also expresses the belief that some people who get a lot of classroom education are at a disadvantage in comparison with someone learning on the job, because they are not learning to apply their knowledge: "Maybe it's because I'm biased in that respect, but I think that experience is probably still better, in a certain sense, experience is still more applicable than education in some instances."

Despite the fact that these men and women had not pursued extensive formal education and were not sure they needed more college for their jobs, some expressed regret about not focusing more on their education in high school. Norma, the forms design analyst who questioned how worthwhile college would have been for her, in retrospect finds some value in college and even shows a hint of regret.

Looking back I think if I had gone off to college, I thought it would probably be a waste of time, not knowing what I wanted to do. But looking back now, I don't think it would have been a waste of time, as far as finding out what I wanted to do. It probably would force you into a field and you would most likely pick one you would be interested in, of course. So I guess it's not as big of waste of time as I thought it would have been.

One of the men also expressed regret about not being serious about school or attending college. Gene is currently working on a five-year apprenticeship needed to obtain his plumber's license. He expressed it in this way:

I always kick myself for not trying harder at school, not trying to set a career goal early in my life. . . . I had no idea of going to college. But now I'm older and I see that a college education would have done me a lot of good.

For these rural women and men, education functions primarily as a pathway to obtain job-related skills. Even the two who earned four-year degrees got those degrees in very practical fields in which the degree led to a specific profession. For example, Nathan got his degree in welding engineering and now works as an engineer. Joyce also has an interesting story. During her senior year of high school, she also attended vocational school. Her high school did not offer a computer course and this was an area of interest for her. She went to the vocational school where she could gain some computer education and experience. However, the vocational track was not challenging or helpful to her, so she pursued her interests further at a community college. Ultimately, she earned a bachelor's degree from a technical institute. This education prepared her for her desired and current career—computer programmer.

As the research presented at the beginning of the chapter indicates, rural students obtain less formal education than their nonrural counterparts. For the young men and women in this study, this information holds true. They did not focus on their formal education but focused on the skills they needed for their future jobs. Some of the attitudes they express help us understand their point of view. It is important that regret about the lack of educational experience in their lives was also revealed by some. In these cases, prior exposure to the potential value of formal education might have expanded the educational options they considered.

Significance of Work in Their Lives

The lack of emphasis rural individuals place on education in no way undermines the valuable role of work in their lives. For both the men and the women included in this study, their jobs hold considerable meaning for them. Work serves several purposes, the most important of which seems to be enjoyment. It also provides a challenge, money, friends, and security. The following section contains the voices of the women and men telling us what an integral part of their lives work is.

Enjoyment seems to be the primary reward of working. Joyce, the computer programmer, got the message that she should find work that she liked from the teacher of a career-related course in high school. She explained how this philosophy affected her choices:

I know the teacher stressed to us to do something that you liked, not make it work. I guess that really hit me. But I guess that motivated me to go to school. And I wanted to do something I liked. And I wanted to enjoy my work. She made me realize that whatever I do, I've got to work for a long time in my life. And it's going to, you know, take up most of my day. And I want to be happy. And I mean that's most important.

Matthew got the same sort of message at a high school career day. People in different professions came to talk about their work, and he recalls a chemist emphasizing how much he enjoyed his job and liked to get out of bed to go to work every morning. Matthew has applied this to his own life.

I really enjoy what I do, I like to get up, but I enjoy—it's not a struggle to come to work and it's not at all a hassle. I can say at this point, at least in life I enjoy what I do and I like to get up. To me that's very important. I just, I've done things that I don't like to do and they make me not want to get up in the morning or regret it the night before. . . . I think it's a privilege, myself, to enjoy what I do and so I feel real privileged to be able to say that especially at this stage of . . . I mean I feel like I'm fairly young to be able to say that.

Through her experience, Norma has also realized the value of enjoying her work. She explained,

The important thing, I don't know, the older I get I just—I think it's important just to be happy. I used to think, I had to make a lot of money to be happy. I don't know, but I think more than anything, it's just, whatever makes you happy I think you should do, because life is too short to do something that you don't enjoy. Even if you don't make a lot of money doing it, I think you should still do it.

When asked what she would want high school students to know about the world of work, she expressed the same message: "I think the most important thing they should learn, choose a career, a job that they would really be interested in and once they get into it, if they're not really interested in it, then that's going to make for a miserable life."

For Elaine, enjoyment of work is also important because she saw her father make himself get up every day and go to a job he hated, and she wanted more than that for herself. In addition to enjoying work, Elaine values several other aspects of her job. She is a people-oriented person and likes interacting with her coworkers. As you may recall, Elaine is a tracking clerk for a large delivery company. She has learned all the jobs in her office and is therefore able to fill in for people on vacation. She enjoys the challenge of learning new tasks on the job. When asked how work fits into her life, she responded,

Well it's a major part, you know, not just the money but, I mean, I actually enjoy going to work because, you know, the friends you have at work and it's a challenge, it's a job. . . . Once you find something you enjoy doing, if it's a pleasant environment to be in—and that's the biggest part of it. And not so much the pay that you get or the benefits, that's just an added bonus.

In addition to valuing work for the enjoyment, challenge, and other characteristics, several comments made by the men and women of this study reveal what a major part of their lives work involves. For example, Nathan, an engineer, puts in whatever time is needed to finish a project even if he is not getting paid for the number of hours worked. When asked how work fits into his life, he responded,

Well, I would say it's definitely entwined in my life, because I definitely take a lot of it home with me. . . . I've always been the type that if you need to work 60 hours, you work 60 hours, even though you are on salary.

Nathan was a hard worker and he demonstrated this in college when some of his courses gave him difficulty. Similarly, Gene, who is mechanically inclined and working toward obtaining his plumber's license, said that work is probably 60% of his life.

Around here, everything I do is related to work. Um, even just mowing the yard, if something happens to my mower I have to fix it. Something goes wrong anywhere, I have to fix it. . . . The other 40% would probably be my fiancée. Gee, that sounds terrible: 60% in my work and 40% for her. But I work five days a week and sometimes six, so it involves a lot of my life.

Finally, Norma expressed the same thought. She said her work as a forms design analyst "takes all my time. It is my life."

Some of the women explain that despite their desire to be with their children, work is still very important. Rachel has two daughters and occasionally does temporary secretarial work. She explained that work is meaningful to her, and likes the fact that it gets her out of the house. She is also looking forward to resuming her full-time work. When asked how important work is in her life, she responded,

Most of the time I would think that it's pretty high priority. Yeah, I think it is pretty high priority. Even with the kids, I'd [don't do it] so much for the money, just for the chance to get out of the house, to get away from dealing with myself. Yeah, you know, it puts it, it helps me to see things better. . . . When both my girls, my youngest is now two and my oldest is five, and when they are both in school, unless I'm home schooling, I would like to go back to work. I really miss working. I've done it since I was in eighth grade in one form or another. And so I like it, I miss it.

Joyce finds her computer programming career very rewarding. However, with her new son, she feels pulled toward being home more. Despite the multiple demands of home and career, she remains in her position. She feels that a part-time position would be ideal, allowing her to stay involved with both of these important aspects of her life.

I do get satisfaction. Um, I do enjoy my job. I guess now it's, you know, sort of hard because I am sort of pulled. I like my work, but you know, now I have this new son and I want to be with him and so now, I mean, I'll always feel that, I think, tugged towards my son. But I'm happy with my job, but you know, I think I'd like to work, if I could work part-time, that would just be perfect. And I think that's something I'll look for.

From the finding that rural men and women seem to value education less or for different purposes, and the fact that they earn less income and experience more unemployment than their nonrural counterparts, we might be tempted to draw the conclusion that they do not value work and do not work as hard. The comments about the role of work, however, reveal that conclusion is far from the reality. The men and women included in this chapter are adamant about the value of work for enjoyment, challenge, social interaction, and money. Furthermore, work occupies a large amount of their time and effort. Even those women feeling a pull toward being home with the children are making work fit into their life plans, because they value that work.

The Fit Between Family and Work

If work is one side of the coin of importance in the lives of these men and women, family is the other. The women, and to a lesser extent the men, make many of their career-related decisions, such as decisions about promotions and relocation, based on how those decisions would affect the family. Not only are the spouses and children considered by these men and women, their parents and siblings also are taken into account. Family in this broader sense shapes career and other aspects of their lives. These men and women seem to form plans that incorporate both family and work in one package.

Elaine, the successful tracking clerk, had the opportunity to move into the management track at work. She and her husband are also currently trying to start a family. Faced with these two important life events, Elaine decided not to go into management at this time. Although work remains an important aspect of her life and she plans to head toward management further down the road, the value she gives family is currently directing her life plan. She expressed her situation and decision in this way:

So, now we're getting serious about it and wanting to, you know, start to have a child or two. And, as far as work, if I were to go into management, that's added pressure and added time away from home. So that's why I wouldn't want to go into that right now. And, plus, you know, the pressures of learning more and, you know, having to be responsible for more things. You need to adjust your mind just on your family at that time.

Joyce is in a similar position. She has a new son and a career as a computer programmer that is very worthwhile. She also finds that opportunities for career advancement have diminished in their importance.

But [with] marriage and now the birth of the child, [career opportunities] are not quite as important, though, you know. I think before, money was a lot more important, but now it's not. Before, like I probably put in extra at work where now it's like well, I want to get home with him. I don't want to work any overtime. I don't want to stay, you know. I can do that tomorrow.

Norma's attitude about fitting family into her life has changed. Her mother stayed at home full-time with Norma and her brothers. Although

Norma appreciated this, she remembers thinking she would never give up her life like that for her children. Norma is worth quoting again on this.

> She stayed home with us. I remember thinking as a kid even, look at her life, she had given up her own life to take care of us. I remember thinking, I'm never going to do that. I felt bad because I thought she had ruined her life to do that, but I enjoyed having her home, and I wouldn't have that any other way. I thought that was great. But I remember thinking if I have kids there is no way that I'm going to give up the rest of my life just to take care of those kids. But as you get older you realize, there's things in life you want and make sacrifices.

When faced with combining family and work, how Norma will incorporate her family's needs into her work life remains to be seen.

The men also talk about changes they have made or will make for their children in their careers and lifestyles. Matthew is married, has one child, and has turned down job advancement partly due to his desire not to travel and be away from his family. Planning for job security has been another factor of importance since the birth of his daughter. Similarly, Gene plans on being home a lot more and planning his lifestyle around his family if he and his fiancée have children.

Career decisions are made not only with children in mind but also parents. Many of the rural individuals consider this broader family environment important. Matthew expressed it best with respect to why he wants to continue living near his parents:

> Just because my family is much more important to me than that. In fact, this—the location of my family, my immediate family, then my mom and dad—those have been a pretty big influence as to where we stay or where we move, things like that. Moving to another state that would be hours and hours away isn't all that good, even though I think it's probably because I'm the oldest child and I've seen my mom and dad aging a little bit, and knowing someday they'll be needing someone to be around for them and feeling that responsibility since I'm the oldest. I guess why that ties in is I don't feel like I need to or want to move a great distance away. . . . I like to think my little girl will have her grandparents close, even though we can't be close to both grandparents, we hope that will happen sometime. I think we in an American society don't have a very big extended family anymore like we used to and it's important for me to have an extended family.

Furthermore, Matthew's devotion to his family is seen in his actions. His father and mother own and manage their own business. At one point, Matthew quit a job he enjoyed to try to join his parents' business.

I wanted to make sure that my father knew that I was proud of him, that what he did was not second class or anything like that and I figured really the only way to do that was to work with him. To tell him that is one thing, but to give up a job and go do it is a little different. . . . My mom works at the business as well. I wanted them to know that I felt it was important, what they did and that I wanted to really try it and make sure that I liked it or that I didn't like it.

Although Matthew did not enjoy this work and eventually reentered his previous job, it was very important for him to show his parents how much they, and what they did, meant to him.

The rural men and women seem to successfully combine their work and family lives. The women generally appear to be making more accommodations in their working lives for their families. This is probably due to modeling the traditional or somewhat traditional roles of their mothers. These mothers stayed at home full-time, worked part-time, or worked full-time for a limited time while raising their children. Despite the greater frequency of compromises often made by the women in the study, both the women and the men seem satisfied with their plans for fitting work and family together.

Need for More Support for Their Careers

In looking back on the educational and career paths they traveled, support or the lack thereof for their careers was a significant factor in the lives of some of the rural men and women. In some cases, traditional beliefs about the roles of men and women create a null environment (Betz & Fitzgerald, 1987; see Chapter 1), which may not be explicitly discouraging, but its lack of direct support yields an overall effect of discouragement for women's academic pursuits. In other cases, the men and women in the study talked about the kind of support they might have benefited from more and what they would like to share with future youth.

Rachel may be one of the people affected by the traditional beliefs in her family. Although she reports that her father was probably disappointed that she dropped out of college, neither she nor her two sisters were particularly encouraged to attend college and obtain degrees. However, her brother, who was the youngest in the family, was expected to pursue a higher education. When asked if it was an expectation for her to go to college, Rachel responded, "Not with my parents. Now with my youngest brother, it has been. It's been very important that he goes. And actually gets a degree. But for us girls, I don't think so." Rachel's parents did not prohibit her from attending college or set any particular obstacles in the way of her educational success; however, neither did they actively support her pursuits, which created a null academic environment.

In addition to the null environment, modeling can be another powerful influence. For example, Elaine's parents were supportive:

They wanted me to go back to school and they had paid for my schooling at community college and, you know, said I could live there at home and not worry about paying bills. They'd give me money I needed.

However, Elaine's father did not want her mother working outside the home and insisted she quit her job when the children came. Her father told her mother that because they had a farm, she was needed for work at home and on the farm. Despite the fact that he did not expect Elaine to stay home and take care of the house, she learned a powerful message from this.

I mean, I think an education is important in most jobs or if you want to have and support a family, you know. For a man maybe it's more important. They need to support their family and maybe if they lose their job for one reason or other they have that to fall back on.

The stories of Rachel and Elaine reveal how a lack of support for a career from family members can be conveyed in some subtle and indirect ways such as these.

More explicitly, Matthew wishes that someone had encouraged him earlier to think about his future and what he wanted to do.

My parents—in one respect they didn't push me to do anything I didn't want to do, as a rule at least. And I really respect that, that's difficult to do. But on the other hand, I sometimes, I wonder if I should've had a little bit more prodding and should've had them tell me, you know, sit me down and say, "Matthew, what are you going to do in ten years? What do you think you'll be doing in twenty years?" I never, I didn't have anybody really do that. . . . It would have been very nice to have somebody, even other than my parents, talk to me about what I wanted to do, and I suppose, I can't think, I can remember talking to some counselors about college and what I wanted to do for college . . . but I can't really remember anybody ever really saying, "What do you want to do? What kind of job do you want to have?"

Similarly, Norma wishes she had have received more guidance. Her parents did always encourage her to do her best, but in retrospect, she sees that some aspect of encouragement was missing: "But as far as guiding me in careers, they really didn't give me the options. They didn't sit down and talk about what I could do." When asked what kind of assistance she needed to plan her career and what future students may need to facilitate their development, Joyce responded,

I think our youth need to be motivated more in self-worth. If you have the self-worth and believe in yourself and have a positive attitude, you're not easily influenced, you know, into maybe having sex or doing drugs or following the wrong people. . . . If you believe in yourself.

Support and guidance is one thing that men and women from a variety of backgrounds, not only the rural individuals, felt they were lacking in high school. Many people express regret that they were not pushed harder in educational and career pursuits. The rural men and women included in this chapter are affected both by subtle messages that convey the lack of support for their efforts and by a more explicit lack of guidance or direction.

Summary and Implications

By tying the research about the education and employment of rural youth presented at the beginning of the chapter to the common themes of seven rural men and women, our previous understanding of their experience can be enriched. First, we heard about why they did not work toward more formal education. The fact that rural youth obtain less formal education than their nonrural counterparts, on average, has been established (U.S. Department of Education, 1994). However, from the stories, we can see that perhaps it is not a matter of valuing education less, but valuing it for different purposes. The men and women of this chapter value education for the job-related skills it provides. Previous research has shown that, in 1980, seniors in rural high schools valued their part-time jobs more than academic courses (Cobb et al., 1989). The themes of both education and work further support this finding. However, perhaps more than was shown in the previous research, work is a major factor of life enjoyment, challenge, and enrichment for theses rural individuals.

The next important factor in their lives and careers is family. The past research does not address how family influences the careers of rural men and women. However, we have seen from their stories that promotions and relocations are turned down and jobs are even quit based on a desire to remain close to the family.

Finally, rural individuals, even more than their nonrural counterparts, suffer from a lack of encouragement for college attendance (Cobb et al., 1989; U.S. Department of Education, 1994). The men and women we have learned about here also mention that they would have benefited from more guidance in defining their interests and formulating future plans. Therefore, support for a greater focus on education, as well as for exploring interests and developing "self-worth" as Joyce puts it, is needed, especially in high school.

The themes and the experiences of these rural women and men attest to the applicability of social learning theory. Role models, or vicarious learning (Bandura, 1978), seem to be an important mechanism in their learning to value education for the job-related skills it provides and to see work as being something they should truly enjoy. Furthermore, these young adults may have had less exposure to a variety of jobs that could have otherwise served as occupational role models. Traditional gender roles and sex role socialization (Astin, 1984; Farmer, 1978) have had a powerful impact on both the men and the women discussed in this chapter. The roles they learned influenced how they fit their families and working lives together. Ultimately, what these people learned in their families and society about who they were, and, in turn, the way they influenced their families and environments, comes together to form the complex career paths they followed.

Part IV

Complex Interplay of Career and Family Roles

12

Career Development in the Context of Family Experiences

JANICE H. ALTMAN

There has been little research directed toward the understanding of the impact of family on career development (Schulenberg, Vondracek, & Crouter, 1984). One area that has been particularly ignored is the effect of family inter- actions. This chapter will focus on how *family of origin* relationships and ex- periences influenced the *process* of career development for our interviewees.

Some interviewees talked about their families of origin a great deal, and family was clearly a dominant influence in their career process. The influence of family for some was direct and focused on career (i.e., support for or con- flict about career choice); for others, it was indirect yet pervasive (e.g., the need to survive or escape family chaos). Our interviewees talked about both negative and positive influences of growing up in their families, including support and guidance (or lack thereof), family structure and relationships, significant family members, and dysfunctional environments. With the words of our participants, I will illustrate each of these influences. Although I am drawing themes from all 21 interviews that I personally conducted, this chap- ter will focus on the stories of Darlene, Tad, Wendy, Mathew, Miguel, Terry, Vanessa, and Jim, supplemented by a few brief quotes from others. All names used are purely fictitious, and some other details have been changed to ensure the anonymity of our interviewees. The themes presented in this chapter arose from the interviews with *all* participants, but I chose to use illustrations only from those whom I knew personally through my inter- views.

I would like to share some of my own personal experiences and perspec- tives so that the reader may gain some understanding of my subjectivity. As the former founder/director of a parent support center, and as a parent, I have been very interested in and involved with families, child rearing, and parent- ing issues. I also have a deep commitment to prevention efforts, and this book is particularly meaningful to me for its potential to help young women de- velop careers that are relevant and rewarding. My clinical training in graduate school introduced me to family systems theory, which continues to strongly influence my conceptualization of the problems that individuals encounter (in both their work and their personal lives). I believe my own career path has been affected by low self-efficacy, and my experience of struggling with this issue has provided me with insight into the lives of women whose choices are inhibited by barriers of various kinds. My roots in counseling psychology have influenced me in numerous ways, including recognizing the importance of career issues, forming a holistic view of a person, using a contextual perspective, appreciating differences, emphasizing wellness, and maximizing people's potential.

Support

One of the most common themes that arose in talking with our interviewees about their families was the concept of support or guidance (Blustein, Prezioso, & Schultheiss, 1995). Some participants got a lot of support from their families while others were lacking in support. What do they mean by *support*? Sometimes they referred to specific career or educational guidance and suggestions. For example, Darlene describes how her thinking about careers was stimulated early by her parents; she says, "My parents were very supportive when I was a kid. They would always offer suggestions, give me books to read."

Darlene's family's participation in career planning was simply a part of ongoing family life: "My dad would always take us on family vacations to a place that had some historical significance. And it was always fun."

In this very natural and comfortable way, career planning started long before it was time for Darlene to begin making some career decisions as a young adult. Sometimes direct assistance and specific suggestions are needed in late adolescence as well, but these do not substitute for the early family experiences that provide support for later career planning. Both women and men talked about how their ongoing family life had an important influence on their career paths; Tad's story illustrates this well. Tad was a man who as a child wanted a career in banking; he had good math skills and loved working with people. Tad's parents had wanted to get divorced for as long as he can remember, but they told the children that they would wait until the children were grown. Tad spent weekends and summers with his grandparents, who lived nearby, and they met his needs for a supportive, cohesive, stable family. He was very fond of his grandmother, who became a significant influence in his life as well as a role model. Tad describes how he first got the idea to work in a bank:

> I always liked going into the bank where my Grandmother worked. It was so impressive—the old bank with the big ceiling and the pictures and the paintings. And . . . it just smelled, you know how money smells? And it just had that smell, and then I saw Grandma, and so it was happy. I guess subconsciously it felt like this was a fun place to be. And so I suppose that was one of the reasons why I wanted to go that direction.

Tad's experience is a good illustration of Blustein et al.'s (1995) view of the importance of "the relational context in career-development" (p. 418).

Some families participated in more direct and intentional ways, even early in the child's career planning process, with varying results. For the child who experienced their parents' suggestion as a good fit, the early assistance provided strong identity formation and consistent support for a rigorously demanding career. In addition, research has shown that connectedness between parent and adolescent "facilitates the kind of risk-taking and exploration that is central to the developmental tasks of identity formation and career development" (Blustein et al., 1995, p. 420). Linda's description is a good example:

> As I said, for me it was a very simple decision process. I was exposed to medicine early on during my childhood. I knew exactly what I wanted to do, medicine. In fact, I also knew I wanted to be a surgeon and that kind of ended up being very consistent and despite minor negative influences, my father's support really helped me so that I ended up achieving what I wanted to do.

But for Wendy, who decided *not* to go into the profession defined for her when she was young, the *specific* guidance was experienced as intense pressure, which led to deep and long-standing conflict with her father.

> I can remember when I was 5 years old, my father saying that when I grew older I was going to be a doctor. And it wasn't like you see on *Sesame Street*—some people are plumbers, some people are electricians . . . It was always—you are going to be a *doctor*. That was just the way it *always* was.

And then in high school,

> I had a battle with my father because I told him I wanted to go into Journalism and not medicine. And he said, "What are you gonna waste your time doing that for? You are never going to make it" . . . My father even told me, "If you go into Journalism, you will pay for your schooling on your own. I won't help you. I won't support you."

This example shows how the *lack* of support from a parent, in the form of conflict, can be very difficult. Fortunately, Wendy knew very clearly what she wanted, and she learned to persevere through every obstacle to achieve her goals. At the time of the interview, she was very satisfied and successful in her chosen profession.

Conversely, several interviewees who floundered in their career paths complained about the *absence* of any such guidance from their families. Mathew, introduced in Chapter 11, ultimately settled into a science career that matched his interests, but he floundered through high school, did not stay with college, and in his early twenties had a string of jobs. He reflects on high school with regret. Like Wendy, Mathew's story illustrates *lack* of family support, but without the conflict. He perceived that nobody pushed or encouraged him in high school, so he didn't get the guidance he needed.

I didn't take the advanced math courses that a lot of people took, and I didn't take any of the science classes that were beyond what was required. . . . I didn't do much that was beyond what was required. At this point I know I should have done that; I should have applied myself more. No one was really prodding me or pushing me to do some of the more difficult things, so I could get by pretty easily by getting Bs. . . . Nobody ever really pushed me. . . . My parents encouraged me to do some things, but not anything that would really stretch me as a person I guess. And I really honestly believe that they didn't want to push me to do something that I didn't want to do, but almost to the point where I didn't do *anything* because I didn't have anybody pushing me.

Mathew was shy and hesitant to try anything, so he concluded from this experience of *not* being pushed that he had little value and it didn't really matter whether he worked hard or not. What might have been helpful for him at the time was for someone to help him set goals for the future, to specifically ask him what he would be doing in 10 years. Mathew's thoughts bear repeating:

I never really thought of what kind of job I would like to do in that very specific sense. I thought about different things of what it might be fun to do but never really, specifically what I'd like to do for 8 hours a day for the next 30 years or whatever. I wonder . . . if someone had sat me down and said, "Mathew, what are you going to *do* in 10 years?" I didn't have anybody really do that.

Although he still has self-doubts, Mathew finally found his place in the work world in a hands-on job with built-in goals and immediate feedback. He cares about doing his best and draws a sense of accomplishment from his work.

With mechanical design or engineering, I could see the goal and all I had to figure out was how to get there. . . . The thing that kept me going was that there was a goal. There were parameters, guidelines which I could judge how good something was. A product either works or it doesn't. I was never good at judging those kind of things. I'm a very goal-oriented person, and I need to have some pretty well-defined objectives. That's what I like about [my job].

For Mathew, feeling supported includes being motivated as well as having specific ideas and suggestions and well-defined goals. It is important here to make the distinction between feeling loved by one's parents and feeling supported by them. It is not uncommon for our interviewees to report good relationships with their parents and feeling loved, but also to have unmet needs for support, encouragement, and/or guidance. Our participants' stories highlight what an important role the parents play in their children's developing career identities.

Most of our interviewees are *still* quite concerned, even as adults, with how their parents feel about their career decisions. They want their parents to be proud of them, and they look for signs of interest and involvement. Again, this underscores the important influence of the family throughout the process of career choice and development. For example, Tad, at age 30, still looks at himself through his father's eyes:

Oh yeah, he is *very very very* proud of me now, very proud. It is nice. It is a good feeling to know that that person, who raised you and was disappointed by you so many times, is actually so proud of you. That is a good feeling. You know, to see the smile on his face when he introduces you. It is like, "Wow! The kid is all right!"

Other participants as well commented on the continuing support they receive from their parents even now, in their late twenties, and how much it means to them. This example is from Darlene:

Dad tries to keep up on things that are happening in all the different fields [that his children are in]. He's always asking me if I've read such and such articles in the *Tribune* and tries discussing them with me. He tries to participate, and he does it with everybody.

For Wendy, the woman who defied her father's wish for her to be a doctor and forged a bright, successful career on her own, his subsequent support carried tremendous meaning:

It is *so* different now. For the last few years he's been like my biggest supporter, but he never *said* anything to me. He never said, "I'm proud of you."

Then one time recently he finally told me. You know I've never told you this, but of all my children I'm proudest of you. And I think my heart broke! Because he finally said he was proud. He finally said that he was wrong.

Young people feel supported by their parents when they know their parents are proud of their accomplishments. They want to hear it from their parents directly, and it *still* matters to them as adults. The importance of a *current* social network that provides felt security is consistent with attachment theory (Bowlby, 1982) and with social learning theory (Bandura, 1986).

Sibling Influence and Family Structure

Next we'll focus on the influences of family structure on careers; by *structure,* I mean the number of children, age order and spacing, loss/addition of a family member, shifts in living arrangements, marital status, and so on. Our interviewees came from all kinds of families, and some of them talked about the connections they experienced between the makeup of their family, relationships between family members, and their career process. This chapter is limited to discussing *one* of the most striking themes: the role of siblings and sibling relationships. Quite often siblings provided challenge and competition for one another. For example, for Susan, the competition was made explicit:

My sister is two years younger than I am but she skipped a grade in elementary school. She used to tease me and say, "I made a double, I'm going to skip again, I'm going to pass you up."

In other cases, the challenges supplied by siblings were completely unintentional. Younger children often try to follow in the footsteps of their older siblings but may experience undue pressure when their siblings excel. Wendy said,

Both of my older siblings were straight A students, and both were at the top of their class. Both of them went to prestigious universities and were at on the top of their class. And I knew that when I went to college I would also have to be on the Dean's List, or else there would be problems. I mean, there was always a lot of pressure.

Family experiences with siblings can begin to influence one's career choice process very early on. Math self-efficacy, an important variable in women's career development, is affected by comparisons with one's peers. Wendy's math self-efficacy was boosted by her performance in math as well as by feedback from her classmates, but simultaneously torn down by measuring her perceived ability against her older sisters. She ultimately chose a career that did not involve math.

> I was very good in my classes in math, you know. I did very well in math. All the other kids always said, "What did you get for this one?" You know, always. But when I compared myself to my brothers and sisters I knew I wasn't good in math. I think I've done that a lot. Too much in my life.

As a child, Wendy concluded that she would never measure up to the sister who was several years older, and she subsequently decided to pursue a completely different career path despite formidable obstacles. In this story, she dramatically describes an incident that affected her early thoughts about careers:

> When I was a kid my neighbor fell on some ice and broke her hip. She was lying on the ground, and it was an emergency situation. I walked by with my sister and we saw her there, and I felt panic stricken. "Oh my God she's really hurt." My sister was cool as a cucumber. She took off her coat, put it over her, and said, "Go call the ambulance." I'm running back to the house going, "Oh my God, what's the ambulance number, what's her name?" And I knew then I wasn't cut out for that kind of thing. There was some blood near her head, and that just emphasized to me that she was in pain, and I just hated that look on her face. I hated the sight of her in pain. That really drove things home to me early on. My sister, on the other hand, knew everything down to the question of whether or not to move her. And she sat with her, and talked to her, and calmed her down.

Wendy experienced pressure, suffered self-doubt, and was clearly influenced by her siblings. It is not actually possible to judge whether these experiences were ultimately positive or negative influences, but it is evident that they affected her career process in many ways. Although she herself did not make the connection to the impact of these early competition-laden experiences, she commented during the interview on the importance of having a competitive spirit to survive and succeed in her profession. Surely her experiences with her siblings helped to prepare her for the challenges she now faces:

> I know a lot of people who are good at what they do—strong skills. But a lot of times it comes down to who you know, how persistent you are, how *competitive* you are, and just plain how much you are willing to work. Because I'm in an extremely competitive field. It's very competitive! . . . I hate

to say it, but sometimes you never know who is gonna stab you in the back. I have developed a very thick skin.

Miguel, the oldest of four in a Hispanic American family, specifically noted the *benefits* to his career that resulted from his lifelong competition with his younger brother. For both Miguel and his brother, their competition stimulated greater effort and achievement:

The reason for us always overshooting our goals is the fact that we've always been in competition with each other. I mean I can think down to day one playing stupid games like Hang on Harvey. We would always, I mean literally, bicker to the end. Before the game was put away, he wanted to be the one who was able to say, "Oh I beat you last." You know? [But] that sense of competitiveness . . . was always a driving force for the both of us, both academically and in sports, as well as in other things. We kind of pushed each other along. . . . And it's good competition, because obviously we strive for the best. We've served as a kind of reality check for each other. Because I think that's how we're able to measure our progress is in respect to one another, comparing ourselves to each other. I think that's what keeps us going.

However, there was also a cost for Miguel. He was motivated to succeed, and grew impatient with a science career that didn't provide the immediate rewards that would allow him to compete successfully with his brother (who was getting an M.B.A. from a top-rated university). Miguel recently changed positions within his company, crossing over from a technical job in product development to sales and marketing to "get on the fast track to senior management." The ultimate outcome of this choice remains unknown until the future. Sibling competition serves a seemingly beneficial role of encouraging one to do one's best, but may also motivate some unwise choices. For example, is this move one that Miguel will later regret? Will he be more satisfied in a marketing management career than a technical one? Even if there is a difference in the inherent satisfaction these careers would provide for him, only Miguel can decide which he values most highly—satisfaction or economic success. Because these issues are so complex, it is impossible to objectively judge the outcomes.

Just as one's environment and relationships play a role in the shaping and development of personality traits, sibling and other relationships contribute to one's unfolding career identity. Young people learn about who they are, as well as who they are not, in the context of their relationships with their family members and others. For example, Wendy was aware of being different than her siblings, and she learned to define herself in contrast to the people close to her. She then applied this self-knowledge to the world of work in identifying a career that would fit her own unique personality:

Unlike my other family members, I'm very people oriented. I really love my work where I get to meet people and talk to them. I really do love working with people, and I've always gotten along with people better, say, than other people in my family.

Although we did not make a direct comparison of women with siblings to those without siblings, the things we learned from our interviewees may prompt one to ask such questions. My sense is that siblings are simply very handy peers, and it may be easier for a young girl to confront questions about her identity by comparing herself with other young people than with her parents.

In addition to providing challenge and comparison, as well as a context for identity formation, we learned that siblings also serve other roles that may facilitate (or inhibit) career development. For example, Miguel's younger brother literally followed in his footsteps. Miguel passed on his first summer job to his brother. They attended the same Catholic high school, and his brother also followed him to the same college. In this way, older children may offer access to important resources (information, job offers, networking contacts) and other advantages to their siblings. Older children often adopt a nurturing role toward their younger cohorts as well, trying to support, encourage, or motivate them in their educational and career pursuits. Further research is indicated to examine the complex interrelationships of siblings with career development processes. Another interesting question for further research is to study how parents might intervene on behalf of their children to buffer them from negative influences and expose them to positive ones.

Stressful Family Environments

In some families, certain realities prevailed (i.e., poor economic conditions, death of a parent, parental alcoholism, child abuse, marital instability, or teenage pregnancy) that impinged on the child's career development in some way. The remainder of this chapter examines the family lives of some of our interviewees and the ways in which their careers were affected. My intent is to be descriptive, not explanatory, about the influences of stressful, chaotic, or dysfunctional family environments. Again, we may turn to attachment theory to understand these influences. A basic premise of attachment theory is that close affectional ties that provide individuals with the experience of felt security reduce anxiety, and tend to promote exploration and facilitate the career development process by providing a secure base (Blustein et al., 1995). Without felt security or a secure base to return to, one's career development may be disrupted. Bandura has also demonstrated that self-efficacy, whether learned in the home or the larger community, provides a person with the necessary self-confidence to initiate new behaviors (Bandura, 1986). An example of the negative effect of a dysfunctional family environment is the story of a young woman, Terry, whose stepfather was an alcoholic.

My mom and stepdad, they—and I really feel sorry for them because I know they can be good people, because I've seen them when they weren't drinking. That's what influenced my whole life.

All of her energy was focused on surviving her circumstances and finding an escape. She describes her high school experiences:

[One time] the day before the test my stepfather got drunk and [had an accident with the Jeep]. It had a fiberglass top on it. He drove holding onto the fiberglass top . . . [but then] the top blew off and he couldn't hold on to it any more and it was lying in the middle of the road. He called me to come and get him, and the police eventually came, you know. We had to talk to the police and all these things. . . . I spent the next day at the hospital. . . . It just made it more difficult to do anything. My stepdad used to encourage me to skip school. . . . He wouldn't understand that I've got other things that I had to do [than] to make lunch for them. No big deal—it was just sandwiches, beer, and groceries. I know I missed a lot of school 'cause of my stepdad.

I did not have anybody in high school that I could have talked to about family. A lot of my friends didn't even know [my parents] drank as much as they did until years later when I would mention it. [Then] they'd say, "I remember you coming up, being upset over this or that or something happening; you would never let us come over, you wouldn't let us talk about it, you would cancel things at the last minute. We didn't know what was going on." But there is . . . I guess I've got the need to protect myself.

For the child who has a career focus, energy may be funneled in that direction. But Terry had little chance to dream or discover her own talents. She also believes that she never would have excelled in college because her experience consisted of parties and drinking. In the absence of a "quick career," she married to get away from home. She explains her priorities:

I did not picture myself being a housewife and mother at the age I am. That wasn't important. I didn't want to be what my mother was. I wanted to be able to get away from that situation and I thought the only way I could do it was to come across a career real quick and get out. You know, just leave. I could not be at home much. I didn't feel like I had any counselors at school that I could talk to. I really didn't know what I wanted to do or what I was good at.

So Terry married young and worked hard to create a secure family life, with great success. She is a survivor, but now that she is no longer consumed by her need to escape, she is searching for a career focus. She was floundering when we interviewed her, like many of her peers did when they were in high school or starting college. She has since reported that she went back to college, earned an A.A. degree in interior design, and is currently employed in that line of work. She is very happy with this turn of events.

Another example is Vanessa, described in Chapter 3, whose family life was simply too complicated and full of obstacles for her career to get off to a good start. Vanessa is a Hispanic woman who lived in a fairly traditional American household as a child, but her mother died from a terminal illness when she was 13 and her adolescence was full of turbulence and conflict with her father. She had to leave school at the end of her sophomore year when she became pregnant (at age 16). When she tried to resume high school a year later, the Catholic school that she previously attended would not admit her, so for various reasons she ended up attending three different high schools. She courageously attempted college at a prestigious university, but dropped out after only one semester. It was simply too hard to manage school along with a preschooler and a job, and she felt indebted to her father who supported her and her child. Vanessa is now 29 years old, divorced, earns a meager income in a dead-end clerical job, and is the sole supporter of two children. She still hopes to work with computers, but a college degree remains elusive, and her life continues to be survival oriented. She doesn't talk about what she'd *like* in a job; instead, she remains focused on what she so desperately needs—good pay and benefits, stability. Here is what she said when I asked her what life would be like if she had a magic wand to change *anything*:

I would still want to work. I would want a good paying job to take care of my family, make sure that I have enough money for them to go to college. Not much would change . . . just that I would have the good paying job, and I would know how to do everything the job required.

Vanessa is a remarkably strong, enthusiastic, upbeat woman who had little opportunity to rise above her circumstances. I was struck by her limited, yet realistic perspective about the world of work. Her options had been constricted long before by a chain of events that continue to direct her life.

Another example is a young white man, Jim, whose mother and father each remarried twice during his childhood. His family moved at least 11 times, and he was clearly affected by all the disruption and instability. Jim simply has had trouble putting his life together. Personality and motivation difficulties, along with self-doubt, have plagued his work history as well as his personal life. Several events in recent years have contributed to a new outlook on life: marriage, the birth of a child, the death of a close friend, and severe injuries from an accident. He has just made a radical career change from production to sales and is finally motivated and making progress toward a degree in his third attempt at community college.

In sharing their difficult childhood struggles, Vanessa and Jim, as well as other interviewees, mentioned someone who was a significant positive influence in their lives. Quite often, this person was an extended family member, such as a grandparent or aunt, who was always there for them or supported them in a time of need. These relatives provided a refuge for children who needed to get out of their homes or a buffer from chaotic circumstances. Blustein et al. (1995) suggested that felt security may be derived from the availability of other attachment figures in one's current life. Vanessa felt that when she got pregnant in high school, her aunt helped her turn her life around. Her aunt took her in, offered to raise the baby if needed, persuaded Vanessa to get group counseling with other pregnant teens, and helped her work through her anger toward her father so she was able to finish high school. This was a good example of how extended family members served as significant sources of support for young people when their families were in crisis. For Jim, it was his grandmother who provided substantial emotional support as he lived through one family crisis after another. Linda, who suffered family trauma, puts into words here what we heard over and over again from our interviewees:

My grandma has a big heart. She loves you unconditionally. Grandma was very helpful because when she came to live with us, my sister and I were probably very very withdrawn from everything, just having been through the divorce and all that. She kinda opened us up and helped us out a little bit. . . . It's not so much what she did. It's that she always loved us no matter how much we tried to push her away.

Blustein et al. (1995) proposed that attachment theory, largely based on the theoretical premises of Bowlby (1982) and Ainsworth (1989), may serve as an organizing framework for many of the "self" and "relational" perspectives that have been applied to career development in various ways. An underlying assumption of attachment theory is that individuals are optimally prepared for developmental tasks (such as the career development process) when they experience "felt security" in their family and other relationships. Many of the highlights of attachment theory, in its application to career development, are particularly relevant to this topic of the influence of families. For example, attachment theory focuses on the real-life experiences of individuals and acknowledges the contribution of *early* childhood experiences but also "highlights the importance of more recent events and relationships" (p. 418). Similarly, social learning theory views early experiences as a basis for developing career self-efficacy and interests as well as career goals and choices throughout life (Lent et al., 1996).

The stories from these interviewees about the support they did or did not receive from their parents may shed some light on the conflicting findings of researchers (O'Brien, 1993; Blustein et al., 1995) about the effects of a close connectedness between parent and adolescent. O'Brien found that high school women's attachment to mother was related to career decision-making self-efficacy, corroborating the Blustein et al. findings, but that attachment also predicted incongruent career choices. Perhaps there is an optimal level of connectedness that provides adequate resources for the necessary career exploration and risk taking but also facilitates the separation-individuation process for young women. Attachment theory is also very useful in understanding the negative impact of dysfunctional family environments and the counterbalancing effects of significant family members or other positive relationships. It seems that this aspect of attachment theory can be placed within a social learning framework (Bandura, 1986).

Summary and Implications

In conclusion, I think that these stories have important implications for career counseling. The big message is that family experiences may be quite relevant to a person's career development and should not be ignored. In some cases, the career process may be completely inhibited by other family stressors, and counseling that addresses these more personal issues is needed before any career interventions can be successfully implemented. But with all clients, it seems important to ask about messages they received in their families about career choice, the role of work in one's life, and sex role expectations. Once these messages are uncovered, then it may be possible to confront any beliefs that may inhibit the client's career path and personal growth and development. Another level of intervention, primary prevention efforts that target parents and/or children, also may be effective, for example, in moderating any negative impact of siblings and peers. Further research is suggested to examine these complex relationships as well as the effectiveness of counseling and other interventions.

I have focused on the *past* influences of the family of origin, particularly what happens when support is missing, how siblings and dysfunctional environments affect the career process, and extended family members who made a significant difference. It is important to remember that family of origin continues to have an influence throughout the life span. In addition, when a person starts his or her own family, experiences from the past are often triggered and rehashed. This is yet another way in which the family of origin continues to have an impact. Lenore Tipping in Chapter 13 explores the influences of one's present family (i.e., spouse, children). Often, current family experiences present learning opportunities and promote the possibility of new understandings about family of origin experiences. It is likely that women will tend to seek counseling at these junctures, and a sensitive, informed response is indicated to help them understand the meaning of these experiences in their lives and free them to make new choices for their future.

13

Work and Family Roles

Finding a New Equilibrium

LENORE M. TIPPING

Young people in beginning career and family stages are both enabled by recent societal changes and inhibited by residual gender role stereotypes. In this transitional situation, they face both challenges and opportunities.

The first of their two-part challenge is to blend the old and the new, sifting through both inherited gender role information and current observations—deciding what to reject and what to retain—to discern their personal role values.

Second, they must learn to structure their work and family roles in a comfortable yet potentially fulfilling manner so as to establish role equilibrium. This second challenge is also their opportunity.

Social learning theory, emphasizing the social origins of behavior, the significance of cognitive processes, and the construct of self-efficacy (Bandura, 1977b, 1982; Farmer, 1985; Hackett & Betz, 1981), provides a valuable framework for understanding how these young women and men came to perceive and enact their work and family roles.

I personally interviewed all of the 24 women and men who contributed to the findings presented here as part of our career motivation and achievement study. The interaction of work and family roles emerged early in our study as a significant topic deserving further, in-depth analysis. To guide this further analysis, I asked the question: "How do women and men in beginning career and family stages perceive their family and work roles?"

Of the 24 persons contributing to this chapter, 15 were women and 9 were men. They ranged in age from 27 to 30 at the time of the interviews. One third were parents, one third were married with no children, and one third were unmarried with no children. All were engaged in paid employment, with all but one working full-time. The majority (19) had some college education, with 10 holding bachelor's degrees and an additional 2 holding master's degrees. Of those who attended college, most were first-generation college students.

All but three of the participants were Caucasian. Juanita and Norman were of Mexican descent and Paul was part Native American and part Filipino.

Participants came from urban, rural, and suburban high schools. They represented a rather narrow socioeconomic strata, with predominantly middle-class and some lower-middle-class families of origin.

Given that qualitative research is experienced through the lens of the researcher, a description of my personal subjectivity will be helpful to readers. As a professional woman, wife of a role-sharing husband, and mother of two preadolescent sons, I understand firsthand the issues involved in combining home and family roles. I experienced combining graduate school and half-time work with mothering infants. I also experienced the need to modify work and school roles when necessary for personal well-being, without losing sight of career goals. I strongly value both family and career, and I support women's needs both to combine the two roles and to fully enjoy each role. I believe this can be done without detriment to either role, but not without some compromise and sacrifice. These experiences and values likely color my interpretations of my interviewees' stories.

I will describe the findings of this study in three main sections: participants' perceptions of their work roles, perceptions of family roles, and views related to combining work and family roles. A final section suggests interventions for counseling.

Perceptions of Work

These women and men inherited from their parents some very clear attitudes and beliefs about work. Some of these they have accepted and have incorporated into their own work role behavior. Other beliefs seemed more open to challenge and to modification.

Three major perceptions about work emerged from the interview data: (a) the philosophical view of work as "earning one's keep," (b) work as a source of identity and/or fulfillment, and (c) work viewed as one's responsibility in providing for family (the breadwinner role).

Work as Earning One's Keep

The participants' parents, born either during or immediately after this country's Great Depression, were guided in their work by a need for job security and by a sense of pride in their ability to earn a living. An added dynamic was that the parents of Chad, Donald, Juanita, and Norman were immigrants to the United States from Ireland, Italy, and Mexico, and had built their lives here through hard work and sacrifice. The participants observed, and were influenced by, these work values and beliefs.

Cindy described this parental influence:

My Dad was a workaholic and to this day he still is. . . . I know the value of a dollar bill. . . . That is one thing I will say for my parents—they raised us to make us realize where money comes from and how much there is and what you do when you don't have it. I really do appreciate my parents for that.

The only way I'm going to get what I have is by working for it, and when I get it, it makes me feel proud to know that I worked for it. Because I don't want anything given to me.

Steve has adopted his father's view of job security: "My Dad worked at the same place for I think 42 years. And I foresee myself working where I am now for the rest of my life."

Donald, whose father had immigrated from Italy, described work expectations that reflected his father's example:

My Dad never missed a day of work. He never missed a day of work in his life. And that's—I think it went out to all of us, because we are all the same way, all four of us are. You know, I have never missed a day of work. . . . I have never missed a day of school.

Let's put it this way: If I lose a customer, it's like I have nightmares at night, you know, "What did I do wrong?" But then again it's like learning from mistakes, because when I lost a customer, I said, I'm not going to do that again. I'm going to go about it a different way.

Elaine's strong sense of work responsibility was, she believes, inherited from her mother:

It must be from my Mom. I mean, she's the hard worker at home, as far as keeping everything organized. They live on a small farm and she takes care of the animals and the yard and stuff like that, so I guess I would have to say it comes from her.

Although these young people seemed to accept their parents' work ethic, they also believed they faced different economic challenges than did their parents. In particular, they noted the high cost of housing, the difficulty of becoming established financially, and the need for two family incomes.

Both women and men spoke with some nostalgia of the days when one partner's job could support a family, but there were differences in their thoughts about the need for two incomes. Women, although clearly valuing the work role in their lives, also knew they lacked choice about whether or not to work outside the home. Men were aware of the necessity of their wives' incomes and seemed to regret their own inability to carry the ball alone, as their fathers had done. Zena's statement summarizes the group perceptions: "There's just no way, in this day and age, unless you marry a Howard Hughes type person, there's no way that two people cannot work."

Paul's perceptions reflect the frustration felt by many:

People used to be able to come out of high school and find these easy jobs and buy a house and settle down, and you can't do that any more. I mean, after college, to get your career to take off by the time you're 30. . . . I mean if you look at the whole society, it takes two incomes nowadays. Child care, that's a big booming business . . . because both people have to work in order to make it. You can't afford a house, no one can buy a house nowadays on one income unless you're really doing fantastic. I mean, how many people are making, you know, $100,000 a year?

While perceiving greater economic pressure than their parents had, many participants also noted their upward mobility. Fred knew his economic potential exceeded his father's:

My father was happy. He was surprised that I got the job I did. . . . My first job was more than what he was making, you know. He knows I've got a lot more potential. He's never said it, but I can see it.

In summary, the work philosophy of these men and women reflects both observational learning from parents and current economic realities (Bandura, 1982). Although expecting to be upwardly mobile, they also view the dual-career lifestyle as a necessity.

Work as a Source of Fulfillment and Identity

Fulfillment and identity are different but related concepts apparent in the participants' perceptions of their work roles. Fulfillment as described here denotes the psychological rewards gained from work, including recognition, challenge, a sense of accomplishment, enjoyment and satisfaction, self-efficacy, and self-esteem. Identity as described here is a broader, more fundamental concept, encompassing the workers' images of who they are.

An interesting finding is that although participants' working parents gained a large portion of their identity through their work roles, they often did not feel fulfilled in their work. Particularly significant here is the influence of fathers who, with concern for job security superseding their desire for job satisfaction, got up every morning and went to work at jobs they hated, sometimes for 20 or 30 years.

Elaine expressed astonishment at her father's persistence in an unfulfilling job:

And you also notice, like my Dad who hated, who had nothing nice to say about his job . . . I mean he went to work everyday, didn't call in sick, but the fact of knowing that he did not enjoy what he's been doing for 20 years, and will be doing for the rest of his life, just did not make any sense to me.

I don't think that I could do it. . . . If I hadn't liked my job I probably would have given it up by now, even though the pay is good.

Fred's career aspirations were influenced by his father's frustration and lack of job satisfaction:

[My father] has never been satisfied with what he's doing. He's been cooking for all his life, but he still can't become a chef because he doesn't have that degree.

I could see he was stagnant, even early on. He didn't like what he was doing and, I mean, it just kind of affected me to think to myself, "Well, I don't want to get into a dead-end situation where I have no place left to go."

Vicarious experience through parents (Bandura, 1982), that is, observing their persistence in unenjoyable, dead-end jobs for financial security, and noting the negative consequences to parents' well-being, influenced both the career self-efficacy and the aspirations of these young people. They tended to be more planful and selective in their career choices than were their parents, often gaining additional education to increase their options.

Mothers taught very powerful lessons about both work fulfillment and identity. Both women and men noted their mothers' fulfillment from their parent role, but also noted a lack of fulfillment as the demands of parenting decreased. In addition, some regretted their mothers' lack of positive work identity.

Cindy reflected on her mother's life as a homemaker:

At the time, you did nothing but stay home and raise your kids. That's how [my mother] was brought up and I know she doesn't regret it, but I know now that the kids are gone and . . . I think she feels inferior at times, and feels like she's not capable . . . but that's not what you did back then.

Her number one goal was for us kids to get an education. And she's happy that I have my degree . . . just happy to know that it's there and that it can be of use to me. And I think there's just times that she wished she had that opportunity.

Barbara noted the change in her mother's self-image over time:

[My mother] never worked when we were growing up, when she was raising us . . . and when they ended up getting separated she had gone to work, which was something that she didn't do for a real long, long time. . . . She started out being a wimpy lady and went to being really, really tough.

My Dad was the king of the house. We always joked my Dad had the Fred Flintstone syndrome, you know, when he came home he wanted dinner on the table within five minutes, that type of thing. . . . I think I'd want my husband to respect me more than she ever got respected. Back then she never fought for what she wanted. She never fought for what she believed in, I don't think. She never stood up for herself. . . . Towards the end, that's when she finally started to get tough and started to fight back, like "I'm not going to do this." And she didn't, and she had two kids that lived at home, and it was tough on her.

Fred's awareness of his mothers' identity struggles have led him to think more about his own gender role attitudes:

My mother was a homemaker by choice. I mean, she decided not to go to college and I was a big reason for that. I don't know if she regrets it. I think she does a little bit. Because she could do a lot more. She feels that she could be doing a lot more. . . .

She was fresh out of high school. In 1965, I know the flower movement was coming up and all that stuff, and I think there was a lot of choices that she passed up. . . . I think she did it because she felt being a housewife was the right thing to do at the time. It was still basically a big image. And there's nothing wrong—there was nothing wrong with it at the time.

Although research in women's career development consistently documents the positive influence of working mothers in their daughters' career success (e.g., Betz, 1993; Hoffman, 1986), the present findings suggest the influence of nonworking mothers as well, both through observation and through mother-daughter communication. Further, the experiences of nonworking mothers tended to influence nontraditional gender role attitudes in their sons.

In summary, women and men learned about the importance of work fulfillment and identity by observing parental role models, including fathers persisting in secure but unsatisfying work and mothers who struggled with negative self-concepts during their empty nest stage. A particularly interesting finding is that nonworking mothers positively influenced their daughters' career motivation, both vicariously and through verbal persuasion (Bandura, 1982).

Work as a Way of Providing for Family

Both women and men saw their personal work contribution as necessary in providing for their families or potential families. This sense of responsibility as provider was consistent among both parents and people planning for parenthood, regardless of education or work commitment.

Women and men differed in the way they perceived this breadwinner role. Women, although assuming provider responsibility, perceived their breadwinner role as secondary to that of their male partners. Men internalized the role of primary breadwinner, no matter how significant their wives' financial contributions were.

Both men and women experienced stress and anxiety related to their provider responsibility. However, for men, who tended to assume primary responsibility as provider, this role represented the major source of role-related stress and conflict.

Paul's comments reflect concern about both his financial future and his breadwinner capabilities:

Right now I look at my job and—if I have a kid I want to have a job where I could say, "OK, I know I can be here ten more years." Right now I doubt if I make it five in this company. I think I'm going to want out. And changing a job, this can be very dangerous. And I'd hate to have a kid in the middle of it and worry about a kid. I try to keep my stress level low.

Steve worried about his career progress and his economic stability:

Basically the only time I get real emotional now is at work when I get depressed sometimes thinking, gosh—I'm looking at the other people I work with that are my age and they're doing this, they're making that much money and they're getting real close to partnership here and I've not even got the title of a kid out of college yet. I get more emotional over those things.

Yeah, I'll worry myself to sleep about how I'm going to be able to afford my next car or buy a house, but I don't lose any sleep over [family issues].

Although both women and men took seriously their provider responsibility, they differed in that women were more likely to negotiate mentally both the provider and the family roles, preparing to lessen the provider role (e.g., work part-time, work from home) if they should have children. Men tended to think of increasing their provider role (e.g., working more overtime, working harder to gain promotions) when becoming parents. Betz (1993) notes a similar pattern in research findings during the mid- to late 1980s, concluding the family role limits women's occupational investment while increasing men's, giving them "a strong rationale for achievement-related behavior" (p. 649).

Ophelia, currently focusing on her provider responsibility, notes the possibility of modifying her work role for family:

All my plans right now are actually revolving around getting money and saving for the future. I'd like to get into a condo, hopefully soon, then at least start saving for a house. . . .

I've always been a working person since probably even 16 years old. And I could see myself working part-time, you know, trying to raise a family. . . . One of us has got to definitely work full-time, so that—that's the big decision that's still off in the future, I guess.

Paul, who is newly married, predicted his breadwinner role would intensify with parenthood:

Would work change [if I have children]? Yeah, I'll probably take on more overtime. Right now I don't take on that much overtime. I tell them I don't want it. I say I can live with or without the money. The money goes somewhere and I don't have a life.

Although lacking the prestige inherent in primary breadwinner status, some women found freedom in their ability to rely on a male partner's income if necessary. Cindy, who highly values her career, was able to take a low-paying teaching position that she enjoys:

My situation's good. I mean, I'm married and my husband does work. It would be nice to have more money but you know, financially it's not like I have to be out there making a certain amount of money, so it makes it easier.

Perceiving men's provider role as inflexible, however, women were left to figure out the logistics of incorporating the parent role into their lives. Both partners expected that the woman, and not the man, would make any career sacrifices deemed necessary to accommodate family. Husbands supported their wives by deferring to wives' decisions about family roles and agreeing to stand by them in those decisions.

Kathy and her husband Ralph are looking ahead to having children. Kathy has a master's degree in business and holds a respectable position as human relations manager for a manufacturing firm. Ralph has an established career in sales and is taking evening courses toward his master's degree. Kathy struggles with whether and how to sacrifice her career role to be home with her children while they are young. Clearly, the career-family decision making is her responsibility:

I don't think [my husband] would really have a problem with it either way. I mean, if I decided to stay at home, I think he'd be fine with it and if I decided to go to work, I think he'd be fine with that too. I don't think he really feels strongly either way. I think he thinks it's more or less my decision, because I'd be the one giving something up, you know? He's still going to be working no matter what.

Asked if Ralph might also consider making career accommodations, Kathy replied:

Well he could, sure, because of his field. He's in sales and I'm sure he could start later every day or something if, you know, in terms of maybe taking the baby somewhere, to a baby-sitter, or something. Yeah, I'm sure that he would be able to do that, to adjust his schedule.

Some men also expressed willingness to make career sacrifices. Isaac, cited later in this chapter, made a major job change to gain more flexibility and more time with his family. Lorna's husband worked a second shift, tending to the children and household during the day.

Women increased their commitment to the provider role when observing mothers who were suddenly thrust into the role of sole provider. Mothers' frequent mandate to their daughters was to have "something to fall back on." Eileen related her mother's dependency to her own situation:

My Mom—you know, my Dad died at 55 years old. We were young and so was my Mom. And you know, she had to deal with making it on her own. And she was totally dependent upon him. My God, she couldn't do a checkbook even. And I'm dependent upon my husband a lot, but not nearly as much as she was.

When Cindy's father became seriously ill, she realized the fragility of her mother's situation:

What if something would have happened to my Dad? My Mom is only 51 years old—what is she going to do with her life? . . . Now she's seen why I've always been such a big fanatic about working. I mean, if anything would ever happen to my husband and if I have a job, at least I can still hopefully make things go smoothly here.

In summary, although women and men shared the provider responsibility, men assumed the role of primary provider. Both men and women experienced provider role stress, men from concerns about their abilities as providers, and women from both provider concerns and the relative inflexibility of men's work in accommodating the family role. Women's work motivation was enhanced by observing mothers who found themselves unexpectedly in the role of sole provider.

Perceptions of Family

Family perspectives centered on three main concepts: valuing the family role, expectations for child rearing, and parenting responsibility.

Valuing the Family Role

Although clearly demonstrating the significance of work in their lives, nearly all men and women described family as their priority value. Much of the information about role values and priorities emerged naturally as women and men talked about their lives; some very specific information came from asking the question, "How does work fit into your life?" I asked the participants to picture their lives as a pie and to think about what piece work would be for them. Some described their pie in terms of time spent in different life roles, others spoke of their life values, and some talked about the relationship between the two.

Both women and men typically described work as the major piece of their time pie, usually about 50%, with less time devoted to family. Many noted this time allocation was disproportionate to their valuing of the family role, and for some this discrepancy was a source of role conflict.

Barbara made a distinction between time obligations and role values:

Well, time—I spend more time at work than I do anywhere else. So as far as time, I'd say the majority of time I spend is at work. As far as priorities, I wouldn't say it's a priority. I mean my family is really, really important to me. Oh my son's really important to me. If I could I would spend every minute of the day with him. But it doesn't always work that way. But I would say if I had to prioritize, work would come second and family would come first.

Fred spoke for the majority in describing his comparative values:

Well, if [work] was ideally the piece I wanted it to be, somewhere at the bottom of the pie. I don't think I would want it to be important. . . . I'd just want it to be there for financial reasons. At the top I would probably have my family, my friends. And I mean, I think that's more important than any job or anything you could ever want.

Lorna, who highly values her work role and describes her husband as "Mr. Mom," felt strongly about her family priority:

Work will come second or third. My family comes first. My kids are my number one priority. And I have made it very clear, you know, at my job. If there is something wrong at home, I'm gone. I am with my kids. And I've always made it that way.

Prioritizing family, while maintaining high career salience, provided many participants with a method of structuring roles to find a comfortable equilibrium. Lorna's early arrangement with her employer, for example, enabled her to engage fully in her work role without anxiety about meeting the needs of sick children.

There is some support in the literature for the relationship between family priorities and coping. In a study of career-family conflict and conflict resolution in married couples with children, Kinnier, Katz, and Berry (1991) found the most frequent theme among those who had resolved their conflicts was "my family comes first," a theme expressed equally by women and men.

Although prioritizing roles was a first step in preventing role conflict, time-value discrepancies remained troubling for some men and women, particularly those perceiving a lack of control over the structuring of their work and family roles.

Discomfort over time-value discrepancies is related to the high salience of both family and work roles for these women and men in beginning work and family stages. Super (1980) addresses this issue of role salience in his "life-career rainbow," with each band of the rainbow representing a particular life role. The brightness of each band increases during times of increased role demands, such as early family and career stages. It is likely that participants will be less concerned with time-value discrepancies as the demands of parenting decrease (e.g., when children enter school) and as work roles become more established.

To summarize, nearly all informants viewed family as their priority role. Prioritizing family and work roles facilitated comfortable role structuring for some women and men; others felt conflicted over time-value discrepancies. Time-value discrepancies likely will become less troubling with changes in role salience over time.

Child Rearing Expectations

Both women and men preferred a strongly supportive early environment for children, with emphasis on imparting parental values. Most believed this happened best when one parent remained at home during children's preschool years.

The majority of these men and women had mothers who stayed at home during their early childhood years. Some mothers never worked outside the home; many began working when their children were in late grammar school or junior high school. Memories of secure and comfortable early childhood experiences influenced their own views of child rearing; they wanted the same positive upbringing for their children.

Natalie, with plans for a home accounting business, weighed financial concerns with the need for quality parenting:

Well, nowadays it's like, unless you win the lottery, or marry a million-aire [she laughs], you have to have two incomes. . . . And when you start with a family, there's extra expenses, and you've got more mouths to feed, and you're going to need extra income coming in. And I realize that. But on the same token I don't want my kids to have to grow up in a preschool or a nursery school, that type of thing. Because that's like taking away from them. I mean, all of a sudden they're there. You don't see them growing. You don't know what's going on. They could become this person you have no idea—where at least here you know, you might do something with them at home, or even do a part-time job. And you have the kids, and you are molding them, not some-body else.

Parents and potential parents expressed concern about children's moral development, particularly in a society where they believe moral values are given low priority.

As a junior high school teacher, Cindy has seen the results of different parenting styles. She planned to have children in the future and talked of her concerns for their moral development:

I personally think a lot of parents are forgetting that it's not what kind of tennis shoes your son or daughter has on [she laughs]. It's what kind of person they are and how they feel about themselves. . . . Who cares if they're wearing Nikes as long as they're happy and they understand the difference between right and wrong, and that they're a good person.

Nate, whose wife has chosen to stay home during their children's early years, made a connection between parental employment and children's moral development:

I appreciate [my mother staying home] a lot more now than I did as a kid. You know, as a child you don't ever think about those things. As an adult, you start to be able to put two and two together and you figure out why, and you start looking back at the guys that you grew up with, and where they're at now, and how their lifestyles are going. And who knows if because mom and dad both worked . . . if that ever had any bearing on the way they are now. But it's just something that we felt real strong about from the get-go. And if we—if our lifestyles had to change because of only one person working, well then so be it. We just felt real strong about somebody staying home with the kids.

Consistent with these early parenting beliefs was a predominantly negative view of day care and the tendency to eliminate day care as an option for their children. This opinion came not only from parents but from married people planning for families, single people thinking of future family roles, and from those who had decided not to have children.

Several parents had tried putting their children in day care facilities. Of these, two were unhappy with the arrangement and had found other child care methods. Two continued the arrangement, but with some discomfort. Parents spoke of negligence in day care settings, frequent illnesses contracted in day care, concern about too much structure and too little spontaneity, and the stress and inconvenience of meeting rigid time demands. This perceived lack of quality day care is troubling, particularly in light of research linking consistent, quality day care with the increased mental health of employed women (Green & Russo, 1993).

Participants' negative views of day care stemmed not only from the lack of adequate day care options but also from the perceived inconsistency of day care with their personal beliefs about what constitutes good parenting. Good parenting, as noted above, was perceived as providing both quantity and quality time to one's children and as being the child's primary source of moral guidance. For many young women and men, the term *day care* symbolized parental neglect.

Although participants were uncomfortable with the day care scenario, they were very comfortable with family child care arrangements, and perhaps the biggest relief to parents and potential parents was having extended family nearby. Some spoke with gratitude about willing family members (e.g., mothers, sisters) who cared for children regularly and thus alleviated the day care anxiety. For some, childhood experiences with extended family caregivers tended to increase their confidence in family child care arrangements.

In summary, participants were consistent in their desire for both quantity and quality parental participation in early child rearing. Positive memories of their own early childhoods, with mothers at home, seemed to influence this child rearing preference. Participants held generally negative views of day care, with the exception of family child care arrangements.

Caretaking Responsibility

Women orchestrated the caretaker role, and both women and men tended to view the caretaker role as primarily the woman's responsibility. A general theme was that although both women and men believed parental contact was important during children's early years, both also assumed the mother would provide most of that contact.

Wanda's early experiences growing up in a single-parent family and her perception of gender role expectations in caretaking contributed to her decision not to have children:

Children require your undivided attention, I feel. If I was to have a child I would want to devote my time to them, which would mean not working, and shaping them as a little individual. I don't know how women do it when they have a career and the kids, and the husband, and the house. It's crazy, you know, and you're killing yourself. I mean, because no matter what kind of guy he is, you are basically responsible for those children. So I think that when women make that choice to have children, you're making it for yourself whether you're married or whatever, because you are ultimately responsible.

Women's tendency to assume traditional caretaker responsibility, like men's assumption of the traditional provider responsibility, is a consistent finding in the career development literature. Although societal attitudes reflect increased acceptance of nontraditional roles, gender role stereotypes have tended to remain stable over time (Deaux & Kite, 1993).

Women planned ahead for the caretaker role. Many began this planning quite early, before making decisions about jobs or relationships. As they approached the family stage, women's plans became increasingly detailed and specific.

Elaine and her husband want to start a family as soon as possible. She described very concrete plans for altering her work role to accommodate a child:

> I've thought about this a lot. Working at my company, if a part-time job comes open you could take a part-time job, and then go back to full-time when you're ready. . . . Plus I'd get six weeks off, you know, maternity leave.
>
> There's quite a few part-time openings that come up, so I would wait until closer, till I actually needed the part-time job before I would take it. I mean, there are jobs that you work maybe 3:00 in the morning till 10:00, or 5:00 to 10:00, where you could get those early morning hours in and then be home practically the whole day. And that's what I think I would be interested in. And then my husband would be home until 7:00, so the child wouldn't be in somebody else's hands for most of the day, just a few hours. So that's probably what I would do.

Juanita engaged in complicated planning to accommodate her nursing job, her home business, and her 5-year old son:

> Immediately I told my boss, "I have to be home for my son." And he was more than willing. . . . So I thought, well, [picking him up from school] just two days a week, plus the weekends—that's plenty of time [with my son], and then I'll see him after 5:00 on Monday, Tuesday, and Fridays, and we'll be OK. So I kind of planned my life to be there enough for him but yet be away from him so that I could still have my, I don't know, my identity? You know, I can go to work and come home like another working person, but I thought because my Mom was such a wonderful mother and always has been, I thought I wanted to be the same way.

Men did not plan for combining roles in the way that women did. In planning for family, most tended to focus on building a financially secure future (the breadwinner role) rather than on caretaking plans. These men, although very responsible as breadwinners and caring deeply about parenting, found it difficult to focus simultaneously on work and caretaking roles.

The finding of gender differences in planning is consistent with studies of career and family expectations. Gilbert (1993) found that men were less likely than women to consider their spouses' employment or family realities in their career plans. Spade and Reese (1991) found no gender differences in expectations for marriage and family, or in commitment to work, yet found significant differences in plans to combine the two roles. They note that men reconciled the demands of work and family by "reverting to the traditional definition of father as provider" (p. 319).

Chad is a single father with both a full-time professional career and a part-time coaching job that he greatly enjoys. He worries about earning money to buy a house for his daughter and also worries about her long hours in day care. Feeling conflicted, he focuses on his breadwinner role:

My main reason for wanting to get a house actually is for [my daughter]. . . . And the other thing is to try and find a way to not have—right now she goes to day care, day care takes her to kindergarten and then they take her back to day care. So I want to try to find a way so that she does not have to do that, spend 90% of her time in one form of a school or another.

Asked how he might lessen her time in day care, Chad responded,

I have no clue [he laughs]. That's something I'm working on. The first step for her at least is that house, more space for her to run, more room for her to do things she wants to do, you know, to have her own swing in the back and so on. I think that is important.

Norman plans his life "like a chess game," thinking several moves in advance. Despite a very clear career plan, however, his plan for incorporating the family role is quite vague:

So right now it's an eight-hour day. But I do know that here in the future . . . I may be looking at another job. And I do expect that this other job, if I want to climb the ladder, I'm probably going to be spending 10 to 12 hours a day, if not more. But that would only be for another five years, and it would come back down to the eight hours again.

And I really hope that when I try to climb up the corporate ladder, that I don't do what happened to me, that I spend time with my daughter. That I spend time with my wife, you know. That is very important to me. It's going to be a hard balancing act but I think I can handle it.

There is evidence that gender differences in caretaking stem partly from men's perceived lack of competence in the caretaking role (Baruch & Barnett, 1986; McBride, 1990). For the men in this sample, it seems that planning for the caretaker role is similarly limited by a lack of perceived competence in combining roles, or work-family self-efficacy, despite the value of family in their lives.

Men's strong valuing of the family role stemmed partly from observing their fathers' lack of family participation. Many described their fathers as distant, unable to express affection, and unable to relate to them as children. The majority of men saw in their fathers negative parenting role models, inspiring some to become more involved in the lives of their own children.

Steve regretted his inability to talk with his father:

You just sit there and watch TV with him 'cause he doesn't talk about things. He doesn't—you know, like my personal life, buying a house, getting a job, any of these things—he rarely talks to you about it. After you leave he'll go talk to Mom and say, "Well, why is he doing this?" or "I think this is a good idea." But when the topic is on the table he rarely ever says his opinion.

Paul's troubled and distant relationship with his father has led him to think about his own parenting preferences:

Our relationship wasn't as close as I wish it was, because you just couldn't open up and talk to the guy, because he'd blow his top. He couldn't—I mean, if you had certain problems, it's like he couldn't deal with them.

It got to the point where it was sports and small talk, you know, and I figured as an adult, I mean, we should be able to talk about anything. And I wanted a relationship where he's my father and a best friend, like I had with my mother, and I could never have that. . . .

Well, even like when we were younger, my mother would kiss us as little boys and he'd—my mother told me this—that he's like, "Why do you always got to be kissing the kids and being like that?"

I remember when I was 12, and he's trying to be that father figure and do something with me. . . . And he said, "Let's go to a baseball game." And I was like, "I hate baseball," and he's like, "You do?" That made us both think, that he didn't even know I didn't like baseball.

Actually, I take it as a lesson learned, so when I have kids I think I want to try to be a better father, because of problems I had with my father. . . . I think if I have kids, I'll probably support them no matter what.

Isaac, whose parents divorced during his early grammar school years, was both angered and motivated by his father's neglect:

All through high school, he lived about one block away, but didn't want anything to do with myself or my two brothers and sister. He just didn't really want to have too much to do with us. . . .

I played baseball, basketball, football when I was growing up, in grade school and what not, and not once did he ever come to a game of mine.

I didn't realize a lot of the family values that I had up until I had my son, and then after I had him, I'm like, "Man oh man, I can't believe this!" It's like a ton of bricks that hit me, that I just can't believe—to not care about a kid that he had, and not provide any direction and stability and future for someone that he had responsibility for bringing into the world!

I see a lot of stuff with my son that I do, things that I never had when I was his age. Going out sledding and playing, whatever good stuff and that's just, God I just love doing that with him! And after work we play and all that, so there's lots of things I know that I missed that I don't want him to miss. And just enjoy having kids.

I guess in terms of family values and what not, I know how *not* to do it.

The finding of men's commitment to good parenting is consistent with a pattern in recent studies describing men "who are deeply connected to their families and whose subjective well-being is significantly related to the quality of these connections" (Barnett, Marshall, & Pleck, 1992, p. 359).

To summarize this section on caretaking responsibilities, women assumed primary responsibility for the caretaker role, including actively planning to combine family and work roles. Men's planning tended to focus on their provider role, perhaps due to a lack of work-family self-efficacy. Learning from inadequate relationships with their fathers, however, men wanted to be good fathers to their own children.

Combining Work and Family Roles

As noted early in the chapter, the challenge of this cohort lies both in determining their own gender role beliefs and role values and in applying these beliefs and values to create a balanced life. This section focuses on the issues arising for participants in their attempts to combine work and family roles: their quest for quality lives and life balance, their experience with role conflict, and their coping styles.

Finding a New Equilibrium

Just as parents taught these men and women about the value of work, they also taught them, both verbally and by example, about the need to set limits on their working.

Steve recalled his father's advice to find a career that would allow for other life roles:

The one thing I remember the most about my Dad was, he always told me to try hard at school and do your homework and get good grades so you wouldn't have to do what I do. He didn't want to see me working 12-15 hours a day, seven days a week, which he does a lot in the fall and spring, you know, to try and pay the bills. "There's an easier way to live, and you don't want to live the way I do." He really meant it and I really wish I would've listened to him.

Nate admires his father's motivation and energy, which he emulates, but also sees a need for more family time than his father had:

My Dad is, I guess if you want to call him, a real motivated person. He's always been on the go. I can remember as a kid, for a long time it used to bother me that he was never around and probably, well hopefully when my kids get a little bigger, we won't have to do that. He's always been painting and bricklaying and this and that. He's always been doing something.

Juanita, quoted earlier as planning time for both work and family, regrets her father's sole focus on his work role:

My father was the hardest working man, always away from home, working. . . . All I know is that he would work all day long and sometimes come home at 9, 10 o'clock at night, eat dinner real late and go to bed and just start another day like that. And when he retired, I told my husband, "You know it's so nice to meet my father and to know and talk to him now. I can appreciate him!"

Both women and men learned, from both mothers and fathers, that giving all to one life role can result in regrets and lost chances. This lesson influenced their desire for a comfortable life balance, or equilibrium.

Cindy's desire for life balance motivated her career decisions:

I've interviewed for some positions and seriously thought about making a big career change, you know, because I was going through this stage where you want to make fifty to sixty thousand dollars a year. But when it boils right down to it, it's not what I want to do. I don't want to work from 7:00 in the morning till 8:00, 9:00 at night and have no holidays, I don't want that. So my job right now really makes me happy.

Isaac, whose job-related travel and other demands greatly limited his family time, left a prestigious investment firm and took a position with a lesser known, local company. He described his decision to find a more comfortable role balance:

I enjoyed the work and I enjoyed working with the people. The work was real challenging and it was probably the primary reason I was there. But just in terms of being responsible, and helping my little guy along, and being home with him, and being able to go to a ball game in an afternoon and what not, that's more important than the work. . . . It wasn't worth it. They're only young once and I need to enjoy it.

This desire for role equilibrium is consistent with trends noted in recent social science and business management literature. Orthner, Bowen, and Beare (1990), for example, describe "shifts in the values and beliefs of an increasing number of workers who are beginning to question the cost of success in the work place, especially when this success compromises their opportunities for other meaningful life experiences" (p. 30).

In summary, a trend among the participants in this study is to seek a comfortable role equilibrium. Many described setting realistic limits in their work roles to allow enjoyment of the family role.

Role Conflict

For women and men who combined work and family roles and those expecting to combine roles, role conflict seemed inevitable. Farmer (1984) describes home-career role conflict as a psychological state resulting from beliefs about the incompatibility of work and family roles. She distinguishes this psychological conflict from the concept of role overload, or time-based conflict.

Perceiving work and family roles as incompatible, women found that work-family decision making was an emotion-laden process. They experienced guilt over the possibility of neglecting a child, sadness at the prospect of giving up a valued career, fear of losing needed income, and, ultimately, frustration at their inability to reach a firm decision about how best to accommodate both roles. The following two examples are typical of this process.

Kathy's inner struggles provide insight into the competing emotions involved in planning for children:

I guess I feel pretty strongly about a career now, which can start to be a problem, for a woman especially because you start to think, "Gee, it would be nice to have a family, but do I want to keep working or do I want to stay home with the baby?" And I don't know yet which way I'd want to go.

A lot of people around me that have had babies are not working. And it's almost like you feel like if you did go back to work, they'd think you were a terrible person.

But my girlfriend who is staying at home—I don't think she really feels very fulfilled by just staying at home. I think she has the guilt thing that she doesn't really want to go back to work, but I think that eventually she probably will because she's—I think she's having kind of a hard time with it.

I really don't know what it would be like to just be at home, you know? And maybe I would like it. I can't see myself just staying at home though with a baby. I just can't see it. But then like my sister-in-law, I could never have seen her doing it either, and she's doing it [she laughs].

I kind of feel like, you know, you went through all this school, I mean six years of college and graduate school. Do I want to—it almost feels like you're putting all that in the garbage can or whatever.

Cindy's comments speak to the variety of issues influencing the perceived incompatibility of work and family roles:

I feel like the first five years are really formative years and I also feel like they're the years that you really can help set good moralistic values into your children. And I struggle with it because I think well, if I work, then someone else is going to be here at home taking care of my child, and I'm going to be missing out on a lot of things that he or she may do, and of course I want them brought up a certain way.

But on the other hand I think, well, I went to school for four years and I've worked hard to get it. And I feel like if I do work it'll make me a better person because I am not a homebody. I am not one to sit home. I feel like I am a better person if I'm outside working.

And I also know that if I do work, of course, a lot of my salary would go to child care, but on the other hand it would provide us with more of an income and it would allow me to probably provide more things for my child. It's just something that I battle back and forth with.

While prospective parents imagined the conflicting situations, parents lived them. Most parents already had negotiated the major decisions about combining roles, yet their continued experience of conflicting emotions occurred with an intensity unknown to those still in the planning stages.

Barbara worries about her son's emotional well-being as he enters kindergarten. She described her decision to leave her current secretarial job, with its inflexible hours, and instead work two part-time jobs:

Right now it's, some days it's a real hassle to leave my job right at five and get [to the preschool]. So I kept thinking, this is going to be even worse—I mean, now he can stay at preschool, nothing's going to happen to him, there's going to be people there to take care of him, it's just a matter of paying more money [if I'm late]. But what I kept thinking was, in kindergarten, what's going to happen? All the other kids are going to go home at the same time, and I kept thinking that must be an awful feeling for Todd, if one day I couldn't get there on time. I'm sure the teacher wouldn't leave him alone, but what an awful feeling he must have thinking that Mom abandoned him or something. And it's just not something I want to have him go through. So he's the major reason why I'm quitting working full-time.

Chad's conflict results from breadwinner demands that infringe on his time with family:

I'd say right now work is probably, at this point, it's about half [of my time]. And I don't want it to be about half. It has to be about half at this point. . . . I spend more of my waking hours with people I work with than my family! But I still think it should maybe be a quarter of it, at the most.

Role conflict for both men and women was likely to involve both the family and the work roles. The conflict-related emotions, however, differed according to traditional gender role expectations. That is, women's guilt and anxiety centered most on the caretaker role; men's guilt and anxiety centered most on the breadwinner role.

Participants also experienced role overload resulting from time constraints in trying to meet the competing demands of different roles, although this was a minor concern relative to their experience of home-career conflict. All the participants led very busy lives, and those with children experienced the greatest time pressures.

Of Gilbert's (1985) three types of dual-worker couples—traditional, participant, and role sharing—most couples described here appeared to be the participant type; that is, they shared home and family tasks but women assumed the greater share of these tasks. Two relationships appeared to be of the role sharing type (i.e., more egalitarian) and at least one fit the traditional model.

Juanita, who has a participant marriage, accepted with resignation her unequal share of household tasks:

[My husband] helps out some, not as much as I would like. I think he helps out about 35%. But if he would do a little bit more, 50%, we would be perfect. But he doesn't, and I think that's because that's him. You know, to him it's very important to sit down and watch a movie three times a night, or it's real important that he comes home from work and reads the paper and does nothing. And I would love to do that too, but I just think it's impossible.

Super (1980) recognizes the inevitability of both stress and enhancement in multiple role enactment; Sieber's (1974) theory of role accumulation emphasizes net gratification as the benefits of multiple roles outweigh the stressors. In this sample, as well, it is true that although role conflict greatly challenged the women and men, at times presenting major obstacles, clearly the rewards in combining roles more than compensated for the detriments.

In summary, both women and men experienced home-career conflict, the most vulnerable being those with children and those planning for combining roles. The greater stress, for both men and women, was linked to their traditional gender role. Participants also experienced but were less concerned about role overload, and most described relationships fitting Gilbert's (1985) participant category. The stresses of role conflict were offset by the benefits of combining work and family roles.

Coping With Role Conflict

Consistent with their quest for role balance and for quality lives, most women and men were creative in their use of strategies for coping with role conflict. These included planning, clarifying role values, modifying roles, reframing, and the use of support systems.

Planning. Women participants, in particular, actively planned in advance for combining roles by exploring opportunities and making decisions that set the stage for later multiple role functioning. Through early planning, women gained some control over the process of structuring work and family roles.

Clarifying role values. Clarifying and prioritizing role values, as the informants did when describing their lives as a pie, was an important first step in finding a comfortable role equilibrium. This strategy has also received consistent support in the work-family literature (Farmer, 1984; Kinnier et al., 1991; Poloma, 1972).

Effective values clarification led to structuring roles in accordance with the prioritized values. For those unable to match role enactment with prioritized role values, conflict persisted.

Modifying roles. Nearly all women in this study planned some modification of their work roles to accommodate family. These modifications included switching from full- to part-time work, moving to a different shift, and starting a home-based business. A few of the men also engaged in role modification by making job changes to accommodate family, although all continued to work full-time. The availability of the role modification strategy depended on both occupational and financial flexibility.

Reframing. This coping strategy involves adjusting one's attitude regarding role stress. For example, some men with long work hours, who regretted the loss of family time, reminded themselves of the normalcy of this role pattern in society. In describing this strategy, Anderson and Leslie (1991) note the value of "realizing the normalcy" of stress as effective in decreasing personal blame and guilt. Similar to Hall's (1972) Type II coping, this method was less effective than strategies aimed at prevention.

Making use of support systems. The most utilitarian support for combining roles took the form of flexible employment opportunities and family child care options. Although most women and men described their work as highly demanding, either because of inflexible schedules or because of travel requirements or extended work hours, a fortunate few described accommodating work situations that offered flexible schedules and/or shortened hours. Two of these were small businesses; one was a major corporation with family-friendly policies.

Several parents arranged for family members (usually mothers) to help with child care while they worked. This was a prime benefit for working parents and very effective in preventing both role conflict and role overload.

In summary, these men and women were creative in finding effective ways to prevent or alleviate role conflict. Long-term, preventive strategies, such as planning and modifying roles, were more effective than short-term, remedial strategies such as reframing. Only three participants had the benefit of flexible employment opportunities, and some parents benefited from family child care situations.

Implications for Counseling

The findings described here suggest several interventions for clients expecting to combine work and family roles. Perhaps most important are societal changes (e.g., accessible quality day care, increased employment flexibility) to bring options into line with current role expectations. Individual interventions, described below, include helping clients to understand the effects of socialization, facilitating values exploration and clarification, educating clients in combining roles, and enhancing clients' work-family self-efficacy.

Understanding Socialization

The current findings suggest the social origins of work and family role behavior, lending support to Farmer's (1992) suggestion that counselors "begin by talking with the client about the effects of socialization" (p. 31). Exploring the origins of gender role beliefs and values, from both cultural and personal perspectives, is a prerequisite to prioritizing role values.

Prioritizing Role Values

Findings in the current study both support and further illuminate the findings regarding the benefits of prioritizing role values. Helping clients to explore their conflicting emotions surrounding work and family roles, as Granrose (1985) has suggested, would be an important part of this process. I further recommend communicating role values and priorities to partners, to clarify and/or modify shared or conflicting role expectations.

Education in Combining Roles

For these participants, understanding the realities of combining work and family roles tended to encourage and facilitate both preparation and role management. To this end, education in combining roles might include information on (a) the positive effects of multiple roles on well-being (Helson, Elliott, & Leigh, 1990; Sieber, 1974; Super, 1980), (b) the myths of role incompatibility (Betz & Fitzgerald, 1987; Farmer, 1984), (c) the practical realities of combining roles, (d) role conflict and coping, (e) options for combining roles, (e) role salience theory, and (f) ways to plan and prepare for combining roles.

Enhancing Work-Family Self-Efficacy

Bandura (1982) notes that "if self-efficacy is lacking, people behave ineffectually, even though they know what to do" (p. 127). This was true for some participants in the current study, particularly men, unfamiliar with structuring work and family roles. Increased work-family self-efficacy could lead to men's increased participation in the process of combining roles.

Other findings consistently relate women's family commitment (but not men's) to lower career achievement (Betz, 1993; Farmer, 1985). Women with increased work-family self-efficacy might be more inclined to maintain commitments to both career and family.

Consistent with self-efficacy theory (Bandura, 1982; Hackett & Betz, 1981), enhancing work-family self-efficacy might best involve facilitating multiple role accomplishments, encouraging connections with role models in multiple role situations, helping to alleviate anxiety regarding combining roles, and both legitimizing the multiple role lifestyle and encouraging relationships supportive of that lifestyle.

Conclusion

The young women and men in this sample are freer in their role expectations than those of dual-worker couples in previous decades, yet they continue to struggle with some of the same issues and challenges. Having learned from parents the consequences of traditional gender role limitations, and following on the heels of the "superwoman" decade, they seek for themselves a new role equilibrium.

Part V

Where Do We Go From Here?

14

Career Counseling for the Next Decade and the Twenty-First Century

This chapter focuses on career counseling and suggests several approaches that would strengthen the career planning and choices of young women today and in the coming decades. First, there is a need to strengthen career education curriculum and resources in elementary and high schools. A revitalized career education would emphasize teaching life planning skills that would help women and men to plan their futures in light of their various future roles. Young women today need to be provided with the experiences that lead to career self-efficacy, that is, confidence in their career preparation and planning skills. School administrators and teachers need to change the classroom environment from one that is largely indifferent to women's career planning needs, and often sexually harassing for women, to one that actively encourages women to achieve their potential through their careers.

Tiedeman and O'Hara (1963) believed that parents, counselors, and educators should give children who are growing up the expectation that their career choices are not permanent; rather, children should learn to expect to change careers several times and to engage in learning new skills throughout their lives. These authors suggested that career decisions need to be held tentatively and that career choice should really be viewed as career choices over a life span. Tiedeman and O'Hara were responding to the technological revolution of the 1950s and 1960s when computers were being introduced into business and industry and when many tasks formerly performed by a person were being taken over by automated machines. In a similar vein today, downsizing in large corporations and businesses resulting from improved technology as well as changes in industry, such as the movement of many U.S. manufacturing firms to places outside the United States, make it necessary for many adults to change their career fields in midlife and to engage in retraining. The challenge of tentatively holding a career choice is relevant for both women and men in our society for the foreseeable future.

I begin with a brief overview of the counseling and career guidance that our participants experienced. In light of their generally inadequate counseling experiences, I then outline suggestions based on theory and prior research for career education in the schools and for reducing sexual harassment in the workplace and in higher education.

Counseling and Career Guidance Experienced by Our Participants

What in the experiences of these women and men did they feel was important for a new generation of high school students to hear? Many of our interviewees told us that they had not received adequate guidance from their parents or their schoolteachers and counselors to prepare them for college and/or employment. Many ended up in the wrong majors based on misinformation or lack of information about the major and about themselves. Others found that they were in a major they liked but that they lacked the academic training to handle the course work. Lack of preparation in high school for college calculus for engineering majors was a serious obstacle for many. Others did not go to college until they had been out of high school several years because they had no idea when they were in high school how important it was for their future. This was so not because college wasn't emphasized in most high schools. Rather, it was because many students were never turned on to academics in high school; instead, they were turned on to sports or partying with their friends. These women and men wanted the current generation of high school students to hear the message: "Get serious; don't wait too long to think about your future and make plans."

As noted in the chapter by Janice Altman, families are probably the most powerful influence on the career development of young people. However, when so many gifted young people in our country grow up with parents who lack a college education, it is necessary that society step in with the public school system to help these young people optimize their career potential.

Family experiences other than lack of exposure to higher education were also noted among our participants. For example, some participants experienced a parent losing her or his job, as many in the shrinking steel industry did, which left a lasting impact on their view of work. Parents cannot be blamed for not passing on knowledge and experience that they themselves did not possess. Nor can parents be blamed for a lack of resources and money to support their children's career goals. None of our participants had parents who withheld information or resources that would have helped these women and men plan better for their careers. Tom, a geologist from Country school, had this to say,

The unfortunate thing in my case was that my parents never even sat down with me and—my parents, neither one of them, completed high school, and they really didn't help us get through college—but they always said you should go to college because we didn't and look where we are at.

Teachers and counselors likewise cannot be blamed for not providing adequate help to students in planning future careers. The funds available for career guidance are very limited. The schools we studied typically held career days that presented career role models to students, and counselors had college catalogs available for students to study. Some of the schools also invited college and armed forces recruiters to present their training options to students once a year. At least one school had students take an interest inventory to help them explore how their interests matched those of persons employed in various career fields. There were some supplemental programs available to some students in some schools. As mentioned in Chapter 1, special programs in the inner city for minority students introduced them to engineering. An example was the INROADS program in which students with promising aptitudes were invited to spend Saturdays and summers learning about engineering careers and, at the same time, learning some of the necessary prerequisite skills. Another program involved minority students in journalism and was sponsored by the *Chicago Tribune*.

All of these efforts were not enough, however, to give this generation of high school students adequate career guidance. At the end of each interview, we asked the question, "Why did you agree to be interviewed?" The answers were surprisingly similar. Most said that they wanted to help future high school students plan better for their future careers. Some added that they wanted their story told because they felt there was a message in it for future generations of high school students.

In 1980, we asked the participants some questions about their perceptions of counselor support for their career planning. Responses to these questions were from 1, strongly disagree, to 5, strongly agree. High scorers viewed their counselors as supportive of and interested in their career plans and their academic achievements. The mean score for women and men was 3.2, which suggests that, on average, these women and men viewed their counselors as only somewhat supportive. Some of the comments in the 1990s from our interviewees help in understanding how these young people felt. Nathan, an engineer described in Chapter 11, who had attended Farmerville High School, told us:

> I graduated from high school here in Farmer City, and didn't really know what I wanted to do. I was going to go to a local community college [instead, he went to a four-year college after talking with a friend of his dad). I found out very quickly that Farmerville was not with the times in terms of mathematics. I was in a class for calculus; there were 35 of us in the class my freshman year. There was another gentleman, another good friend from high school that was in the same college class, and out of the 35, we were the only ones who had never had precalculus. So my freshman year at college was extremely difficult. Yeah. Well, the math teacher said that as long as I didn't give up, he wouldn't flunk me. And I got a D. I wasn't proud of it. but I passed. . . . I had three semesters of calculus, and the last one I either got a B+ or an A. In high school, I was ranked fifth or sixth out of a class of 105. My GPA was like 4.85 out of 5, and I was used to being able to skate by in school and classes.

Nathan had played football in high school, even after injuring his leg his junior year. Looking back, he said he would tell high school students today to work hard and not to pick the easy way but pick a career that is challenging and then to stick with it. Nathan exemplified this message himself by sticking with it even though calculus was hard.

Linda, who attended Country High School, had a negative experience with her counselor. Her story was told in some detail previously, especially in Chapter 5. She is Chinese American and also experienced a lot of ethnic discrimination in this rural school. She was a very good student and is now a surgeon. Linda said,

> I met with our counselor once. I told him what I wanted to do (i.e., be a doctor) and he told me I'd be more suited to something else. I seem to think it was something that wasn't quite such a position of responsibility, I guess like, I don't remember exactly but I keep thinking of that stewardess position.

Gary, who grew up on a farm, was a senior at Garden City school in 1980. As a result of his experience in high school with counselors and test results, he said he would encourage current high school students not to take test results too seriously. By 1990, he had earned an A.A. degree in chemistry and was employed as a chemist. He was given a college placement test in high school by his counselor and, based on the results, the counselor said he should consider engineering. However, Gary didn't like engineering and instead chose chemistry.

Darlene, who is now a biochemist, also attended Garden City High School. During her interviews in 1990, Darlene said,

> My high school didn't help me very much, I didn't feel. Then again, I never really asked. So I mean I'm partly to blame you know. I'm one of these type of people who believe, "Well hey you should know what I'm thinking!" "Read my mind." Maybe if they had presented me with more college opportunities, informed me a little bit more about scholarships that were available. . . .
>
> There was one counselor in particular who was really into high school stuff, I mean the college stuff. But it just seemed like she was always very busy, you know I mean with doing other things, and she also had her group of students, like an adviser type of thing and so I was kind of like, "Oh well you're busy OK." I'm sure that if I would have extended any amount of effort you know then I probably would have gotten something out of it but I didn't.

In summary, the career guidance and counseling received by our participants in high school was limited and was judged inadequate by those we interviewed. However, the career guidance available in high schools in the 1980s and 1990s is better than that available 50 years ago. When I attended high school in the 1940s, there were no school counselors and no career education programs. My lack of guidance from teachers or counselors in high school led to my floundering in college and the waste of several years before I found my career niche. Although I graduated from college in 1952, I didn't earn my Ph.D. until 1972. I was always among the top 3 or 4 in a high school class of 150, but I was never given any advice or guidance by my teachers about college or career plans. Only 5 members of my high school class went to college. I was crushed when I found out the summer before that I had been declared ineligible for a big scholarship I had applied for because I had not taken enough English and foreign language classes. Instead, I had taken all the math and science classes available because I liked them and I was good at them. I did qualify for a smaller government scholarship that paid tuition costs.

It is also important to point out that although our participants did not receive adequate career counseling or guidance in high school, some of our participants did receive help from their high school counselors for personal concerns, for example, Vicky, an African American woman who attended City High School, and Wendy, a Hispanic woman who attended Farmerville High School. Their stories are presented in Chapter 3.

Sexual harassment was experienced by several of the women in our study. The women who persisted in a science career reported experiencing sexual harassment both at school and later at work. However, they typically shrugged these experiences off, or were inspired by the "sexual putdowns" to do better, to achieve in spite of harassment. Gena is an example of a woman with this kind of attitude, and Chapter 4 by Susan Giurleo illustrates this attitude further. However, other women in our study were put off or discouraged by sexual harassment. One woman quit taking science in high school because of overt sexual advances to her by her science teacher (see Chapter 3). Beatrice, described in Chapter 3, was in the same class with Gena when a teacher said, "There's only one thing on earth stupider than horses, and it's women." Beatrice, unlike Gena, found this very insulting and discouraging and avoided math and science thereafter.

Career Education Revitalized for High School Students

It has long been known by those who specialize in career development (Super, 1957, 1990) that career planning requires both a wide range of information about the "self" and the "world of work" and in addition requires skills in decision making and planning. The federal-level career education legislation of the 1970s supplied funds for schools at both the elementary and the secondary levels to provide students with these kinds of information and skills. Special semester- or year-long classes were provided for students. However, not all schools benefited from this federal support. Of the six school in our study in 1980, none offered such semester-long classes. When funds for career education dried up in the 1980s, very few of the demonstration schools continued the programs they had established with federal funding (Farmer & Seliger, 1985).

It may be useful at this point to recall what these same young people told us they would want to get across to high school students today with respect to careers. They had four primary themes in their stories, which were reviewed extensively in Chapters 3 and 6. First, they emphasized that it is important for students to choose careers that they really like, that make them happy and excited about getting up in the morning. Second, they would encourage young women and men to explore and try out a variety of career-related activities, to collect information on careers, and to talk to persons in careers of interest to them. Third, they would encourage young people to plan ahead, to have long-range goals to sustain them in the face of obstacles. Finally, some emphasized perseverance, "hanging in there," when some obstacle stands in the way, such as a lack of money, a failing score on an entrance exam, a person in authority being discouraging.

Interestingly, none of our interviewees suggested that schools hire more counselors who would devote time helping students plan for their careers. Nor did anyone suggest that a special career education class in high school would be useful. Perhaps they assumed that the high school itself wouldn't change, so it was important to encourage young people themselves to choose wisely and to plan ahead and persist.

With what is known about career development from prior theory and research, as well as from the voices of these women and men, I have come to the following conclusions. I believe that high school personnel could help young people figure out what interests them and how these interests could lead to viable and satisfying careers (Super, 1980). State boards of education and high school administrators could make policy decisions to ensure that career education is provided in high school, preferably a semester-long class in both the freshman *[sic]* year and the senior year. This class could provide exercises designed to increase self-knowledge related to abilities, aptitudes, values, interests, needs, and goals. Such a class could provide information on a wide range of occupations as well as some hands-on experiences to help young people decide whether or not they would like some of the careers and have an aptitude for them. This combination of self-exploration and career exploration should provide the basis for making an informed and congruent career choice, one that makes full use of their potential.

I asked myself if such a class would have helped me plan better when I was in high school. It seems to me that if a teacher had sat me down after physics class one day and talked with me about my future plans, it would have made a powerful impression on me. I might have taken physics my first year at college and not Greek. Instead, I remember reading the college catalogue description of the introductory physics class when I was trying to decide between physics and Greek my first week in college. When I was 16 years old I had decided to study theology, the queen of sciences, so when I entered college, although I planned to take physics, I put my long-range plan first, and when the physics class conflicted with the Greek class, I chose Greek. I didn't find the description of the physics class very appealing and I didn't understand it very well. I might have trained to be a scientist instead of a theologian if someone knowledgeable about physics had talked with me in high school about my career plans. As it turned out, theology was not a good fit for me. For women and for men who are raised in families whose parents never went to college, the high school can provide information and career education that could lead to less floundering in adult life and less loss of talent to our society.

Career Education to Increase Sex Equity

In a review of the career education programs offered in high schools in the first 10 years following affirmative action legislation, Farmer and Seliger (1985) identified programs that had been evaluated as effective in teaching career decision-making and planning skills and increasing interest in and self-efficacy for careers nontraditional for women. Most of these programs were semester- or year-long experiences that combined introducing girls to a wide range of careers through hands-on experiences as well as observing and talking with role models in these fields. They also included self-awareness experiences and practice in decision making and planning. An example was the Women in Nontraditional Careers (WINC) program conducted in Portland, Oregon, with high school women. This program lasted a full semester, and evaluation evidence indicated that women ended up with more flexible career and life plans than women in a control group. Evidence also indicated that the women in the program increased their understanding of the way sex role stereotyping limits women's career planning and preparation.

Another example was the Career Internship Program conducted in New York State, which placed high school women as interns in 25 nontraditional work sites. A majority of the participants increased their sense of competence, or self-efficacy, in their ability to perform well in these nontraditional careers and also learned life planning skills in the program.

EQUALS, an in-service program for high school teachers, administrators, and counselors, was developed by staff at the University of California, Berkeley, and intended to help these professionals use materials to promote the participation of women and minorities in mathematics (Klein, 1985). Educators participate in 10 to 30 hours of training. Students of teachers who are trained in the use of these materials exhibit more interest in taking advanced and/or elective mathematics and exhibit more interest in entering math-related career fields.

The federal government enacted the Women's Educational Equity Act (WEEA) in 1974, which continues to fund various programs aimed at increasing women's career and life planning skills and exposing high school girls to careers nontraditional for their sex. One such program, Options: A Curriculum Development Program for Rural High School Students, was found to be effective in achieving its goals with rural girls. The WEEA Resource Center

(1996) publishes an annual catalogue describing curricular materials developed by projects supported by them that have been evaluated for effectiveness in increasing career development knowledge and skills.

Programs that facilitate school-to-work transitions are important, especially for students who are not college bound. Given that approximately 22% of young people today graduate from four-year colleges (National Science Foundation, 1994), the vast majority of young people either are not college-bound or will earn two-year rather than four-year college degrees. The suburban and inner-city high schools in our study had work-study programs that some of our interviewees participated in. For many, these were useful ways to learn about various careers in a hands-on fashion. The programs were aimed at exposing students to the trades, not the professions, and sometimes college-bound students were placed in them and resented it. Provided that care is taken not to send high school students who might profit from college to these programs, work-study programs provide useful training for high school students. Congress recently renewed continuing funding for these work-study programs (Goetz, 1996).

Career Education to Increase Women's Participation in the Sciences

In the current decade, many federal and state dollars have been invested in increasing the number of women who choose a career in science (National Science Foundation, 1994). Special programs have been introduced at the elementary and secondary levels to encourage girls to view nontraditional careers in science more positively. One of my graduate students who is also a second-grade science teacher has been doing science experiments with her pupils. When she asked her students to "draw a scientist," her results contrasted sharply with those often reported by teachers at higher grade levels. Instead of girls drawing a nerdy man, several girls drew women scientists doing experiments, making "poisons," examining cell structures, putting dinosaur bones together, and so on (Figure 14.1). The results this teacher obtained suggest that starting early with curricula that provide hands-on experiences in science to girls makes a difference.

There are several bridging programs sponsored by universities that invite high school women to campus annually to learn about women scientists firsthand. Examples include the University of California, Berkeley; the University of Illinois, Champaign-Urbana; and Indiana University. Some of these bridging programs are sponsored by the national organization of Women in

Figure 14.1. A Second-Grade Girl's Drawing of "a Scientist"

Science and Engineering. You may recall that Gena, one of our participants who is now an engineer, was actively involved in this organization during her entire college training program. Gena reported that many of the high school girls they brought to campus ended up choosing a science or engineering major in college.

Project WISE, funded by the National Science Foundation, supports programs that involve high school women in science activities at three centers: the University of Stony Brook, Brookhaven National Laboratory, and Cold Spring Harbor Laboratory. This project involves women for three years. Beginning in 10th grade, each woman selected to participate spends one day a month at one of the three institutions. Each summer, they are involved in a two-week science experience. In addition, participants engage in special workshops for skill training and counseling for college. Criteria for selection to participate in this program are that candidates are ninth-grade girls enrolled in accelerated science and math courses at their local high schools, earning B+ average grades or better in these courses, who are sponsored by one of their high school science or math teachers. Project WISE publishes a booklet called *The Future Is Yours—Get Ready!* This booklet describes 250 different occupations within the science and engineering fields and is available, free of charge, from the Brookhaven National Lab, Upton, New York. Another important project sponsored by the Girl Scouts of America is called Bridging the Gap. This project helps involve girls in science and engineering activities at a young age.

Many college campuses that offer engineering and science degrees have set up special resource centers for women who enter these majors. These centers are designed to help retain the women in science and engineering majors and offer personal and career counseling, financial aid planning, and skill training related to prerequisites in these majors. Important factors in keeping girls in the science and engineering pipeline are faculty role models, mentors, and positive attitudes in the faculty and in other students. These resource centers also help women in engineering combat the "chilly climate" found in many of these classrooms (Sandler & Hall, 1996).

Handling Sexual Harassment

Sexual harassment in the workplace is not well understood. A few years ago, media attention to the accusations leveled at Clarence Thomas by Anita Hill during his Supreme Court confirmation hearings raised the level of public awareness. In recent years, there have been several firings at high levels in government and the armed forces for sexual harassment behaviors. Federal government guidelines (U.S. Equal Employment Opportunity Commission, 1980) make it clear that sexual harassment is any behavior—verbal or physical—that interferes with a woman's work performance or that creates an intimidating, hostile, or offensive work environment. Since these guidelines were disseminated, university and college administrators have developed guidelines for sexual harassment that apply not only to relationships among employees but also to relationships between faculty and students. The "chilly climate" found in many nontraditional college majors for women and for women faculty (Sandler & Hall, 1996) has many negative effects on women.

The rare instance in which the perpetrator is fired or punished in some way makes headline news. The reasons for this are many, including difficulty in obtaining evidence that will stand up in a court proceeding and the continuing attitude of most men that women ought to be "good sports" and take sexually explicit jokes as harmless social repartee. Enforcement of the government and campus guidelines on sexual harassment to date has been unsatisfactory. The major gains made are that behaviors formerly viewed as a woman's problem are now viewed as a societal problem, and victims are increasingly turning to grievance staff in employment or campus settings where they find some validation and acknowledgment of the seriousness of the sexual harassment behaviors they are experiencing.

Riger (1991) contends that the low rate of reporting harassment is a result of gender bias in the harassment grievance policies rather than an absence of harassment or lack of assertiveness by victims. For example, courts have ruled that behaviors classified as creating an intimidating, hostile, or offensive work environment must be repeated to constitute evidence of harassment. Some have held that these incidents must be shown to affect the victim's mental health. Further, the "reasonable person rule" has been invoked to establish whether a reasonable person would be offended by the behavior. The problem is that the definition of a reasonable person is different in the view of most men compared with that of most women. Riger (1991) suggests that grievance policies that begin with informal dispute procedures, provide an advocate for the victim, and permit repeat offenders to be identified appear most effective in settling sexual harassment grievances. Riger also argues that prevention policies are more effective than retribution or punishment policies. In the prevention approach, education about harassment is aimed at helping men think like a woman. Also in the prevention approach, institutional policies are examined, especially where persons in authority are not accountable for their behaviors, so that policies for greater accountability can be put in place. An institutional climate that actively promotes equal opportunities for women is needed to discourage behaviors that are hostile to women's positive growth in the institution.

A Life Planning Perspective: Career Counseling for Women

Today, a majority of adult women, including those with preschool children, are employed (U.S. Bureau of the Census, 1990). The majority of working women are married, and the dual-worker couple has become normative. Women who are single heads of households, those in lesbian relationships, and those choosing a single lifestyle make up a sizable percentage (approximately 20%) of working women. The multiple roles that adult women find themselves filling, including worker, partner, spouse, and parent, require a different kind of planning today than in previous decades when multiple roles were not the norm but the exception.

To avoid confusion, I will note that some authors use the terms *dual-worker couple* and *dual-career couple* interchangeably. However, *dual-worker couple* is the more inclusive term because it encompasses all employed couples, whereas *dual-career* couple includes only those couples who view their work as a career, usually at the professional level. I will use the term *dual-worker couple* in this chapter.

Donald Super (1980), one of the outstanding career development theorists of this century, proposed a "career rainbow" to depict the multiple roles persons, both men and women, are likely to engage in at different time points in their life cycle. In Super's theory, conflict between demands from these multiple roles is not envisioned. Instead, multiple roles are identified as a way of describing the variable investment most of us make in our different roles as life circumstances change. For example, the adolescent invests primarily in the student role, with some investment in relationship roles and personal roles such as leisure, whereas the young adult woman invests in her work, family, and leisure roles. Super built on these ideas to develop a measure of Career Salience (Super & Nevill, 1985). This measure assesses the importance to a person of each of five roles: worker, student, parent, citizen, and leisurite. Use of this measure with a person provides information on the current importance of each role, that is, a snapshot of where the person's current priorities lie. Because priorities may change with the passage of time, the results of such assessment should be viewed as temporary. A companion measure was developed by Super and Nevill (1985) to assess work values. The results of this assessment may provide a more permanent description of a person's values, because these are less likely to change with time. When counseling a person about her or his career plans and choices, these measures may be useful in combination, especially for women who are considering their values and how these fit their long-term career plans.

Career-Family Role Conflict

For most women, an easy shifting of emphasis between career and family roles is not very possible, especially when they are required to engage in parenting, homemaking, and employed work. Chapter 13 provides ample evidence of this for our participants. If, in addition, the role of parent is added to career, women have a difficult time balancing their multiple roles with any degree of comfort. Sekaran (1986) described the quality of life experienced by dual-career couples and the degree of satisfaction people experience in each of the roles they engage in. In contrast to Super, Sekaran recognizes that interrole conflicts exist and that life satisfaction depends on the resolution of these conflicts. For women, stresses develop from role conflict, the division of labor at home, the need to find adequate child care, and the distribution of power and responsibility within the marriage. Amatea, Cross, Clark, and Bobby (1986) developed a measure to assess the work and family role expectations of career-oriented men and women, which they call the Life Role Salience scales. Their measure is intended to assist dual-worker couples with long-range career planning that takes into account the couples' priorities for other life roles. Farmer (1984) developed a Home-Career Conflict measure to assess the extent of conflict between these roles that a woman is experiencing. These measures should be useful to counselors working with women as well as with men and women who are part of dual-worker couples.

Why do women who are part of dual-worker couples experience more conflict and difficulty in handling multiple roles compared with men? There are at least two reasons for this. Both men and women are socialized to expect women to be primarily homemakers and mothers and to expect men to be primarily breadwinners. These sex role stereotypes continue to be operative in the expectations, attitudes, and behaviors of men and women in dual-worker relationships. Such expectations and attitudes create stress for women who are part of a dual-worker couple because they are expected to take responsibility for homemaking as well as work, whereas men take responsibility primarily for work, not homemaking.

Recently, some research has been designed to assess the readiness of young women for their multiple roles of wife, mother, worker, and leisurite. Weitzman (1992) designed a measure to assess multiple role realism in planning with a group of high school and university women. The measure has four scales: Independence, Involvement, Commitment to Multiple Roles, and Knowledge/Certainty about combining roles. Reddin (1996) adapted the Weitzman measure in an attempt to increase its validity, and used it with women in a variety of graduate study majors. Of interest, Reddin found that women with nontraditional career majors also had nontraditional homemaking plans with respect to the number of children they planned to have and expectations for working while the children were young. Similarly, women in traditional career majors had traditional homemaking plans and expected to work part-time or quit working when they had children. The women interviewed by Lenore Tipping (Chapter 13) are like the women who choose more traditional child rearing plans. The women who are highly career committed, as were those presented by Jana Reddin (Chapter 5), had "transitional" plans with respect to child care. Those women planning to have children also plan to continue working full-time so as not to interfere with the accumulation of equity in their positions, and they use various plans for achieving this. Some opt for arrangements to work at home part of the time (i.e., Gena); still others have husbands whose work allows them to share child care responsibility (i.e., Tonya). These women describe their relationships with their husbands as strong in terms of their communication, shared values, and shared coping strategies. Linda's husband has sacrificed his career for her and moved to another city to be with her during her medical residency. These couples are providing patterns of role sharing that will have strong effects on their children. If one thing was clear from our interviews, it was the powerful influence of family experiences on future values and behaviors of young people. The influence of the school and community were important but hardly as powerful. In light of this reality, efforts by education institutions should be viewed as potentially providing a positive influence on values and behaviors but not a source of radical change.

In the past two decades since sex equity legislation was passed, changes in the participation of men and women in homemaking and parenting roles have been observed. Men are now more interested in and willing to be involved in parenting (Gilbert, 1994) and most are willing to help their partners with homemaking chores. However, few men view parenting and homemaking as their responsibility; they are available primarily to help out. Equitable sharing of homemaking and parenting is still very rare.

On September 9, 1994, Supreme Court Justice Ruth Bader Ginsburg visited the University of Illinois to rededicate a law building on campus and was quoted as saying that there will be no equity for women in the workplace until men assume equal sharing of homemaking and parenting roles. This is not a new idea, women have been saying this for at least two decades, but it cuts to the heart of the matter. The lack of role sharing by men in the home combined with the continuing wage gap between working women and working men (still approximately 66%) attests to a continuing lack of sex equity in the United States.

The response of working women to their multiple roles was at first an attempt to do it all. Women tried to be supermoms and executive managers at the same time. The literature reflects this trend in the 1970s and early 1980s. More recently, women have backed off from attempting to do everything and have compromised some roles to benefit others. Counselors have worked with women to help them with their career planning, to help them think through their values, and to help them make hard choices in light of these values.

Gottfredson's (1981) theory of career choice as circumscription and compromise has informed some of these efforts. This theory is based on research indicating that girls learn early in life what career roles are acceptable for girls and what career roles are not acceptable. These sex role stereotypes circumscribe the range of careers girls consider when it is time to make career-related choices. Gottfredson further proposed that girls have limited their career aspiration levels early in grade school, based in part on the career and work values learned in their homes and also on their perception of their abilities learned through their achievements at school. In combination, career sex role stereotypes, career values, and self-perceptions of ability lead girls to circumscribe and compromise their career potential.

It is my view that helping women to plan for multiple roles by emphasizing circumscription and compromise ignores the role men play in our world in relation to women and assumes that men are not going to change in ways that would increase sex equity. A more futuristic approach to counseling today, I believe, would focus on career planning programs in elementary and secondary schools that engage both boys and girls in experiences as well as in discussions that would lead them to expect to share responsibilities in the home and the workplace more equitably.

An interesting finding in a study on home-career conflict (Farmer, 1984) was that when women thought their husbands were sharing in child care to an extent that enabled the women to travel on work-related activities while their children were preschoolers, the women experienced less stress and anxiety. Gilbert (1994) reported such activities by fathers in her research on dual-career couples, but such activities were rare rather than the norm.

Adequate child care is a continuing need in our society. The United States lags behind most European countries in terms of the amount of available quality child care facilities There are some large business institutions that now provide on-site child care for their employees. Also, many higher education institutions now have policies that permit tenure rollbacks for faculty who are parents who need to take time to raise small children (Hyde, 1995). Most women take primary responsibility for raising their children (Gilbert, 1994).

With a newborn, finding quality day care is a major task that confronts mothers who plan to continue working. Adequate quality day care available to mothers of newborns would drastically reduce the stress these women experience. Tipping (Chapter 13) reported that the women she interviewed in our study were generally negative about using day care. Many women reject the use of day care, preferring to make arrangements with family members or friends to care for their baby if they continue to work. Yet it is these very arrangements that add considerable stress to child rearing in the early years of the child's life and lead women to compromise their career potential.

Table 14.1 Decision-Making Styles for Dual-Worker Couples

Traditional
  Sex role stereotypes rigidly adhered to.
  Women are homemakers.
  Men are breadwinners.
Transitional
  Women's work is important.
  Men help with homemaking.
  Men's work is more important, takes priority.
Equal
  Women's and men's work are equally important.
  Men take active responsibility for and an equal share of homemaking and parenting roles
Egalitarian
  Decisions are based on individual interests, abilities, and personality.
  A variety of patterns of role sharing evolve.

SOURCE: Based on L. Smith (1981).

Career Planning Skills

An aspect of life planning is having decision-making and negotiating skills. L. Smith (1981) conducted a study of dual-worker couples' decision-making style in relation to homemaking and work roles. She defined decision-making style as a continuum from traditional (decisions based on a traditional view of sex roles) to egalitarian (decisions based on equitable valuing of needs, talents, and interests of each individual) (Table 14.1). The distinction between a style that emphasizes equality and one that is egalitarian is a subtle one. Basically, the difference is in the emphasis on each partner as a person. An egalitarian style provides equal opportunity for each person to develop her or his potential and to express an individual personality. In contrast, an equal style emphasizes a 50-50 partnership in which each one does an equal amount of, for example, the homemaking tasks. It is more challenging to negotiate an egalitarian partnership in which, first, each person chooses the task she or he likes and performs best, and then partners select the leftover tasks based on a 50-50 rationale.

An underlying assumption that I am making is that it is desirable for women to be able to achieve their full potential in their work and family roles. If one accepts this viewpoint, one will also agree that our educational system could play an important part in furthering women's achievement in these roles. As noted earlier, attitudes related to sex roles change very slowly, Therefore, beginning in elementary school, special courses in social studies could introduce girls and boys to experiences and ideas related to their future roles in the family and the workplace, emphasizing how these roles are inter-dependent. In high school, students could be provided with experience in planning ahead for these roles. Norma, whose story is told in Chapter 3, might have benefited from such simulated planning experiences. Many women make their career choices without considering how these affect their values related to family and homemaking. Not thinking about the conse-quences of their career choices on their family plans often leads to stress, dis-appointment, and floundering. It is important to help children and adolescents anticipate their future multiple roles and to learn decision-making and plan-ning skills while they are still in school. Weitzman's (1992) Multiple Role Realism Inventory might be useful in alerting adolescents to the need to plan ahead.

Career education classes should teach planning and decision-making skills. Several exercises are on the market today that provide simulated expe-riences in life planning (Varenhorst, 1969). These exercises involve young persons in planning their futures, and provide them with feedback on the con-sequences of various choices to help them plan realistically. The computer-assisted career counseling programs available such as SIGI published by Edu-cational Testing Service and DISCOVER published by the American College Testing Corporation provide some of these experiences and help build decision-making skills when used in conjunction with a counselor.

Varenhorst (1969) was aware that high school students are often primarily involved with the present and that future planning was distant and of little in-terest to them. She recognized that life planning experiences would have to in-volve the students so they would begin to feel a need to plan. To plan for the future, they will need to be given relevant information on work, college, and marriage. Students may need help in understanding that how they spend their time now may affect their lives in the future. An important aspect of education and counseling for life planning is value clarification, or answering questions such as these: "How important is having a career?" and "How important is having a family?" Disentangling personal values from normative values is an-other important part of this value clarification. Only in late adolescence are personal values fully formed. Clarification of values involves getting a per-spective on future lifestyle options that are important and then figuring out how to plan to have this kind of future. Skill in making decisions is learned gradually, through practice—by making decisions and experiencing the con-sequences. A review of several current publishers' catalogues that provide career counseling and guidance books as well as career exploration and as-sessment materials indicated that there are no materials currently available similar to Varenhorst's (1969) life planning exercise. This is a serious gap in the career counseling field, and I hope someone will take up the challenge to remedy it.

Self-Efficacy and Role Models: How to Increase Career Persistence

The fourth message that our participants had for young people today with respect to career guidance was to persevere in the fact of obstacles. How can counselors and school systems help young people do this? One way is to increase self-efficacy, especially with respect to career development and career tasks. Studies have shown that self-efficacy is related to persistence at a task until it is mastered as well as engaging in a task, that is, choosing to try it (Bandura, 1989).

The importance of performance self-efficacy has been demonstrated by Hackett, Esposito, and O'Halloran (1989), who found that self-efficacy beliefs (i.e., I can do it) were more determining of career choices than actual abilities. That is, even when a woman had the necessary grades for entry into a particular college major, she was unlikely to choose that major unless she believed she could perform well in it. In this study, performance self-efficacy was found to predict career commitment, educational aspiration, and nontraditionality of career choice. Similarly, these researchers found that having had positive experiences with career role models also predicted career commitment and educational aspiration. It was surprising that role model influence did not predict choice of college major, whereas performance self-efficacy did. This finding suggests that role model influence is not enough to stimulate interest in a career area; rather, a person's interest must be backed up by belief that she or he can perform well in that career. Vanessa, the single mother in Chapter 3 who found it difficult to juggle her multiple role responsibilities of student, worker, and mother, might have been helped if she had been given some training in planning and provided with a group experience with other women who were experiencing similar difficulties.

Bandura (1989), whose research on the influence of role models on learning dates back to the 1960s, has found that role models are more effective if the learner/observer can identify with the role model. A role model representing career success will not be identified with if the behaviors or successes are too far removed from observers' beliefs about themselves. Thus high school students listening to star athletes in their high school auditorium are unlikely to identify with them unless the students themselves have won praise for their athletic abilities. Similarly, high school women listening to a woman who won a Nobel prize for physics are not likely to aspire to be a physicist unless they have already found they both like and perform well in physics classes. For example, my successful experiences with high school physics and my interest in taking a physics course in college, inspired in part by a film about Madame Curie, were not enough to make me choose physics in college when I was confronted with a choice between physics and Greek (a prerequisite for theology). I was familiar with and admired several theologians and felt confident that I could do what they did. No one had ever talked to me about being a physicist, so when I had to make a choice, I chose theology instead of physics. Madame Curie was an inspiration but was not very real to me and was too far removed to have a determining influence on my career choice. A high school woman who had never thought about taking physics might be inspired by the Nobel prize winner to sign up for a class in physics, and to that extent role models can stimulate exploratory behaviors that could lead to career choices later on. But role models presented in a career day are not likely to change beliefs and behaviors of young people without the additional information and experiences provided in a career education class or in hands-on experiences.

How Self-Efficacy Is Learned

If performance self-efficacy is a critical ingredient in generating continuing interest in a career, how is it engendered and fostered? Bandura (1989; see also Lent et al., 1994) has found that self-efficacy is learned by a person as a result of four basic influences or experiences. Primary among these are performance accomplishments, namely, successfully engaging in a task—thus the importance of hands-on experiences. Next in importance are vicarious experiences, that is, observing others perform a task or describe their experiences related to a career. This, of course, is the effect of "role models" on self-efficacy. Third is the influence of verbal persuasion by others who tell a person that she or he can accomplish a task and encourage her or him to try. We have noted the effect of the "null environment" (Betz & Hackett, 1983) on women's career aspirations. A null environment at home, as well as in the school and the community at large, that is indifferent to women's career aspirations and related achievements does not foster commitment to or persistence in a career. What is needed is a kind of affirming action to provide encouragement from significant others for girls' and women's career aspirations and achievements. Bandura's fourth influence is the absence of

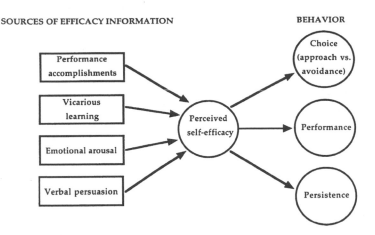

Figure 14.2. Bandura's Model of Perceived Self-Efficacy
SOURCE: Adapted with permission from Betz (1990).

anxiety, or feeling comfortable about trying out a new behavior. Figure 14.2 illustrates Bandura's theory related to self-efficacy. If I had had extended exposure to a successful woman physicist, and been engaged in some of the kinds of research she conducted, similar to the girls in project WISE described earlier, I might well have chosen physics instead of theology in college. On reflection, the Madame Curie movie had a broader impact on me and a continuing positive effect—not in terms of identifying with her role as a scientist but in terms of my identification with her perseverance in her search for a cure for cancer in spite of great odds.

Summary

This chapter has focused on career counseling and suggested several approaches that would strengthen career planning for young women and men today and in the coming decades. First, there is a need to reintroduce a more extensive career education curriculum in the high schools. Current practices that provide "career days" and occasional group-based career assessment were found to be highly inadequate by the young people we interviewed. Revitalized career education would emphasize life planning, an approach that would help young persons plan their futures in light of their various role commitments (i.e., work, family, leisure). Women cannot plan for their futures without considering the interdependence of work and family roles, and it is desirable that men begin to plan with this in mind as well. A third theme for career counseling in the coming decades was noted. Young people today need to feel confident that they can be successful in whatever career they choose to enter. Research has indicated that this kind of performance self-efficacy is more important in determining career choice than actual ability. Educators and counselors can plan programs that enhance career and performance self-efficacy, which in turn should lead to career choices more congruent with ability, especially for women. Finally, reducing the "null environment" in the classroom, one that is indifferent to women's achievements, is essential to increasing the likelihood that women will begin to realize their potential. In higher education settings, it is essential to reduce the "chilly environment" and sexual harassment present in many classrooms, especially those in physics, engineering, and other majors nontraditional for women.

Some of the changes in career counseling that I have proposed require extensive changes at the policy level for their realization. To provide semester-long career education in high schools, state boards of education will need to establish a policy requiring it and at the same time make funds available to implement the requirement. Within higher education and the workplace, review and revision of the sexual harassment guidelines are needed to make procedures more "user friendly" for victims. On the employment front, there is the continuing need for more quality child care subsidized by government and by employer agencies. Unless women are confident that sufficient quality child care is available, they will continue to compromise their career goals to ensure that they have adequate time to raise their children.

15

Future Directions for Research on Women's Career Development

This chapter reviews the research needs related to women's career development. I focus on a review of the gains based on social-cognitive theory testing and on what remains to be done. The design and evaluation of some of the programs needed to evaluate social changes in the family, school, higher education, and the workplace are described. A qualitative interview-based follow-up study in the year 2005 is recommended.

Research Needed to Extend Evidence for a Social-Cognitive Basis for Women's Career Development

As discussed in Chapter 1, Bandura's social-cognitive theory formed the basis for the theoretical model used to test the quantitative data collected for this study in 1980 and 1990. These tests provided some evidence supporting this theoretical approach but were more comprehensive in supporting an explanation of men's career development than they were for women. Below I explore ways to strengthen future research to more fully explain what happens in women's career development. The reader may want to refer back to Chapter 1, where a fuller description of social-cognitive theory is given. Recall that Bandura proposed that cognitions (i.e., personal beliefs, feelings, and attitudes) affect and are affected by social experiences (both interpersonal and contextual) and that each of these affects and is affected by behaviors (e.g., choices, performance). Further, these three dimensions exist in a dynamic, reciprocal relationship.

I adapted Bandura's social-cognitive theory in certain ways. First, for model testing, I separated the effect of background factors such as gender, ethnicity, and socioeconomic status from his three dimensions. Bandura does not ignore these background factors; rather, he assumes that their effect is subsumed by the cognitive and social factors. Second, the particular cognitive, social, and behavior variables I assessed were unique to the focus on women's career development and included potential positive and negative influences. For example, for women, discrimination in the environment and women's gender role socialization often have a negative, deflating effect on their career motivation. Positive effects include support from parents and personal self-esteem and self-efficacy.

Evidence for the Effects of Gender, Ethnicity, Socioeconomic Status, and Genetic Disability

As noted above, Bandura does not separate the influence of given background variables such as gender, ethnicity, socioeconomic status, and genetic disability from the influence of personal beliefs in his conceptual model. I disagree with his theoretical framework on this point. For model testing, I have separated background variables from personal beliefs, such as self-esteem, self-efficacy, values, and conflicts (see Figure 1.1).

Gender. There is convincing evidence that gender differences exist in the career choice process. As noted previously, my research colleagues and I have found differences in the pattern and strength of factors influencing men and women's career motivation and choice. Farmer (1985) found that, for women, the pull between home and career roles dampened their long-range career commitment. In our longitudinal research (Farmer, Wardrop, Anderson, & Risinger, 1995), we had to examine statistical models separately for men and women because some relationships were nonlinear. We were better able to account for these career choices for men compared with women. For men, we accounted for 97% of the variance in "persistence" in a science or technology career, whereas, for women, we accounted for 34%. In our analysis of models predicting factors that discriminate between men and women in science versus nonscience careers (Farmer, Wardrop, & Crabtree, 1995), the fitted model for men accounts for 74% of the variance, whereas for women it accounts for 36%. Gender differences were also found for experiences and attitudes toward women working (Farmer, 1985). These findings support the view that gender affects certain cognitions, socialization processes, and behaviors.

Our interview data provided a picture of women choosing careers that they thought could best accommodate their family role. Norma (Chapter 3) represents this "circumscription and compromise," and other women, especially those choosing nurse instead of doctor, also illustrate how women planned for their home and work roles. Another continuing popular career choice for women today is teacher, a career viewed as accommodating well to family role responsibilities. It appears that until the perception of their family responsibilities shifts to one that is shared by their spouses, women will continue to compromise their career prospects to fulfill their family role in a responsible fashion, and these behaviors differ from those found for men (see Chapter 13).

Socioeconomic status. We have been less successful in establishing the effect of socioeconomic differences on career development. For adolescent women and men, socioeconomic status (SES) had a small positive relationship with career aspiration level and mastery motivation (Farmer, 1985). For these same persons 10 years later, a small effect was found for high SES indirectly related to both women and men's persistence in a science career. High SES was also related to more liberal views of women's role in the workplace (Farmer, 1985). The model we tested permitted us to access the effect of both high and low SES, and low SES was found to be related to men's persistence in a science or technology career. This finding for men suggests that, for some men, growing up in low SES families was related to persistence in a high-level science career (see also Chapter 10).

Our interview data supported the quantitative findings. For men who were children of first-generation immigrant parents, low SES was related to high motivation to achieve (see Chapters 9 and 10). We conclude that sometimes low SES stimulates commitment to a career and at other times it stifles it. As with our finding on gender discrimination, individual persons and families react differently, and generalities about the negative effect of low SES should be avoided in favor of a more careful look at how low SES persons develop and cope.

Ethnicity. Ethnic differences were found for adolescents, with minority men and women having higher career aspiration levels and higher long-range career commitment than white students (Farmer, 1985). Ten years later, minority women were more persistent in a science or technology career than white women (Farmer, Wardrop, Anderson, & Risinger, 1995). The opposite was true for minority men. Minority participants had higher scores on parent support for careers when they were in high school (Farmer, 1985) and on the need for financial support to attend college (Farmer, Wardrop, Anderson, & Risinger, 1995). Our minority participants were mostly from two inner-city schools in Chicago, and although the proportion of minority stu-

dents (23%) in the first wave of data was comparable to the national proportion at that time, and was 20% in the follow-up 10 years later, the sample size
was small overall and we caution the reader about generalizing from our findings. It is clear, however, from these findings that ethnicity affects cognitions, socialization processes, and behaviors.

Interview findings indicated that minority women and men experienced
powerful negative forms of discrimination at school, in the community, and
in their workplaces (Chapter 7). These experiences had the effect for some of
making them more determined to do well and "make good." Although this
was an uphill battle, they were strongly motivated (Chapter 8). However,
others were sidetracked early in their career development and never caught
up.

Genetic disability. We did not obtain much evidence for the effect of genetic disability on career choice. We did collect data on this both in 1980 and
in 1990 but very few of our participants reported such disabilities. This is an
important and neglected area for research.

Evidence for the Effects of Socialization on Women's Career Development

Following Bandura's social-cognitive theory, a social influence that affects one important cognition, self-efficacy, is verbal persuasion. This relationship was assessed in our study by the measures of support or lack of support from parents, teachers, counselors, and others. Support for Bandura's
theory was found in that experiences in the community, family, and school
that led to a liberal and equitable view of women's place in the workplace
were related to math self-efficacy (Farmer, Wardrop, Anderson, & Risinger,
1995). Experiences with family, teachers, and others were also found to relate positively to career and achievement motivation (Farmer, 1980, 1985).
Farmer and Bohn (1970) found that if women experienced their family and
friends as being supportive of their career choices and, in addition, believed
that they would be treated equitably in their work environments, women
chose more challenging high-level careers such as lawyer, doctor, physicist,
and engineer. These findings support the view that social experiences influence cognitions and behaviors.

Of interest, in 1990 when we tested models to explain why some women
persisted in a science career and others did not, the social support variables

were not significant predictors (Farmer, Wardrop, Anderson, & Risinger, 1995). Also, when we tested models to determine how women in science careers differed from women in other careers, the social support variables were not significant predictors (Farmer, Wardrop, & Crabtree, 1995). Based on these findings, we might conclude that social factors influence women's math self-efficacy, career motivation, mastery motivation, career aspiration levels, and choice of careers nontraditional for women, but not in ways that distinguish women in science fields from women in other career fields.

The qualitative interview data from these same women indicated that their parents were a strong influence on their career development but were less of an influence on the specific occupational field chosen (Chapter 12). Counselors were reported to have had little influence on the career choices of these women (Chapter 3). A few teachers had important influences on some of the women's choice of a science career, but this was not generally the case (Chapter 3). Although the quantitative findings suggest a significant positive relationship between women's perception of support from teachers, our interview indicated that this perception was relatively weak among these women after they had been away from high school a few years. However, the quantitative findings for the influence of parents was strongly supported by the interview data, as were the findings for the lack of perceived support from counselors.

Another social variable affecting self-efficacy in Bandura's theory is vicarious learning through observation of role models in the environment. Role model influence was not successfully assessed in our quantitative studies, but in our interviews we learned that these women were inspired by the example of others to choose challenging careers. One woman referred to an aunt as a role model, another to her mother, and another to her father. A surprising finding was that, for these women, teachers were seldom role models. However, for some women, coworkers in part-time summer jobs were role models.

Our interviews also gave us insight into how different women reacted to the same experiences, especially gender and ethnic discrimination in the classroom. Some of the women felt humiliated by it and avoided further contact with certain teachers and courses (i.e., science). Other women felt challenged by gender discrimination and seemed to thrive in spite of it. These individual differences support Bandura's (1986) concept of personal agency, that is, that persons are capable of reflection on their experiences and of weighing consequences of their behaviors, setting standards for their behavior, and thus shaping who they become. Without the qualitative interview data, we would not be attuned to these individual differences. Quantitative data masks these individual differences in favor of average trends.

In addition to a difference in the attitudes and beliefs of women who have the same experiences, there may be a difference in personality and temperament that affects how they react to their socialization experiences. In our qualitative analyses of interview data, we attempted to assess personality by using a "big five" approach (John, 1989) to rate each person. There is considerable agreement among researchers that personality can be described along five basic dimensions: Introversion/Extraversion, Agreeableness/Disagreeableness, Conscientiousness/Irresponsibleness, Adjustment/Emotional Instability, and Openness/Narrowness. Experts disagree somewhat on how to name these dimensions but agree that research over the past several decades supports such a classification. Analysis of our interview data for these personality dimensions has not been done at the time of this writing. However, such a study could be informative, provided that these personality profiles were compared with the women's positive or negative reaction to similar socialization experiences.

We might conclude that social context and experiences with significant others influenced women's career development, especially their self-efficacy, their motivation to achieve and invest in a career, and their choice of nontraditional careers. Our findings also support a relationship between negative experiences and cognitions and behaviors. These findings are supportive of Bandura's (1977a, 1986) social-cognitive theory.

Evidence for the Effects of Cognitive Beliefs/Attitudes/Feelings

Career self-efficacy (Betz & Hackett, 1983) has been found to be related to choosing higher-level careers in college women. We did not assess career self-efficacy, but we did assess math self-efficacy in our study and found it to be related to persistence in the choice of a science or technology career for women (Farmer, Wardrop, Anderson, & Risinger, 1995) as predicted by Bandura's (1986) theory. Women's beliefs about their ability to perform activities such as drafting, fixing a car motor, repairing electrical equipment, and so on are related in our study to their career interest in and choice of careers such as surgeon versus pediatrician and physicist or chemist versus physics or chemistry teacher (Crabtree et al., 1995). These kinds of self-efficacies or competencies must be nurtured for young girls and women if we are to achieve some form of critical mass in underrepresented career fields such as physics, chemistry, and medical surgery.

Career goals. Bandura's theory also predicts that having a goal, such as a career goal, is related to persistence in related behaviors. In our study, career goals were assessed by the level of career these women aspired to, and, indeed, these goals were important predictors of persistence in a science career. Also, having high career goals in 1990 was more characteristic of women in science than of women in other career fields (Farmer, Wardrop, & Crabtree, 1995).

Outcome expectations. Positive outcome expectations related to participating in a task are predicted by Bandura (1986) to relate to persistence at a task until it is mastered as well as choosing to engage in that task. In a related vein, Lent et al. (1994) have posited, consistent with Bandura (1986), that outcome expectations (about rewards/punishments) are related to career choices. In our study, outcome expectations were assessed by the values these women had related to their career expectations. A characteristic of women choosing a science career, compared with women in other fields, was their high valuing of math and science because competency in these academic subjects was viewed as relevant to their future careers (Farmer, Wardrop, Anderson, & Risinger, 1995; Farmer, Wardrop, & Crabtree, 1995).

Androgyny. When this study was first designed in the late 1970s, I was convinced that women's sex role socialization negatively affected their career motivation and choices. I was, at this time, enthusiastic about the possibility that more gender-free socialization might lead women to be more androgynous in their beliefs and behaviors and that such women would be more likely to choose careers commensurate with their abilities and talents. The idea that women are persons first and women second (Farmer, 1955), for me, is based on the work of Karen Horney (1945) and is related to the concept of androgyny (Bakan, 1966; Bem, 1976, 1981). This idea of the desirability of androgyny contrasts with Gilligan (1982) and Bernard (1981), who emphasize the differences between men and women (i.e., in a "different" voice). We assessed androgyny using the Bem Sex Role Inventory (BSRI; 1976, 1981). In Chapter 3, we briefly referred to these data in relation to agentic characteristics of some of the interviewees. Several studies (Gaudreau, 1977; Moreland et al., 1978) have found two factors for this measure. *Expressive* represents the feminine items and *Instrumental* represents the masculine items. Persons scoring high on both factors would be classified as androgynous. We renamed the Instrumental factor *Independent,* in part because we were reporting our findings to the participating high schools, and this label communicated its meaning better. The findings reported in Farmer (1985) indicated that high scores on Expressive and Independent were significantly related to long-range career commitment for women, whereas for men only Independent was significant.

In our 1990 data analyses, we did not find either Expressive or Independent to be more characteristic of women who persisted in a science career compared with women who did not persist or to women in other career fields. Mean scores for men and women in 1990 were similar, as were scores for Expressive and Independent, which suggests that as young adults, these men and women were relatively androgynous—both those choosing science careers and those in other career fields.

Another cognitive gender difference often found is that men have higher scores on a Competitive achievement style, whereas women have higher scores on a Cooperative achievement style (Farmer, 1985). A person with an androgynous achievement style would have high scores on both. In our study of adolescents, both Cooperative and Competitive achievement style preferences were significantly correlated to career and achievement motivation (Farmer, 1985). Ten years later, neither a Competitive nor a Cooperative achievement style differentiated women in science from those in other career fields (Farmer, Wardrop, Anderson, & Risinger, 1995) or women who persisted in science compared with those who did not (Farmer, Wardrop, & Crabtree, 1995). It seems important to note that a Cooperative achievement style was not negatively related to women's career and achievement motivation; rather, it had a positive relationship. Recent research suggests that a Cooperative style, when applied in management positions, is valued by many corporations today (Spence, 1985). Unger and Crawford (1992) have reviewed theory and research related to androgyny and concluded that masculinity and femininity are not yet equally valued in our society. Thus, although women's approach to management may be more valued today than in the past, women's lower social power and status may both impose external constraints on women's choices and behaviors and set up internal conflicts as women struggle to reconcile their personal preferences with differing social expectations.

Value conflicts. Women, because of their socialization, are prone to home-career conflict, which has a dampening effect on their career choices (Farmer, 1985; Farmer & Bohn, 1970). Farmer (1984) distinguished between this conflict as it relates to values and the conflict related to role overload. For the latter, planning and negotiation may reduce conflict. However, for the former, a woman has to become fully conscious of the values that may be in conflict to tease out which values are hers and which are ones she has learned through her socialization but does not truly value for herself. There is evidence (Farmer, 1985) that for women who value both family and career roles, there is a lowering of their long-range career commitment. Whereas, for men who say they value both roles, no effect was evident on their long-range career commitment.

There is evidence that women in engineering majors are more likely to expect to combine home and career roles than women in education majors (Farmer, 1984). Also, the engineering majors evidence less conflict about home and career roles than the education majors (Farmer, 1984). It appears that women who choose nontraditional careers experience less home-career conflict.

Another value conflict experienced by some women is "fear of success" (Horner, 1972). In Bandura's theory, a fourth source of self-efficacy is the lack of negative emotional arousal (i.e., anxiety, fear). We did not assess anxiety directly but we did assess fear of success and found that for the women in science, fear of success was low, whereas their math self-efficacy was high. This finding lends some support to Bandura's theory that self-efficacy is higher when fear of negative social consequences for certain behaviors is lower. More research is needed to clarify these relationships.

The qualitative interviews shed some light on the role of personal beliefs and attitudes and their influence on behaviors and career choices. Some of the women believed it was important to be economically independent, that is, not to have to rely on a man to pay the bills. This belief, or goal, sustained them through obstacles they encountered, and they pursued college degrees successfully. Many spoke of expectations from their parents that they would go to college and obtain training for a satisfying career. This expectation was a strong motivator for many of the women. It seems clear that personal attitudes, beliefs, and values have an important role in a women's career choices and behavior, and that these same attitudes, beliefs, and values have been shaped by their experiences with others and with the particular environment they grew up in—whether rural, suburban, or urban; whether affluent or one of scarce resources.

As noted in Chapter 13, many of the women compromised their career plans so as to combine work and family roles. This behavior does not appear to be androgynous; it does not transcend gender role expectations. It appears from the interviews that androgynous attitudes as assessed by the BSRI do not necessarily translate into related behaviors. More research is needed to assess these relationships.

Evidence for Effects of Behavioral Choices

Performance accomplishments. One of the four sources of self-efficacy is performance accomplishments. These accomplishments were represented in our study by the GPAs the women had in high school math and natural science. Math self-efficacy was significantly correlated with both math and natural science GPA. In a related vein, academic self-esteem was significantly correlated with GPA in these courses.

Initiating behaviors. In addition to investigating choice behavior as a criterion variable, we examined the relationship of certain course-taking behaviors in high school to the choice of and persistence in a science or technology career. We found that taking elective science and math courses (i.e., those taken in addition to the ones required for graduation) was, in the case of science, the most important predictor for women persisting in a science or technology career as young adults. Elective math course taking had an indirect effect on persistence for women as well. Both elective math and elective science had indirect effects on persistence for men, but no direct effects. In terms of the strength of these effects, they were stronger for women than for men, which suggests that it would be useful to encourage women to take more math and science courses in high school than those required, if it is a societal goal that more women choose science and technical careers. Some school districts are now requiring advanced math and science courses instead of leaving it up to students. Research comparing the impact of these two approaches on the number of women choosing a science career is needed.

Summary of Research for Theory Building

Researchers on women's career development for the twenty-first century would do well to focus on theory building. The model we tested, based on Bandura's social-cognitive theory and that adapted by Lent et al. (1994), could form the basis for these investigations. The complexity of these models is somewhat overwhelming, and the fragmentary nature of findings to date could lead to disillusionment. Bandura (1986) has suggested that it may be best for theory building to focus research on discrete parts of a theoretical model, on two sets of interacting variables, for example, rather than three or four sets, and then explore the two in detail. The following list describes some ideas for research on such smaller sets of variables:

1. Identify the ways in which ethnicity, gender, and socioeconomic status (various levels) interact with a set of relevant cognitive variables such as outcome expectations and goal setting.
2. Identify the ways in which personality factors (i.e., the big five) relate to career development and choice.
3. Identify the ways in which androgynous beliefs and behaviors relate to career choices.
4. Identify the role of and relative strength of the social, behavioral, and cognitive sources of career self-efficacy.
5. Identify the role of social variables—interpersonal (i.e., role models) and contextual (i.e., discrimination)—on career choice.

Having said all this, it seems important to sit back and reflect on the whole, what it is we want to know more about. Women's career development from a social-cognitive perspective, as well as a life planning perspective, is a very large slice of the pie called "life space." Will we lose sight of the big picture if we parcel out our research and focus on specific phenomena within the larger whole? The answer is that we will lose sight of the big picture unless we shuttle back and forth between the micro and the macro perspectives. Boris Pasternak, the Russian novelist and author of *Doctor Zhivago,* has described his goal as being a writer who describes existence, and that this vast terrain was more important than any individual story or incident (Pasternak, 1959/ 1996). For Pasternak, that larger whole represented existence as purposeful, purposeful beyond the human condition. So, too, a full conceptualization of career development is a reality beyond its parts. For example, the concept, so important to Bandura's theory, of reciprocal interaction between the theoretical parts, has rarely been demonstrated in quantitative research. My efforts to do this have, so far, failed. Yet common sense as well as theory support the idea that not only do our beliefs (cognitions) affect our behaviors, but, also, our behaviors affect our beliefs. If I want to engage in scientific invention (a belief), I will behave in ways that involve me in scientific activities, and these activities and my experience with them will shape my beliefs about science and about myself (i.e., Do I like doing this? Am I good at it?). To lose sight of this interactive aspect of learning and development would be to lose an important part of our respondents' reality. Qualitative interview data may provide some of the evidence we seek on these interactions and it will be important for the foreseeable future to continue to conduct our research on both fronts. When research is conducted on less than the full theoretical model, it is essential that researchers not lose sight of the "big picture." They will need to involve researchers in other disciplines such as sociology, work together, share findings, and cross-verify findings.

Research on the Impact of Changes in the Family, School, College, and Workplace

Family. More married women are working, and a majority of women with preschool children are now working. This translates into the dual-earner family being normative, whereas 20 years ago it was nontraditional. Within the family in which both parents are working, there are role behavior changes, with either more sharing of homemaking and parenting roles or more purchasing of substitute services. Evidence from various sources indicate that some of these changes are occurring but that women who work still do a disproportionate amount of the work related to homemaking and parenting. Men have added to their family role more parenting responsibilities than homemaking responsibilities (Gilbert, 1994; Hoffman, 1989).

These changes in the home provide somewhat different socialization experiences for children growing up today, typically with both parents working and children receiving more parenting from fathers than previously (Hoffman, 1989). Also, more children grow up with the expectation that women will work. However, the mother usually works at a lower-paying, lower-prestige job than the father so the "vicarious learning" for girls is that women's work is less important. Parents who want to increase equity in the workplace for women need to encourage their daughters to aim as high as possible rather than settling for lower-paying jobs. Parents also need to challenge the idea that women work only because their salary supports the family income/lifestyle. In fact, women work for much the same reasons men do—to earn money, yes, but also to give meaning to their lives, feel pride in a job well done, and contribute to the needs of society. Several of our participants were single parents and this increasingly prevalent family structure needs special attention. Research on the impact of these societal and family changes on career development is needed.

Schools. Changes in the schools in the past 20 years include changes in textbooks, mandated by Title IX equity legislation, to present a more balanced view of men and women in all work roles and include the contributions of women in history, art, and science. Teacher behavior has also changed as more teachers trained in a curriculum responsive to Title IX guidelines enter the school system. Teacher behaviors, such as responding equally to boys and girls who raise their hands in the classroom and giving similar feedback for successes and failures, may become more common (Sadker, Sadker, & Klein, 1991). However, continuing attitudes and beliefs that suggest it is less important for girls to succeed in math and science, and that for girls the most important role is to be future mothers rather than workers, still place girls at a disadvantage. Teachers need to reinforce the current reality that girls typically will grow up to "work" as well as raise a family and that girls should aim at achieving at the highest level they are capable of in their work. Research on the impact of these changes in teacher behaviors and in curricula is needed to evaluate their impact on women's career development.

Universities. In higher education, at both the undergraduate and the graduate levels, women have increased their enrollment in majors nontraditional for them (e.g., law, medicine, engineering, physics, chemistry, business administration, computer science). However, women are still underrepresented in engineering and the natural sciences. Researchers have found that the classroom climate is a chilly one in many of these nontraditional majors—an atmosphere that is lacking in support for women and at times hostile. Professors need to change both their attitudes and their behaviors in these majors to reduce dropout rates for the women who enroll. Research on the impact of these participation rate and classroom climate condition changes is needed to evaluate their effect on women's career development.

Workplace. Employers have made changes in employment policies responsive to sex equity legislation and affirmative action guidelines. For example, most entry level positions give equal access to men and women. Maternity leave is an accepted part of employee benefits. Inequities still exist, however, in the promotion processes, and fewer women than men reach top levels in fields formerly dominated by men. There is a continuing need for more quality child care facilities at or near workplaces. Sexual harassment in the workplace, as in the classroom, is a serious deterrent to the retention and advancement of women in occupations in which they are still a minority. Research on the impact of policy changes in the workplace and the availability of child care is needed to evaluate the effect of these variables on women's career development.

Counselors. Counselors and therapists who engage in career counseling have changed their behaviors since 1970. Most are trained to help women increase the career options they consider and to encourage the choice of careers that are commensurate with the women's potential. The current need, in the 1990s, is for career counselors to conduct their counseling within a life planning framework. Counselors need to help women and men consider the interdependence of their various life roles, that is, how decisions about one role affect other roles. Counselors need to help women and men plan ahead for the best way to achieve their life goals. Research is needed to evaluate the impact of counselor behavior change on women's career development.

A Follow-Up Study for the Year 2005

The women and men we interviewed in 1991-1993 would be important to follow up when they are in their late thirties and early forties. It would be interesting to see how those who married and are part of dual-worker families have coped with their multiple role lifestyles and how these lifestyles have affected their children's experiences and behaviors in school as well as their values and goals. For those who are single parents, it would be important to know how they have coped with their multiple roles. With the rapidly changing economy and changes in economic opportunities, it is important to know how persons who were on a positive career trajectory fared 12 years later. Our study has underscored the usefulness of combining quantitative and qualitative data. Thus a follow-up study in the year 2005 should follow this pattern and collect both types of information with the participants described in this book.

The findings related to optimizing women's career development and ensuring that more women choose careers congruent with their abilities and interests should lead to innovative programs. Evaluation of these programs in the schools, colleges, universities, and workplace is needed if they are to benefit society as a whole. Women are not using their full potential in the workforce for many reasons. Among these are their beliefs that (a) their family, friends, and society in general don't care whether or not they work and (b) they won't be treated fairly/equitably in the marketplace (Betz & Fitzgerald, 1987; Farmer, 1976b; Farmer & Bohn, 1970). This underuse of women's potential is a loss to both society and individual women. Consistent with Bandura's (1977a, 1986) social-cognitive theory, such beliefs can be changed with new experiences or changes in society. And getting reacquainted with Gena, Juanita, Linda, Terry, and Norma, to name a few, when they are about 40 years old would give a fuller picture of their lives and experiences, their ups and downs, and how these have come about.

Appendix A

Characteristics of Participants in 1980

Table A.1 *Number of 9th- and 12th-Grade Women and Men From Three Geographic Locations (1980) (N = 1,863)*

Location	9th Grade		12th Grade		Total
	Females	*Males*	*Females*	*Males*	
Inner City					
Mixed[a]	17	6	7	7	
Black	36	27	58	28	
Hispanic	36	35	39	33	
White	89	99	72	87	
total	178	167	176	155	676
Suburban					
Mixed	10	25	2	8	
Black	1	1	0	0	
Hispanic	9	6	10	5	
White	206	192	183	199	
total	226	224	195	212	857
Rural					
Mixed	7	10	4	4	
Black	0	0	0	1	
Hispanic	0	1	0	1	
White	71	80	72	79	
total	78	91	76	85	330
Grand total	482	482	447	452	

a. Mixed = Native American, Asian American, and others (approximately 6% of totals).

Table A.2 *Percentage Ethnic Distribution in 1980 Compared With United States*

Race	United States[a]	Sample
Black	11.7	8.2
Hispanic	6.4	9.2
White	76.8	77.0
Other[b]	5.1	5.6

a. Based on data from the U.S. Bureau of the Census (1981).
b. Other includes Asian American, Eskimo, Native American, and others not elsewhere classified.

Appendix B

School Characteristics

Table B.1 *Background Characteristics at City High School (N =228)*

Variable	Percentage*
Grade	
9th	51
12th	49
Sex	
male	36
female	64
Race	
Native American	0
Asian American	5
Black American	36
American of Spanish-speaking descent	37
White American	15
mixed	7
Handicap	
absence	91
presence	9
Ability level in English (student estimate)	
A	11
B	32
C	47
D	10
Ability level in math (student estimate)	
A	12
B	21
C	35
D	32
Father's educational level	
less than high school	39
high school diploma	36
junior college degree	9
R.N.	2
B.A.	10
M.A.	3
Ph.D. or professional	3
Mother's educational level	
less than high school	32
high school diploma	40
junior college degree	11
R.N.	10
B.A.	4
M.A.	3
Ph.D. or professional	0
Father's occupational level**	
76-100 quartile	8
51-75 quartile	20
26-50 quartile	35
0-25 quartile	37
Mother's occupational level**	
76-100 quartile	4
51-75 quartile	30
26-50 quartile	38
0-25 quartile	28
Mothers who are homemakers	27

*Percentages may not add up to 100% because of incomplete responses.
**Percentages based on employed mothers or fathers.

Table B.2 *Background Characteristics at Metro High School (N = 498)*

Variable	Percentage*
Grade	
9th	52
12th	48
Sex	
male	52
female	48
Race	
Native American	1
Asian American	0
Black American	15
American of Spanish-speaking descent	14
White American	68
mixed	2
Handicap	
absence	95
presence	5
Ability level in English (student estimate)	
A	10
B	31
C	45
D	14
Ability level in math (student estimate)	
A	12
B	26
C	35
D	27
Father's educational level	
less than high school	23
high school diploma	52
junior college degree	14
R.N.	0
B.A.	6
M.A.	4
Ph.D. or professional	1
Mother's educational level	
less than high school	15
high school diploma	60
junior college degree	10
R.N.	7
B.A.	4
M.A.	3
Ph.D. or professional	1
Father's occupational level**	
76-100 quartile	6
51-75 quartile	18
26-50 quartile	44
0-25 quartile	32
Mother's occupational level**	
76-100 quartile	4
51-75 quartile	44
26-50 quartile	37
0-25 quartile	14
Mothers who are homemakers	35

*Percentages may not add up to 100% because of incomplete responses.
**Percentages based on employed mothers or fathers.

Table B.3 *Background Characteristics at Suburban High School (N = 553)*

Variable	Percentage*
Grade	
9th	46
12th	54
Sex	
male	50
female	50
Race	
Native American	1
Asian American	1
Black American	1
American of Spanish-speaking descent	4
White American	90
mixed	3
Handicap	
absence	94
presence	6
Ability level in English (student estimate)	
A	27
B	36
C	27
D	10
Ability level in math (student estimate)	
A	17
B	31
C	32
D	20
Father's educational level	
less than high school	23
high school diploma	46
junior college degree	14
R.N.	1
B.A.	12
M.A.	4
Ph.D. or professional	1
Mother's educational level	
less than high school	17
high school diploma	57
junior college degree	12
R.N.	5
B.A.	6
M.A.	2
Ph.D. or professional	0
Father's occupational level**	
76-100 quartile	11
51-75 quartile	32
26-50 quartile	36
0-25 quartile	21
Mother's occupational level**	
76-100 quartile	1
51-75 quartile	47
26-50 quartile	29
0-25 quartile	23
Mothers who are homemakers	31

*Percentages may not add up to 100% because of incomplete responses.
**Percentages based on employed mothers or fathers.

Table B.4 *Background Characteristics at Garden High School (N = 324)*

Variable	Percentage*
Grade	
9th	64
12th	36
Sex	
male	53
female	47
Race	
Native American	3
Asian American	0
Black American	0
American of Spanish-speaking descent	2
White American	92
mixed	3
Handicap	
absence	91
presence	9
Ability level in English (student estimate)	
A	10
B	31
C	38
D	21
Ability level in math (student estimate)	
A	15
B	29
C	25
D	31
Father's educational level	
less than high school	23
high school diploma	44
junior college degree	11
R.N.	1
B.A.	12
M.A.	7
Ph.D. or professional	2
Mother's educational level	
less than high school	18
high school diploma	54
junior college degree	14
R.N.	6
B.A.	5
M.A.	3
Ph.D. or professional	0
Father's occupational level**	
76-100 quartile	11
51-75 quartile	26
26-50 quartile	37
0-25 quartile	26
Mother's occupational level**	
76-100 quartile	3
51-75 quartile	37
26-50 quartile	31
0-25 quartile	29
Mothers who are homemakers	20

*Percentages may not add up to 100% because of incomplete responses.
**Percentages based on employed mothers or fathers.

Table B.5 *Background Characteristics at Farmerville High School (N = 196)*

Variable	Percentage*
Grade	
9th	57
12th	43
Sex	
male	55
female	45
Race	
Native American	5
Asian American	1
Black American	1
American of Spanish-speaking descent	1
White American	89
mixed	4
Handicap	
absence	91
presence	9
Ability level in English (student estimate)	
A	43
B	26
C	22
D	9
Ability level in math (student estimate)	
A	27
B	35
C	28
D	10
Father's educational level	
less than high school	20
high school diploma	50
junior college degree	17
R.N.	0
B.A.	6
M.A.	7
Ph.D. or professional	0
Mother's educational level	
less than high school	16
high school diploma	64
junior college degree	8
R.N.	4
B.A.	5
M.A.	3
Ph.D. or professional	1
Father's occupational level**	
76-100 quartile	4
51-75 quartile	18
26-50 quartile	42
0-25 quartile	36
Mother's occupational level**	
76-100 quartile	2
51-75 quartile	34
26-50 quartile	33
0-25 quartile	31
Mothers who are homemakers	31

*Percentages may not add up to 100% because of incomplete responses.
**Percentages based on employed mothers or fathers.

Table B.6 *Background Characteristics at Country High School (N =141)*

Variable	Percentage*
Grade	
9th	44
12th	56
Sex	
male	50
female	50
Race	
Native American	2
Asian American	0
Black American	0
American of Spanish-speaking descent	1
White American	94
mixed	3
Handicap	
absence	93
presence	7
Ability level in English (student estimate)	
A	12
B	37
C	39
D	12
Ability level in math (student estimate)	
A	20
B	38
C	29
D	13
Father's educational level	
less than high school	21
high school diploma	57
junior college degree	6
R.N.	0
B.A.	9
M.A.	4
Ph.D. or professional	3
Mother's educational level	
less than high school	13
high school diploma	63
junior college degree	9
R.N.	4
B.A.	8
M.A.	2
Ph.D. or professional	1
Father's occupational level**	
76-100 quartile	7
51-75 quartile	28
26-50 quartile	33
0-25 quartile	32
Mother's occupational level**	
76-100 quartile	1
51-75 quartile	30
26-50 quartile	40
0-25 quartile	29
Mothers who are homemakers	34

*Percentages may not add up to 100% because of incomplete responses.
**Percentages based on employed mothers or fathers.

Appendix C

Interview Protocol

First Interview Session

Goals: Get to know each other, find out how interviewee thinks/talks about work, determine whether focus is on current job or future job, move into the past to understand the process of career choice/persistence.

1.	Read purpose statement.	(Get to know each other)
2.	What would you like to start with?	(Get to know each other)
3.	Tell me what you're doing now.	(Get to know each other)
4.	Do you expect to continue doing (___)?	(Focus current/future?)
5.	How do you feel about (___)?	(Get to know each other)
6.	How does work fit into your life?	(Meaning/importance of work)

For more info:
What if you won the lottery?
What if you had to choose only one of your roles?
What if working and child sick?
Use pie to demonstrate relative importance of roles.

7. What would you tell a friend who was interested in a job like yours? WHY? (Get to know each other—for person who hasn't said much about her or his work.)

8. What would you tell a friend was the best and worst part of your job? WHY? (Get to know each other—for person who hasn't said much about her or his work.)

9. What would your coworkers/colleagues say about being a (___)? (Get to know each other—for person who hasn't said much about her or his work.)

10. How did you come to be/do (___)? (Move to past; focus on her or his process words. Is there choice? What are the factors?)

11. Did you ever want to do/be anything else? (Gives focal point to move forward and backward from.)

IF NO: Did you ever have any doubts? (Process: What sustained or hindered them?)

12. When did you first want to do/be (___)? (Help with thinking back process. Must at least go back to high school.)

IF NOT HIGH SCHOOL: What about high school?

13. Tell me about how you got from (___). (Process—moving from past to present/future.)

14. What factors led to you being/doing (___)? (Identify important factor for second interview.)

NOTE: At the end of the first interview, you will reintroduce the idea of a second interview. At that time, ask:

(1) You've given me a lot of good information today. I'd like to spend some time thinking about what we've talked about, and what else I need to know. Could we meet again in a couple of weeks?

(2) One additional thing that might help me get ready for our second interview is looking over the answers you gave to the questionnaire you mailed in. I would need special permission from you to do that though—since we promised that your answers would be anonymous. If you don't mind letting me look over your answers, I can ask the project director to look up which questionnaire is yours (they have code numbers, not names on them)—and even bring you a copy if you like. Would that be OK?

(3) Since we'll be meeting again, I am also wondering if there is anything you were hoping we would talk about during our interview?(Get preliminary idea of motivation, respond to her or his agenda.)

Second Interview Session

Goals: Talk more about the factors identified during the first interview as influencing the interviewee's choices, possibly identifying additional factors.

INTRO: Last time we talked a lot about (___). Since then, I spent time listening to our tape and thinking about what parts of your story I feel like I understand and what parts I need to know more about. I'm hoping to focus today's interview more on the parts I need to know more about. I want to explore some topics that came up last time in more depth, and I want to ask you about some additional points in time. It may feel like I ask more specific questions today than I did last time because I want to be sure to fill in the gaps—so that I get as complete a picture of your story as I can. OK?

Personal Factors

1. Last time you talked about (___). Tell me more about that and how it relates to (___).

KEEP REPEATING UNTIL MENTION ALL ITEMS OF INTEREST

2. Are there other things about yourself (e.g., skills, likes and dislikes, physical characteristics) that led you to be/do (___)?
   IF ONLY HEAR NEGATIVE FACTORS: Was there anything about yourself that helped you overcome these doubts/concerns?
   IF ONLY HEAR POSITIVE FACTORS: Was there anything about yourself that caused you to have doubts about doing (___)?

3. How do these things we've just been talking about relate to your change from wanting to be/do (___)?

4. You indicated in your questionnaire that (___). Tell me more about that, and how it relates to (___).

KEEP REPEATING UNTIL MENTION ALL ITEMS OF INTEREST

ALTERNATIVE FACTORS QUESTIONS

1. If I were a student at (___), what help could I expect to get in terms of thinking about or planning a career (e.g., from teachers, counselors, others)?

2. Why do you think somebody who wants to be an (___) ends up
   (a) in something entirely different?
   (b) doing exactly that?

Environmental Factors

1. Last time you talked about (___). Tell me more about that and how it relates to (___).

2. Are there other things about your life situation (e.g., certain people, certain experiences or realities) that led you to do/be (___)?
   IF ONLY HEAR NEGATIVE FACTORS: Was there anything in your life that supported you?
   IF ONLY HEAR POSITIVE FACTORS: Was there anything in your life that got in the way?

3. How do these things we've just been talking about relate to your change from wanting to be/do (___) to wanting to be/do (___)?

4. You indicated in your questionnaire that (___). Tell me more about that, and how it relates to (___).

KEEP REPEATING UNTIL MENTION ALL ITEMS OF INTEREST

1. To wanting to be/do (___)?

(Help person remember an important factor mentioned during first interview and not yet elaborated on.)

(Talk about factors moving person from first/early choice to present/future choice.)

(Get both sides of the picture.)

(Get both sides of the picture.)

(Ask only if person once wanted to be something other than what she or he wants to be now.)

(Use CMAP clues, such as critical incidents, success/failures.)

319

MOTIVATION FACTORS

Goals: Broaden discussion to include motivation. Get high hopes/dreams.

1. OK. We've been spending a lot of time   (Get motivation for choice.)
    talking about (the what), now I want to
    shift a little and talk about why you
    pursued ___.

    a. What was important to you about ___   (Get values, maybe needs.)
        when you decided to pursue it?

    b. What did you think you would get out   (Get needs, maybe goals.)
        of ___ when you decided to pursue it?

    c. When you first decided to pursue ___,   (Get goals.)
        what goals did you think it would
        meet?

    d. What did you hope to achieve?   (Get more specific in terms of goals.)

    e. Any other reasons you decided to   (Get her or his perspective.)
        pursue ___question

2. OK. I have a pretty good idea why you   (Get motivation for persistence.)
    decided to pursue ___. Why do you stay
    in it?

(Other words to use: keeps you going, what do you get out of it, why do you continue, goals, benefits?)

3. If you had a magic wand that allowed you   (Get aspiration information.)
    to change things so that you could do/be
    anything you wanted to do/be, what would
    you want to do/be. Remember, your magic
    wand gives you special powers so that you
    aren't confined by your previous
    experiences or current circumstances. It
    even gives you the power to decide when
    you'd like to start being/doing this new
    thing. (It could be now, 10 or 20 years
    from now—whenever.)

    Or

4. Tell me something that you would love
    to do/be that you really haven't
    considered seriously.

SUMMING IT UP QUESTIONS

1. If the local junior high or high school   (Get her or his ideas about most important
    invited you to talk to their classes about   points.)
    careers, how would you want to present
    it—what would you want to be sure to
    get across?

2. Why did you agree to be interviewed?   (Get context for information.)

Appendix D

Analysis Themes

HyperQual Codes (in alphabetical order)

Filenames

Tags
Country*
City*
Suburban*
Farmerville*
Garden*
Metro*
Q (quote)
neg
pos

COLLEGE

CRIT*ical Incidents*

Family
Inferred
Personal
School*
Work
Work/Family

DECIS*ion Process*

Choices Considered
Plans
Style

EARLYED

EDUC*ation*

Awards
Apprentice
Behavior
Culture
   peer
   school*
Grad
High*

EXPER*iences*

    Hobbies
    Media
    Programs
     church
     community
     school*
     work
    Other

FAMILY

    Exper (for *experiences*)
     neg
     pos
    Tree

GUID*ance*

    Talk (for *school talk*)

MODELS (for *role models*)

MOTIV*ation*

OBST*acles*

    Discrim
     ageism
     racism
     sexism
     other
    Inferred
    Other
     nonevent
     null

PARENT

    Dad
    Mom

SELF

    Abilities
    Behavior
    Beliefs
    Feelings
    Personality
    Physical

SIGNIF*icant People*

Counselors
Family
    children
    relatives
    sibling
    S.O.
    other
    adopt
Friends
    School*
    teachers
Super (for *boss or supervisor*)
Other

TRANS*itions*

Begin
Births
Graduations
Marriages
Miles (for *milestones*)
Other

WORK

Culture
Current
History
Volunteer

Work/Home

World **View**

Interpersonal
Philosophy
Other
    cultural

* Pseudonym for School

Appendix E

Rules for Classifying Occupations/Majors as Science or Technology

This classification uses the Holland Coding system (Gottfredson & Holland, 1989) + the *Dictionary of Occupational Titles* (DOT) Coding system (U.S. Department of Labor, 1991) to identify science + technology occupations. Occupations are classified as science or technology if they fit *either of the two following rules*:

(1) (a) The occupation has an "I" in its Holland Code. The "I" may be in either the first, second, or third place in the code; *and* (b) the DOT Code for the occupation has any number from 00-07 in the first two digits.

For example:	Occupation	Holland Code	Dot Code
	Civil Engineer	*I*RE	*005*.061-014
	Education Specialist	E*I*A	099.167-022
	Residence Counselor	SEC	*045*.107-038

Civil Engineer would be coded as a science/technology occupation because it *fits BOTH criteria*: "I" in the Holland Code; 00-07 in first two digits of DOT Code.

Education Specialist would *not* be coded as science/technology. It has an "I" in the Holland Code, *but it does not have 00-07 in the first two digits of the DOT code.*

Residence Counselor would *not* be coded as science/technology. It has 00-07 in the first two digits of the DOT Code, *but it does not have an "I" in the Holland Code.*

To be coded as a science/technology occupation, the occupation must fit *BOTH* criteria in (1) or it must fit (2)

(2) (a) The occupation has an "R" in its Holland Code. The "R" may be in the first, second, or third place, *and* (b) the DOT Code for the occupation has any number from 00-07 in the first two digits, and (c) any number from 0-3 in the fourth digit.

For example:	Occupation	Holland Code	Dot Code
	Electroencephalographic Technologist	*R*CS	*078.3*62-022
	Credit Analyst	ES*R*	191.267-014
	Recreational Therapist	SEC	*076.1*24-014

Electroencephalographic Technologist would be coded as a science/technology occupation because it *fits all three criteria* for 2. It has an "R" in its Holland Code. It has 00-07 in the first two digits of the DOT Code. It has 0-3 in the fourth digit of the DOT Code.

Credit Analyst would *not* be coded science/technology. It has an "R" in the Holland Code and 0-3 in the fourth digit of the DOT Code, *but it does not have 00-07 in the first two digits of the DOT Code.*

Recreational Therapist would *not* be coded as science. It has 00-07 in the first two digits of the DOT, and it has 0-3 in the fourth digit of the DOT, *but it does not have an "R" in the Holland Code.*

Science Sample Rules: Addenda

1. In addition to the rules outlined above, we added some occupations from the professional category that were excluded by the rules because they had "9" in their DOT code in the second place. These "9" digit codes represented teachers and we decided to include high school and university teachers who had Holland codes with an "I" in the first place.

2. Only DOT codes with a "0" in the first place are included by rule. We reviewed all occupations with a "1" in its DOT code in the first position, and identified from this set four occupations that had Holland codes with an "I" or an "R" in the first or second place. We included these four occupations:

OCCUPATION	DOT CODE	HOLLAND CODE	DUNCAN SEI CODE
Accountant	160167010	CRS	78
Controller	186117014	EIS	56
Estimator	160267018	CIS	62
Research Worker	199364014	IRS	65

We included Duncan codes from 45 to 96 following a review of occupations that fit the rules but had lower Duncan codes. This review indicated that there were only two occupations that fit the rules but had Duncan codes lower than 45. These were Dietitian and Dental Assistant.

Table E.1 *Science Sample by Gender, Ethnicity, and Persister/Changer Status (n = 173, 1980/1990)*

| | Persister | | Changer | | Total |
	n	%	n	%	n
Ethnicity					
Minority					
men	3	4	9	9	12
women	9	13	8	8	17
Majority					
men	32	46	33	31	65
women	26	37	53	52	79
Age					
9th men	15	21	25	24	40
9th women	20	29	38	37	57
12th men	20	29	16	16	36
12th women	15	21	24	23	39
Total	70		103		173

References

Ainsworth, M. D. S. (1989). Attachments beyond infancy. *American Psychologist, 44,* 709-716.

Almquist, E. M., & Angrist, S. S. (1971). Role model influence on college aspirations. *Merrill-Palmer Quarterly, 17*(3), 263-279.

Alper, T. (1974). Achievement motivation in women: Now-you-see-it-now-you-don't. *American Psychologist, 29,* 194-203.

Amatea, E., Cross, E., Clark, J., & Bobby, C. (1986). Assessing the work and family role expectations of career-oriented men and women: The Life Role Salience Scales. *Journal of Marriage and the Family, 48,* 831-838.

Ames, C., & Archer, J. (1988). Achievement goals in the classroom. *Journal of Educational Psychology, 80,* 260-267.

Anderson, E., & Leslie, L. (1991). Coping with employment and family status: Employment arrangement and gender differences. *Sex Roles, 24,* 223-237.

Arnold, K. D. (1993). Undergraduate aspirations and career outcomes of academically talented women: A discriminant analysis. *Roeper Review, 15*(3), 169-175.

Astin, H. (1967). Factors associated with the participation of women doctorates in the labor force. *Personnel and Guidance Journal, 46,* 240-246.

Astin, A., & Astin, H. (1993). *Undergraduate science education: The impact of different college environments on the educational pipeline in the sciences.* Los Angeles: University of California, Higher Education Research Institute.

Astin, H. (1984). The meaning of work in women's lives: A sociopsychological model of career choice and work behavior. *Counseling Psychologist, 12*(1), 117-126.

Atkinson, J. (1978). The mainsprings of achievement-oriented activity. In J. Atkinson & J. Raynor (Eds.), *Personality, motivation and achievement.* New York: Halsted.

Bakan, D. (1966). *The quality of human existence.* Chicago: Rand McNally.

Bakken, L., Hershey, M., & Miller, P. (1990). Gifted adolescent females' attitudes toward gender equality in educational and intergender relationships. *Roeper Review, 12*(4), 261-264.

Bandura, A. (1969). *Principles of behavior modification.* New York: Holt, Rinehart & Winston.

Bandura, A. (1977a). Self-efficacy: Toward a unifying theory of behavioral change. *Psychological Review, 84,* 191-215.

Bandura, A. (1977b). *Social learning theory.* Englewood Cliffs, NJ: Prentice Hall.

Bandura, A. (1978). The self system in reciprocal determinism. *American Psychologist, 33,* 344-358.

Bandura, A. (1982). Self-efficacy mechanism in human agency. *American Psychologist, 37*(2), 122-147.

Bandura, A. (1986). *Social foundations of thought and action: A social cognitive theory.* New York: Prentice Hall.

Bandura, A. (1989). Human agency in social cognitive theory. *American Psychologist, 44,* 1175-1184.

Bardwick, J. (1971). *Psychology of women.* New York: Harper & Row.

Barnett, R., Marshall, N., & Pleck, J. (1992). Men's multiple roles and their relationship to men's psychological distress. *Journal of Marriage and the Family, 54,* 358-367.

Baruch, G., & Barnett, R. (1986). Role quality and psychological well-being. In F. Crosby (Ed.), *Spouse, parent, worker: On gender and multiple roles* (pp. 63-73). New Haven, CT: Yale University Press.

Becker, A. (1985). *The role of the public school in the maintenance and change of ethnic group affiliation.* Unpublished doctoral dissertation, Brown University, Providence, RI.

Bem, S. (1976). Beyond androgyny: Some presumptuous prescriptions for a liberated sexual identity. In J. Sherman & F. Denmark (Eds.), *The future women: Issues in psychology.* New York: Psychological Dimensions.

Bem, S. (1981). *Bem Sex Role Inventory: Professional manual.* Palo Alto, CA: Consulting Psychologists Press.

Bernard, J. (1981). *The female world.* New York: Free Press.

Betz, N. (1990). *What stops women and minorities from choosing and completing majors in science and engineering.* Washington, DC: Federation of Behavioral, Psychological and Cognitive Sciences.

Betz, N. (1993). Women's career development. In F. L. Denmark & M. A. Paludi (Eds.), *Psychology of women: A handbook of issues and theories* (pp. 627-684). Westport, CT: Greenwood.

Betz, N., & Fitzgerald, L. (1987). *The career psychology of women.* New York: Academic Press.

Betz, N., & Hackett, G. (1983). The relationship of mathematics self-efficacy expectations to the selection of science-based college majors. *Journal of Vocational Behavior, 23,* 329-345.

Bloch, D. P. (1989). Using career information with dropouts and at-risk youth. *Career Development Quarterly, 38,* 160-171.

Blustein, D. L., Prezioso, M. S., & Schultheiss, D. P. (1995). Attachment theory and career development: Current status and future directions. *Counseling Psychologist, 23*(3), 416-432.

Bowlby, J. (1982). *Attachment and loss: Vol. 1. Attachment* (2nd ed.). New York: Basic Books.

Brown, D., Brooks, L., & Associates (Eds.). (1996). *Career choice and development* (3rd ed.). San Francisco: Jossey-Bass.

Brush, S. G. (1991). Women in science and engineering. *American Scientist, 79,* 404-419.

Burke, P. J., & Hoelter, J. W. (1988). Identity and sex-race differences in educational and occupational aspirations formation. *Social Science Research, 17,* 29-47.

Burlew, A. K., & Johnson, J. L. (1992). Role conflict and career advancement among African American women in nontraditional professions. *Career Development Quarterly, 40,* 302-312.

Burwood, L. R. V. (1992). Can the national curriculum help reduce working-class underachievement? *Educational Studies, 18*(3), 311-321.

Calabrese, R. L., & Underwood, E. (1994). The effects of school-generated racism on students of color. *High School Journal, 415,* 267-273.

Caplan, N., Choy, M. H., & Whitmore, J. K. (1991). *Children of the boat people: A study of educational success.* Ann Arbor: University of Michigan Press.

Card, J., Steel, L., & Abeles, R. (1980). Sex differences in realization of individual potential for achievement. *Journal of Vocational Behavior, 17,* 1-21.

Cassidy, J. (1995, October 16). Who killed the middle class? *New Yorker,* pp. 113-124.

Cobb, R. A., McIntire, W. G., & Pratt, P. A. (1989). Vocational and educational aspirations of high school students: A problem for rural America. *Research in Rural Education, 6*(2), 11-16.

Commission on the Status of Women. (1970). *Participation of women in the economic and social development of their countries.* New York: United Nations.

Coopersmith, S. (1980). *The antecedents of self-esteem* (2nd ed.). Palo Alto, CA: Consulting Psychologists Press.

Crabtree, S., Farmer, H., Anderson, C., & Wardrop, J. (1995, August). *Gender differences in science careers: Prestige level and Holland type.* Paper presented at the American Psychological Association annual meeting, New York City.

Crandall, V., & Battle, E. (1970). The antecedents and adult correlates of academic and intellectual achievement efforts. In J. Hill (Ed.), *Minnesota Symposia on Child Psychology* (Vol. 4). Minneapolis: University of Minnesota Press.

Crosby, F. J. (1991). *Juggling: The unexpected advantages of balancing career and home for women and their families.* New York: Free Press.

DeAngelis, T. (1995). Ignorance plagues affirmative action. *APA Monitor, 26*(5), 1, 8.

Deaux, K., & Kite, M. (1993). Gender stereotype. In F. L. Denmark & M. A. Paludi (Eds.), *Psychology of women: A handbook of issues and theories* (pp. 107-139). Westport, CT: Greenwood.

Delgado-Gaitan, C., & Trueba, H. (1991). *Crossing cultural borders: Education for immigrant families in America.* London: Falmer.

Dunnell, P., & Bakken, L. (1991). Gifted high school students' attitudes toward careers and sex roles. *Roeper Review, 13*(4), 198-202.

Eccles, J. (1985). Why doesn't Jane run? Sex differences in educational and occupational patterns. In F. D. Horowitz & M. O'Brien (Eds.), *The gifted and talented: Developmental perspectives* (pp. 251-294). Washington, DC: American Psychological Association.

Eccles, J. (1994). Understanding women's educational and occupational choices. *Psychology of Women Quarterly, 18*(4), 585-609.

Eccles, J., Adler, T., & Meece, J. L. (1984). Sex differences in achievement: A test of alternative theories. *Journal of Personality and Social Psychology, 46,* 26-43.

Endler, N., & Magnusson, D. (Eds.). (1976). *Interactional psychology and personality.* Washington, DC: Hemisphere.

Entwisle, D., & Baker, D. (1983). Gender and young children's expectations for performance in arithmetic. *Developmental Psychology, 19*(2), 200-209.

Ethington, C. A., & Wolfle, L. M. (1988). Women's selection of quantitative undergraduate fields of study: Direct and indirect influences. *American Educational Research Journal, 25,* 157-175.

Etzkowitz, H., Kemelgor, C., Neuschatz, M., Uzzi, B., & Alonzo, J. (1994). The paradox of critical mass for women in science. *Science, 266,* 51-54.

Farmer, H. (1955). *The role of the professionally trained wife.* Unpublished bachelor of divinity (B.D.) thesis, Union Theological Seminary, New York.

Farmer, H. (1971). Helping women to resolve the home-career conflict. *Personnel and Guidance Journal, 49,* 795-801.

Farmer, H. (1976a). INQUIRY project: Computer-assisted counseling centers for adults. *Counseling Psychologist, 6,* 122-134.

Farmer, H. (1976b). What inhibits career and achievement motivation in women? *Counseling Psychologist, 6*(2). Also in Harmon, L., et al. (Eds.). (1978). *Counseling women* (pp. 159-172). Monterey, CA: Brooks/Cole.

Farmer, H. (1978). What inhibits career and achievement motivation in women? In L. Harmon, J. Birk, L. Fitzgerald, & F. Tanney (Eds.), *Counseling women* (pp. 159-172). Monterey, CA: Brooks/Cole.

Farmer, H. (1980). Environmental, background, and psychological variables related to optimizing achievement and career motivation for high school girls. *Journal of Vocational Behavior, 17,* 58-70.

Farmer, H. (1983). Career and homemaking plans for high school youth. *Journal of Counseling Psychology, 30,* 40-45.

Farmer, H. (1984). Development of a measure of home-career conflict related to career motivation in college women. *Sex Roles: A Journal of Research, 10*(9/10), 663-676.

Farmer, H. (1985). A model of career and achievement motivation for women and men. *Journal of Counseling Psychology, 32*(3), 363-390.

Farmer, H. (1990). *Dual-career families.* Invited paper at the AERA annual meeting. (Available from the author, Department of Educational Psychology, University of Illinois, Champaign, IL 61820)

Farmer, H. (1992). The influence of early environment and ongoing social support. In N. J. Smith & S. K. Leduc (Eds.), *Women's work.* Calgary, Alberta, Canada: Detselig Enterprises.

Farmer, H., & Backer, T. (1977). *New career options for women: A counselor's sourcebook.* New York: Human Sciences Press.

Farmer, H., & Bohn, M. (1970). Home-career conflict reduction and the level of career interest in women. *Journal of Counseling Psychology, 17,* 228-232.

Farmer, H., Keane, J., Rooney, G., Vispoel, W., Harmon, L., Lerner, B., Linn, R., & Maehr, M. (1981). *Career motivation achievement planning: C-MAP* (A measure and administrator's manual). (Available from the first author, Department of Educational Psychology, University of Illinois, Champaign, IL 61820)

Farmer, H., & Seliger, J. (1985). Sex equity in career and vocational education. In S. Klein (Ed.), *Handbook for achieving sex equity through education* (pp. 338-359). Baltimore: Johns Hopkins University Press.

Farmer, H., Wardrop, J., Anderson, M., & Risinger, R. (1995). Women's career choices: Focus on science, math and technology careers. *Journal of Counseling Psychology, 42,* 155-170.

Farmer, H., Wardrop, J., & Crabtree, S. (1995, December). *Why women persist in a science or technology career.* Presentation at the National Science Foundation, "Women & Science Conference," Washington, DC.

Fitzpatrick, J. L., & Silverman, T. (1989). Women's selection of careers in engineering: Do traditional-nontraditional differences still exist? *Journal of Vocational Behavior, 34,* 266-278.

Frieze, I., Whiteley, B., Hanusa, B., & McHugh, M. (1982). Assessing the theoretical models for sex differences in causal attributions for success and failure. *Sex Roles: A Journal of Research, 8,* 333-344.

Gaskill, L. R. (1991). Women's career success: A factor analytic study of contributing factors. *Journal of Career Development, 17*(3), 167-178.

Gaudreau, P. (1977). Factor analysis of the Bem Sex-Role Inventory. *Journal of Consulting and Clinical Psychology, 45,* 299-302.

Gibson, M. A. (1988). *Accommodation without assimilation: Sikh immigrants in an American high school.* Ithaca, NY: Cornell University Press.

Gibson, M. A. (1991). Minorities and schooling: Some implications. In M. A. Gibson & J. U. Ogbu (Eds.), *Minority status and schooling: A comparative study of immigrant and involuntary minorities* (pp. 357-381). New York: Garland.

Gilbert, L. (1985). *Men in dual-career families: Current realities and future prospects.* Hillsdale, NJ: Lawrence Erlbaum.

Gilbert, L. (1993). *Two careers/one family*. Newbury Park, CA: Sage.

Gilbert, L. (1994). Current perspectives on dual-career families. *Current Directions in Psychological Science, 3*, 101-104.

Gilbert, L. (1994). Reclaiming and returning gender to context: Examples from studies of heterosexual dual-earner families. *Psychology of Women Quarterly, 18*(4), 539-558.

Gilbert, L. A., & Rachlin, V. (1987). Mental health and psychological functioning of dual-career families. *Counseling Psychologist, 15*(1), 7-49.

Gilligan, C. (1982). *In a different voice*. Cambridge, MA: Harvard University Press.

Glesne, C., & Peshkin, A. (1992). *Becoming qualitative researchers: An introduction*. New York: Longman.

Goetz, B. (1996, June). School counselor triumph as Congress restores 1996 education funding. *Counseling Today*, p. 34.

Goldstein, B. L. (1985). *Schooling for cultural transitions: Hmong girls and boys in American high schools*. Unpublished doctoral dissertation, Department of Educational Policy Studies, University of Wisconsin, Madison.

Gottfredson, G., & Holland, J. (1989). *Dictionary of Holland occupational codes* (2nd ed.). Odessa, FL: Psychological Assessment Resources, Inc.

Gottfredson, L. (1981). Circumscription and compromise: A developmental theory of occupational aspirations. *Journal of Counseling Psychology, 28*, 545-579.

Granfield, R. (1991). Making it by faking it: Working-class students in an elite academic environment. *Journal of Contemporary Ethnography, 20*(3), 331-351.

Granrose, C. (1985, March). Anticipating the decision to work following childbirth. *Vocational Guidance Quarterly*, pp. 221-230.

Green, B., & Russo, N. (1993). Work and family roles: Selected issues. In F. L. Denmark & M. A. Paludi (Eds.), *Psychology of women: A handbook of issues and theories* (pp. 685-719). Westport, CT: Greenwood.

Green-Powell, P. A. (1993). Facilitators and barriers to black women's progress toward the principalship: Six case studies. *Dissertation Abstracts International, 54*, 388.

Hackett, G., & Betz, N. (1981). A self-efficacy approach to the career development of women. *Journal of Vocational Behavior, 18*, 326-339.

Hackett, G., Betz, N., Casas, J., & Rocha-Singh, I. (1992). Gender, ethnicity, and social cognitive factors predicting the academic achievement of students in engineering. *Journal of Counseling Psychology, 39*, 527-538.

Hackett, G., Esposito, D., & O'Halloran, M. S. (1989). The relationship of role model influence to the career salience and educational and career plans of college women. *Journal of Vocational Behavior, 35*, 164-180.

Hall, D. (1972). A model of coping with role conflict: The role behavior of college educated women. *Administrative Science Quarterly, 17*, 471-486.

Harmon, L. (1970). Anatomy of career commitment. *Journal of Counseling Psychology, 17*, 77-80.

Harmon, L. (1978). Career counseling for women. In L. Hansen & R. Rapoza (Eds.), *Career development and counseling of women* (pp. 443-453). Springfield, IL: Charles C Thomas.

Hawks, B. K., & Muha, D. (1991). Facilitating the career development of minorities: Doing it differently this time. *Career Development Quarterly, 39*, 251-260.

Hayes, L. S. (1986). The superwoman myth. *Social Casework: The Journal of Contemporary Social Work, 67*(7), 436-441.

Helson, R., Elliott, T., & Leigh, J. (1990). Number and quality of roles: A longitudinal personality view. *Psychology of Women Quarterly, 14*, 83-101.

Higham, S. J., & Navarre, J. (1984). Gifted adolescent females require differential treatment. *Journal for the Education of the Gifted, 8*(1), 43-58.

Hilton, T., Miller, J., & Brown, K. (1991, February). *Tomorrow's scientists, mathematicians, and engineers.* Paper presented at the 1991 annual meeting of the American Association for Advancement of Science, Washington, DC.

Hoffman, L. (1986). Work, family, and the child. In M. Pallak & R. Perloff (Eds.), *Psychology and work: Productivity, change, and employment.* Washington, DC: American Psychological Association.

Hoffman, L. (1989). Effects of maternal employment in the two-parent family. *American Psychologist, 44,* 283-292.

Holland, J. (1966). A psychological classification scheme for vocations and major fields. *Journal of Counseling Psychology, 13,* 278-288.

Holland, J. (1985). *Making vocational choices: A theory of vocational personalities and work environments.* New York: Prentice Hall.

Holland, J., Fritzsche, B., & Powell, A. (1994). *Self Directed Search: Technical manual.* Odessa, FL: Psychological Assessment Resources, Inc.

Holland, J., Powell, A., & Fritzsche, B. (1994). *Self Directed Search (SDS): Professional user's guide.* Odessa, FL: Psychological Assessment Resources, Inc.

Hollinger, C. L. (1983). Multidimensional determinants of traditional and nontraditional career aspirations for mathematically talented females adolescents. *Journal for the Education of the Gifted, 6*(4), 245-265.

Hollinger, C. L. (1991). Facilitating the career development of gifted young women. *Roeper Review, 13*(3), 135-139.

Hollinger, C. L., & Fleming, E. S. (1992). A longitudinal examination of life choices of gifted and talented young women. *Gifted Child Quarterly, 36*(4), 207-212.

Horner, M. S. (1972). Toward an understanding of achievement-related conflicts in women. *Journal of Social Issues, 28,* 157-175.

Horner, M. S. (1978). The measurement and behavioral implications of fear of success in women. In J. Atkinson & J. Raynor (Eds.), *Personality, motivation and achievement.* New York: John Wiley.

Horney, K. (1945). *Our inner conflicts.* New York: Norton.

Hyde, J. (1995). Women and maternity leave: Empirical data and public policy. *Psychology of Women Quarterly, 19,* 257-298.

Ibarra, H. (1995). Race, opportunity, and diversity of social circles in managerial networks. *Academy of Management Journal, 38,* 673-703.

Jagacinski, C. M. (1987). Engineering careers: Women in a male dominated field. *Psychology of Women Quarterly, 11,* 97-110.

John, O. (1989). Towards a taxonomy of personality descriptions. In D. Buss & N. Cantor (Eds.), *Personality psychology: Recent trends and emerging directions* (pp. 261-271). New York: Springer-Verlag.

Jones, E. P. (1991). The impact of economic, political, and social factors on recent overt black/white racial conflict in higher education in the United States. *Journal of Negro Education, 60*(4), 524-537.

Kahn, S. E., & Lichty, J. M. (1987). The career plans of women. *International Journal for the Advancement of Counseling, 10,* 123-130.

Karable, J., & Halsey, A. H. (1977). *Power and ideology in education.* Oxford: Oxford University Press.

Keith, P. M. (1981). Sex-role attitudes, family plans, and career orientation: Implications for counseling. *Vocational Guidance Quarterly, 29,* 244-252.

Kinnier, R., Katz, E., & Berry, M. (1991). Successful resolutions to the career-versus-family conflict. *Journal of Counseling & Development, 69,* 439-444.

Klein, S. (1985). *Handbook for achieving sex equity through education.* Baltimore: Johns Hopkins University Press.

Kluckhohn, F. (1956). Toward a comparison of value emphases in different cultures. In L. White (Ed.), *The state of social science* (pp. 116-132). Chicago: University of Chicago Press.

Kozol, J. (1991). *Savage inequalities: Children in America's schools*. New York: HarperCollins.

Krumboltz, J. (1991). *Career Beliefs Inventory*. Palo Alto, CA: Consulting Psychologists Press.

Lane, M. (1990). *Women and minorities in science and engineering*. Washington, DC: National Science Foundation.

Lent, R. W., Brown, S. D., & Hackett, G. (1994). Toward a unifying social cognitive theory of career and academic interest, choice, and performance. *Journal of Vocational Behavior, 45,* 79-122.

Lent, R., Brown, S., & Hackett, G. (1996). Career development from a social cognitive perspective (pp. 373-422). In D. Brown, L. Brooks, & Associates (Eds.), *Career choice and development* (3rd ed., pp. 373-422). San Francisco: Jossey-Bass.

Leung, S. A. (1995). Career development and counseling: A multicultural perspective. In J. G. Ponterotto, J. M. Casas, L. A. Suzuki, & C. M. Alexander (Eds.), *Handbook of multicultural counseling* (pp. 549-566). Thousand Oaks, CA: Sage.

Lincoln, Y., & Guba, E. (1985). *Naturalistic inquiry*. Beverly Hills, CA: Sage.

Lipman-Blumen, J., & Leavitt, H. (1976). Vicarious and direct achievement patterns in adulthood. *Counseling Psychologist, 6,* 26-32.

Lucas, M. S. (1993). Personal, social, academic, and career problems expressed by minority college students. *Journal of Multicultural Counseling & Development, 21,* 2-13.

Luzzo, D. A. (1993). Ethnic differences in college students' perceptions of barriers to career development. *Journal of Multicultural Counseling & Development, 21,* 227-236.

Maccoby, E., & Jacklin, C. (1974). *The psychology of sex differences*. Stanford, CA: Stanford University Press.

McBride, B. (1990). The effects of a parent education/play group program on father involvement in child rearing. *Family Relations, 39,* 250-256.

McDade, L. (1988). Knowing the "right stuff": Attrition, gender, and scientific literacy. *Anthropology and Education Quarterly, 19,* 93-114.

McDonald, J., Clarke, M., & Dobson, E. (1990). *Increasing the supply of women and minority engineers: An agenda for state action*. Washington, DC: National Governor's Association.

McIlwee, J., & Robinson, J. (1992). *Women in engineering: Gender, power and the workplace culture*. Albany: State University of New York Press.

Miller, G., Galanter, E., & Pribram, K. (1960). *Plans and the structure of behavior*. New York: Holt, Rinehart & Winston.

Miller, J. (1986). *A longitudinal study of the development of adolescent and young adult attitudes toward and knowledge about science and technology*. DeKalb: Northern Illinois University, Public Opinion Lab.

Miller, M., Springer, T., & Wells, D. (1988). Which occupational environments do black youths prefer? Extending Holland's typology. *School Counselor, 36,* 103-106.

Mitchell, L., & Krumboltz, J. (1990). Social learning approach to career decision making: Krumboltz' theory. In D. Brown, L. Brooks, & Associates (Eds.), *Career choice and development* (2nd ed., pp. 145-196). San Francisco: Jossey-Bass.

Mitchell, L., & Krumboltz, J. (1996). Krumboltz's learning theory of career choice and counseling (pp. 233-280). In D. Brown, L. Brooks, & Associates (Eds.), *Career choice and development* (3rd ed., pp. 233-280). San Francisco: Jossey-Bass.

Moreland, J., Gulanick, N., Montague, E., & Harren, V. (1978). Some psychometric properties of the Bem Sex-Role Inventory. *Applied Psychological Measurement, 2,* 249-256.

Morgan, C. S. (1992). College students' perceptions of barriers to women in science and engineering. *Youth & Society, 24,* 228-236.

Murray, H. (1938). *Explorations in personality*. New York: Oxford University Press.

Murray, J. D., & Keller, P. A. (1991). Psychology and rural America: Current status and future directions. *American Psychologist, 46,* 220-231.

Murray, J. D., Keller, P. A., McMorran, B. J., & Edwards, B. L. (1983). Future expectations of rural American youth: Implications for mental health. *International Journal of Mental Health, 12,* 76-88.

National Center for Education Statistics. (1995). *The pocket condition of education in 1995.* Washington, DC: U.S. Department of Education.

National Science Foundation. (1994). *Women, minorities, and persons with disabilities in science and engineering: 1994* (NSF 94 333). Arlington, VA: Author.

O'Brien, K. M. (1993). *The influence of psychological separation and parental attachment on the career choices and self-efficacy beliefs of adolescent women.* Unpublished doctoral dissertation, Loyola University, Chicago.

Okacha, A. A. G. (1994). Preparing racial ethnic minorities for the workforce 2000. *Journal of Multicultural Counseling & Development, 22,* 106-114.

Orthner, D., Bowen, G., & Beare, V. (1990). The organization family: A question of work and family boundaries. *Marriage and Family Review, 15*(3-4), 15-36.

Osipow, S. (1966). *Theories of career development.* New York: Allyn & Bacon.

Osipow, S., & Fitzgerald, L. (1996). *Theories of career development* (4th ed.). New York: Allyn & Bacon.

Padilla, R. (1991). *Qualitative analysis with HyperQual.* (Available from the author, 3327 N. Detota, Chandler, AZ 85224)

Parsons, J., Adler, T., & Kaczala, C. (1982). Socialization of achievement attitudes and beliefs: Parental influences. *Child Development, 53*(2), 310-321.

Pasternak, B. (1996, June). [Letter, 1959]. *New Yorker,* p. 110.

Peshkin, A. (1988). Understanding complexity: A gift of qualitative inquiry. *Anthropology and Education Quarterly, 19*(4), 416-424.

Pollard, K. M., & O'Hare, W. P. (1990). *Beyond high school: The experience of rural and urban youth in the 1980s.* Washington, DC: Population Reference Bureau, Inc.

Poloma, M. M. (1972). Role conflict and the married professional woman. In C. Safilios-Rothschild (Ed.), *Toward a sociology of women* (pp. 187-198). Lexington, MA: Xerox Publishing.

Poole, M. E., Langan-Fox, J., Ciavarella, M., & Omodei, M. (1991). A contextualist model of professional attainment: Results of a longitudinal study of career paths of men and women. *Counseling Psychologist, 19*(4), 603-624.

Psathas, G. (1968). Toward a theory of occupational choice for women. *Sociology and Social Research, 52,* 253-268.

Rakow, S. J., & Bermudez, A. B. (1993). Science is "ciencia": Meeting the needs of Hispanic American students. *Science Education, 77,* 669-683.

Reddin, J. (1996). *The effects of role models on women's multiple role planning.* Unpublished master's thesis, University of Illinois, Urbana-Champaign.

Richardson, M. S. (1993). Work in people's lives: A location for counseling psychologists. *Journal of Counseling Psychology, 40,* 425-433.

Riger, S. (1991). Gender dilemmas in sexual harassment policies and procedures. *American Psychologist, 46,* 497-505.

Rubovits, P. (1975). Early experience and the achieving orientations of American middle class girls. In M. Maehr & W. Stallings (Eds.), *Culture, child and school* (pp. 21-32). Monterey, CA: Brooks/Cole.

Sadker, M., Sadker, D., & Klein, S. (1991). The issue of gender in elementary and secondary education. In G. Grant (Ed.), *Review of Research in Education, 17,* 269-334.

Sala, S. J., Ashton, J., & Fitzpatrick, J. F. (1995). Affirmative action after Adarand: A legal, regulatory, legislative outlook (*Labor Relations Reporter: Special Report, 68*(6), FEP cases). Washington, DC: Bureau of National Affairs.

Sandler, B., & Hall, R. (1996). *The campus climate revisited: Chilly for women faculty, administrators and graduate students.* Washington, DC: Association of American Colleges and Universities.

Savickas, M., & Lent, R. (1994). *Convergence in career development theories: Implications for science and practice.* Palo Alto, CA: Consulting Psychologists Press.

Schulenberg, J. E., Vondracek, F. W., & Crouter, A. C. (1984). The influence of the family on vocational development. *Journal of Marriage and Family, 46*(1), 129-143.

Sekaran, U. (1986). *Dual-career families.* San Francisco: Jossey-Bass.

Sells, L. (1975). *Sex, ethnic, and field differences in doctoral outcomes.* Unpublished doctoral dissertation, University of California, Berkeley.

Sewell, W., & Hauser, R. (1975). *Education, occupation, and earnings: Achievement in the early career.* New York: Academic Press.

Sherman, A. (1992). *Falling by the wayside: Children in rural America.* Washington, DC: Children's Defense Fund.

Sieber, S. (1974). Toward a theory of role accumulation. *American Sociological Review, 39*, 567-578.

Skinner, B. (1953). *Science and human behavior.* New York: Macmillan.

Smith, E. J. (1983). Issues in racial minorities' career behavior. In W. B. Walsh & S. H. Osipow (Eds.), *Handbook of vocational psychology: Vol. 1. Foundations* (pp. 161-222). Hillsdale, NJ: Lawrence Erlbaum.

Smith, L. (1981). *The relationship of interpersonal needs, role of work definitions and occupational prestige to marital structure in dual-career couples.* Unpublished doctoral dissertation, University of Illinois, Urbana-Champaign.

Spade, J., & Reese, C. (1991). We've come a long way, maybe: College students' plans for work and family. *Sex Roles, 24*, 309-321.

Spence, J. (1985). Achievement American style: The rewards and costs of individualism. *American Psychologist, 40*, 1285-1295.

Spence, J., & Helmreich, R. (1978). *Masculinity and femininity: Their psychological dimensions, correlates, and antecedents.* Austin: Texas University Press.

Spokane, A. (1996). Holland's theory. In D. Brown, L. Brooks, & Associates (Eds.), *Career choice and development* (3rd ed., pp. 33-74). San Francisco: Jossey-Bass.

Stake, J. E., & Noonan, M. (1985). The influence of teacher models on the career confidence and motivation of college students. *Sex Roles, 12*(9-10), 1023-1031.

Steffy, B. D., & Ashbaugh, D. (1986). Dual-career planning, marital satisfaction and job stress among women in dual-career marriages. *Journal of Business and Psychology, 1*(2), 114-123.

Stendler, C. (1949). *Children of Brasstown.* Urbana: University of Illinois, Bureau of Research and Service.

Stevens, G., & Cho, J. H. (1985). Socioeconomic indexes and the new 1980 census occupational classification scheme. *Social Science Research, 14*, 142-168.

Super, D. (1957). *The psychology of careers.* New York: Harper & Row.

Super, D. (1963). Self-concepts in vocational development. In D. E. Super et al. (Eds.), *Career development: Self-concept theory.* New York: College Entrance Examination Board.

Super, D. (1970). *Manual for Work Values Inventory.* Boston: Houghton Mifflin.

Super, D. (1980). A life-span, life-space approach to career development. *Journal of Vocational Behavior, 16*, 282-298.

Super, D. (1990). A life-span, life-space approach to career development. In D. Brown & L. Brooks (Eds.), *Career choice and development* (2nd ed., pp. 197-261). San Francisco: Jossey-Bass.

Super, D., & Cuhla, M. (1976). *Work Salience Inventory.* (Available from Helen Farmer, University of Illinois, 1310 S. 6th St., Champaign, IL 61820)

Super, D., & Nevill, D. (1985a). *The Salience Inventory.* Palo Alto, CA: Consulting Psychologists Press.

Super, D., & Nevill, D. (1985b). *The Values Inventory.* Palo Alto, CA: Consulting Psychologists Press.

Tangri, S. S., & Jenkins, S. R. (1986). Stability and change in role innovation and life plans. *Sex Roles, 14*(11-12), 647-662.

Tiedeman, D., & O'Hara, R. (1963). *Career development: Choice and adjustment.* New York: College Entrance Examination Board.

Tinsley, H. E. A. (1993). Construct your reality and show us its benefits: Comment on Richardson (1993). *Journal of Counseling Psychology, 41*(1), 108-111.

Tipping, L., & Farmer, H. (1991). A home-career conflict measure: Career counseling implications. *Measurement and Evaluation in Counseling and Development, 24*(3), 111-118.

Trueba, H., Jacobs, L., & Kirton, E. (1990). *Cultural conflict and adaptation: The case of Hmong children in American society.* New York: Falmer.

Unger, R., & Crawford, M. (1992). *Women and gender: A feminist psychology.* New York: McGraw-Hill.

U.S. Bureau of the Census. (1981). *Supplementary reports: 1980 Census of the Population.* Washington, DC: Government Printing Office.

U.S. Bureau of the Census. (1990). *Who's minding the kids?* Washington, DC: Government Printing Office.

U.S. Department of Education, Office of Educational Research and Improvement. (1994). *The condition of education in rural schools.* Washington, DC: Author.

U.S. Department of Labor. (1972). *The myth and the reality.* Washington, DC: U.S. Department of Labor, Women's Bureau.

U.S. Department of Labor. (1991). *Dictionary of occupational titles.* Washington, DC: Government Printing Office.

U.S. Equal Employment Opportunity Commission. (1980). Final amendment to guidelines on discrimination because of sex under Title VII of the Civil Rights Act of 1964, as amended. 29 CFR Part 1604. *Federal Register, 45,* 74675-74677.

Varenhorst, B. (1969). Learning the consequences of life's decisions. In J. Krumboltz & C. Thorenson (Eds.), *Behavioral counseling* (pp. 306-319). New York: Holt, Rinehart & Winston.

Walker, B. A., Reis, S. M., & Leonard, J. S. (1992). A developmental investigation of the lives of gifted women. *Gifted Child Quarterly, 36*(4), 201-206.

Ware, N. C., & Lee, V. E. (1988). Sex differences in choice of college science majors. *American Educational Research Journal, 25,* 593-614.

Webster's Ninth New Collegiate Dictionary. (1991). Springfield, MA: Merriam-Webster Inc.

Weiner, B. (1974). *Achievement motivation and attribution theory.* Morristown, NJ: General Learning Press.

Weiner, B. (1979). A theory of motivation for some classroom experience. *Journal of Educational Psychology, 71,* 3-25.

Weitzman, L. (1992). *The development and validation of scales to assess realism of attitudes toward multiple role planning.* Unpublished doctoral dissertation, University of Illinois at Urbana-Champaign.

Women's Educational Equity Act (WEEA) Resource Center. (1996). *Gender equity works for all students: 1996 catalog.* Newton, MA: Education Development Center, Inc.

Worton, B. (1996, March 4). Women at work. *Fortune, 133,* 13-19.

Index of Study Participants

Index of Authors and Subjects

About the Authors

Janice H. Altman is on staff at the Psychological Services Center of Mary Washington College and provides individual and group psychotherapy, consulting, and outreach services to students. Prior to this, she did career counseling at Johns Hopkins University with adults and graduate students and taught courses in career planning. She received a B.A. from Hofstra University in psychology, an M.A. from the University of Maryland in community counseling, and a Ph.D. from the University of Illinois at Urbana-Champaign in counseling psychology. Her primary research interests include women's issues and career issues with a specific focus on the antecedents of math self-efficacy.

Amy Carter is a graduate assistant at the University of Illinois Counseling Center and a fourth-year graduate student in the counseling psychology program. She has a B.S. in psychology from Iowa State University and an M.S. in counseling psychology from the University of Illinois. Her research interests include family of origin issues and current adjustment as well as the often unregarded demographic variable of social class issues.

JoAnn Cohn is pursuing a Ph.D. in professional psychology at George Washington University. She received a B.A. from Yale University and an M.Ed. from the University of Illinois at Urbana-Champaign, both in counseling psychology. Her research interests include qualitative research, cross-cultural counseling and therapy, the career development of persons of color, and factors contributing to the success of at-risk youth.

Rebecca L. Conrad is a Ph.D. candidate in counseling psychology at the University of Illinois at Urbana-Champaign. She received a B.S. from Ohio State University in psychology and an M.S. from the University of Illinois at Urbana-Champaign in counseling psychology. She was coauthor of an article in *Journal of Research in Science Teaching*. Her research interests include career development focusing on women and rural adolescents, the relationship between career self-efficacy and women's career achievement, and the role of client and counselor attributions in the therapy process.

Helen S. Farmer is Professor in the Department of Educational Psychology, University of Illinois, Champaign-Urbana. She received her Ph.D. in counseling psychology from UCLA in 1972, her master's in counseling psychology from Columbia University in 1969, and her master's of divinity, in psychiatry and religion, from the Union

Theological Seminary in 1955. She is an APA, Division 17, Distinguished Senior Contributor to Counseling Psychology in 1995 and Distinguished Senior Scholar of the University of Illinois College of Education, 1995. Her current research involves a longitudinal study begun in 1980, with data collected again in 1990 and 1991-1993. She has developed a theoretical model of women's career choice process that focuses on the interaction between personal and environmental factors rather than internal psychological factors.

Susan Giurleo is finishing her doctoral studies in counseling psychology at the University of Illinois, Urbana-Champaign. She received a B.A. in psychology from Connecticut College, New London, Connecticut, in 1991, and an M.Ed. in counseling and guidance from Boston University in 1992. Her research interests include the career development of women, the social and psychological experiences of women who pursue nontraditional/science-related careers, and how psychological attachment influences career planning and choice. She has presented her research at the American Psychological Association meeting and at the Great Lakes Conference for Counseling Psychology. She has accepted an internship position at the University of New Hampshire Counseling Center for fall 1997.

Veronica Lugris is a doctoral student in counseling psychology at the University of Illinois, Urbana-Champaign. She has a B.A. in journalism and Spanish from the University of Connecticut and an A.M. From the University of Illinois. Her research interests are issues of identity development (including ethnic identity, gender identity, and affectional/sexual identity) and social support.

Kirsten Peterson is Sport Psychology Consultant for the U.S. Olympic Committee's Sport Science and Technology Division in Colorado Springs. She has an M.S. in physical education and a Ph.D. in counseling psychology, both from the University of Illinois. She has coauthored articles in *Pediatric Exercise Science, Journal of Sport and Exercise Psychology,* and *Sport Psychologist.* Her research interests include women in sport and the psychology of athletic injury rehabilitation.

Jana Reddin is Helen Farmer's research assistant on both qualitative and quantitative projects. She received a B.A. from Austin College in Sherman, Texas, in psychology and an M.S. from the University of Illinois at Urbana-Champaign in educational psychology. Her research interests include women's issues, career development, and the therapeutic relationship. She has presented her research on women's career development at the American Psychological Association annual meeting.

Lenore M. Tipping is a clinician with the Northeast Occupational Exchange, a comprehensive mental health agency in Bangor, Maine, and an adjunct faculty member at Husson College in Bangor, ME. She has an M.S. and a Ph.D. from the University of Illinois at Urbana-Champaign and completed her clinical internship at the University of Maine. Her primary research interests are home–career conflict and multiple role planning.

DATE DUE

	~~EL GRANDE~~		
	~~MAY 3 0 1998~~		~~AUG 3~~
	~~AUG 1 1 1999~~		
	~~FEB 1 1 2000~~	~~NOV 1 1 2001~~	
~~OCT 1 0 2003~~			
~~JUN 1 4~~			
	~~DEC 0 9 2001~~		
	~~JAN 3 1 2002~~		
	~~MAY 0 5 2004~~		
			Printed in USA